Civil Society and Democracy

Civil Society and Democracy in Latin America

Edited by

Richard Feinberg, Carlos H. Waisman,
and
Leon Zamosc

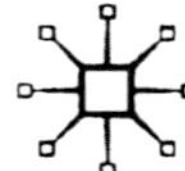

First published in 2006 by
PALGRAVE MACMILLAN™
175 Fifth Avenue, New York, N.Y. 10010 and
Houndmills, Basingstoke, Hampshire, England RG21 6XS
Companies and representatives throughout the world.

PALGRAVE MACMILLAN is the global academic imprint of the Palgrave Macmillan division of St. Martin's Press, LLC and of Palgrave Macmillan Ltd. Macmillan® is a registered trademark in the United States, United Kingdom and other countries. Palgrave is a registered trademark in the European Union and other countries.

ISBN 1–4039–7228–1

Library of Congress Cataloging-in-Publication Data

Civil society and democracy in Latin America / edited by Richard Feinberg, Carlos H. Waisman, and Leon Zamosc.
p. cm.
Includes bibliographical references and index.
ISBN 1–4039–7228–1 (alk. paper)
1. Civil society—Latin America. 2. Democracy—Latin America. 3. Latin America—Politics and government—1980– I. Feinberg, Richard E. II. Waisman, Carlos H. (Carlos Horacio), 1943– III. Zamosc, Leon.

JL966.C58 2006
320.98—dc22 2005056461

A catalogue record for this book is available from the British Library.

Design by Newgen Imaging Systems (P) Ltd., Chennai, India.

First edition: April 2006

10 9 8 7 6 5 4 3 2 1

Printed in the United States of America.

Contents

CHAPTER 1

INTRODUCTION: CIVIL SOCIETY AND DEMOCRACY: THE LATIN AMERICAN CASE

Carlos H. Waisman, Richard Feinberg, and Leon Zamosc

A central feature of the revival of democracy in Latin America in the past two decades has been the awakening, or reawakening, of civil society in the region. The purpose of this volume is to examine the relationship between these two processes. More particularly, we will focus on the extent to which civil society has contributed to the strengthening of democratic institutions.

This question is of major importance, for both theoretical and practical reasons. Since the downfall of Communist regimes in Central and Eastern Europe, the classical concept of civil society has been resurrected, and arguments of Tocquevillean inspiration connecting civil society and democracy have become commonplace. However, this literature is rather vague: different users have defined the term in diverse and even divergent ways and the specific processes that presumably link civil society and politics have not been conceptualized with precision. However, there is a common thread among different versions of the civil society argument: regardless of how the term is defined and of what mechanism is postulated as a link between civil society and democracy, the core idea is that the existence of a dense web of private associations based on all the major classes, interest groups, and value communities constitutes a foundation for a strong and durable democracy.

Conversely, definitions of democracy currently used by social scientists do not necessarily imply an active or strong civil society. Nevertheless, there is little doubt that a high-quality democracy presupposes one. In broad terms, contemporary social scientists have understood democracy in three different, albeit related, ways. First, in the Schumpeterian tradition, the term democracy refers to a political regime characterized by fair elections and toleration of the opposition (Schumpeter 1987:250–283).[1] This definition is unsatisfactory, because it does not include the extent and range of citizens' inclusion in the polity. On its basis, a competitive oligarchy would still qualify as a democracy. Second, we have Robert Dahl's (1971) classical definition, according to which democracy requires high levels of inclusiveness and competitiveness, and a strong institutionalization of civil and political rights. The problem with this set of criteria is that it does not take into account the intensity and functions of citizens' participation. A polity whose citizenry is demobilized and disorganized or, on the contrary, is mobilized against democratic institutions, would still be considered democratic. Finally, the civic or republican democracy advocated by Alexis de Tocqueville and other classic theorists (and brought into current popular debate by Robert D. Putnam) would involve Dahl's traits, plus a highly organized civic community.[2] This kind of high-quality democracy is the one that, according to one of the oldest lines of argument in social and political theory, presupposes a strong civil society. We hope that this volume, beyond its geographic and temporal focus, will contribute to our general understanding of the ways, positive and negative, in which processes involving citizens' collective action and organizations outside the state affect the quality of democracy.

There are also very practical reasons for undertaking this study at this time. Civil society mobilization has been an important factor in the decay and eventual collapse of the authoritarian regimes that ruled almost all the countries in the region in the decades preceding the 1990s. The centrality of this determinant in relation to others (such as economic failure or success, delegitimation of coercive policies, external influences, even defeat in war) varied from country to country. However, the activation of groups and associations that pursued economic demands, the protection of human rights, and the establishment of a democratic order was a salient aspect of the political process in the final phase of all these regimes.

On the other hand, an examination of the question of the quality of the democracies being activated across Latin America reveals the central role of civil society in this regard. In a region of the world plagued by extraordinarily high levels of social and economic inequality, and in which a very large proportion of the population faces economic, political, or cultural exclusion, it would be hard to establish and sustain a high-quality democracy. However, there are important differences among these newly democratic regimes, in relation to critical matters such as the extent to which the rule of law is upheld; whether underprivileged classes, women, or indigenous groups can effectively exercise civil and political rights; and whether a welfare state, even at a rudimentary level, is in place.

These outcomes are explained, in part, by what happens in the realm of associations and movements in which citizens come together to protect and advance their own and shared interests and values. When these groups operate as vehicles for the exercise of citizenship, as agencies that make demands, offer contingent supports, and audit governmental activities, there is a strong civil society, which produces a republican or civic democracy. This does not imply, of course, that a civil society would simply acquiesce to the existing distribution of power and privilege; on the contrary, many of its organizations could become central agents, together with some of the democratic political parties, in reform processes oriented toward producing a more egalitarian and participatory social order. On the other hand, social organizations could be sparse, weak, and dependent; and operate as channels for clientelism or state corporatism. In so doing, they would be passive actors in a process of democratic stagnation or decay. Further, as Latin American history painfully illustrates, social organizations could also be the carriers of political polarization that, if it were very intense, might contribute to the breakdown of democracy itself. This can happen when there are powerful civil society organizations in societies with strong cleavages and weak adhesion to constitutional and legal norms, where the pursuit of particular interests weighs more heavily than the preservation of the democratic rules of the game. In such situations, social organizations could be the gravediggers of democratic institutions, even if this consequence is unintended and unwanted. In short, when it comes to the quality of democracy, social organizations could be either part of the solution or part of the problem.

Contemporary Latin America comprises a variety of situations in this regard. In some countries there are large and active organizations representing all major interests and value communities while in others the organization is a monopoly of the privileged, or the governments control organizations representing nonelites. In some cases, a relatively strong civil society can be said to exist while in others cases associations and movements have played a more ambiguous role. Even by international standards, the region includes some solid and well-functioning democracies such as Chile (this in spite of high levels of inequality and the persistence of authoritarian enclaves), Costa Rica, and some polities in the English-speaking Caribbean, where civil society has been a vehicle for the exercise of citizenship. At the other extreme, Venezuela, Bolivia, and Ecuador are polarized societies where while some sectors of the society may behave civically others are subject to clientelistic mobilization from above, and still others may revolt. Venezuela is fragmented between a pole subordinated to the state and another bent on removing Hugo Chavez from office by whatever means, legal or not. In Bolivia and Ecuador, and also in a relatively more "civic" society, such as Argentina, mass protests spawned by social organizations and movements have forced elected presidents to resign. This volume will discuss several of these instances as well as theoretical and comparative perspectives.

Theoretical Frameworks

Part I discusses major conceptualizations of civil society, their application to Latin America, and the contemporary articulation between society and the state in different countries of the region.

Carlos H. Waisman's chapter, "Autonomy, Self-regulation, and Democracy: Tocquevillean-Gellnerian Perspectives on Civil Society and the Bifurcated State in Latin America" takes the conceptualization of civil society in sociological theory as his point of departure, focusing on Alexis de Tocqueville's classical analysis and on Ernest Gellner's contemporary approach. In this perspective, civil society refers to the web of associations that are representative of interests and values existing in a society as long as its constituent units are not controlled by the state. Waisman then operationalizes the diffuse concept "strong civil society" as one characterized by three properties of the web of associations existing in a society. In strong civil societies, this associational web is dense, highly autonomous from the state, and has a high level of self-regulation; that is, a demonstrated capacity to resolve conflict within the institutional channels of the democratic system. In the second part, Waisman applies this concept to contemporary Latin America. He concludes that economic liberalization has intensified social dualization, so that civil society is strong in some regions and areas of society, and weak in others. This increasingly segmented society has a selective affinity with a two-faced (split, Janus-like) state, one of whose faces is liberal democratic, and the other nonliberal, either clientelistic / corporatist or authoritarian.

Leonardo Avritzer's "Civil Society in Latin America in the Twenty-First Century: Democratic Deepening, Social Fragmentation, and State Crisis" discusses the trajectory of the concept of civil society, and its recent revival as a central tool for understanding the process of democratization. Avritzer begins by examining the different processes of emergence, or reemergence, of civil society in Latin America in the past three decades. This phenomenon has taken different forms in Brazil, the Southern Cone, Mexico, and the Andean countries due to the various characteristics of their authoritarian regimes, patterns of economic liberalization, preexisting political traditions, and the degree of transformation experienced by their key social actors. Later, he conceptualizes three types of civil society in contemporary Latin America: the preliberal (in Andean countries) where civil society is in turmoil and the state in crisis; the liberal-democratic (exemplified by Argentina and Chile), in which state–society boundaries have not changed but the system has became more accountable; and the civic-participatory (Brazil, and perhaps Mexico), in which local participation has been expanded in the process of democratization. These tiered models are dynamic and each has the potential to either fall into noncivil patterns or to accede over time to "higher" levels of civicness and participation.

The last chapter in this section is Philip Oxhorn's "Conceptualizing Civil Society from the Bottom Up: A Political Economy Perspective." It argues that contemporary definitions of civil society, which originated in the liberal tradition, are excessively individualistic, normative, and based on a rigid state–society dichotomy. For this reason, their relevance to the understanding of contemporary social and political processes in Latin America is limited. In turn, he proposes an alternative perspective, one that is "from the bottom up" and based on the analysis of the groups and communities that make up society. These units both resist subordination to the state and demand inclusion into national politics. Therefore, civil society cannot be understood independent of the state. This conceptualization focuses on the social construction of citizenship, a process located in the political system and characterized by conflict, negotiation, and compromise. His discussion of transitions from authoritarian rule, the establishment of the rule of law and basic rights, and the effectiveness of educational systems illustrate the usefulness of this approach. In any case, Oxhorn contends that the two theoretical traditions, the liberal and the collectivist, complement each other.

These contributions strongly suggest that the concept of civil society is useful for understanding the social foundations of democracy in contemporary Latin America as well as the differences between democracies in this region and those in industrial societies. The case studies further highlight the pertinence of this approach.

Country Case Studies

The chapters in part II discuss civil society processes in specific countries. In "Citizenship and Civil Society in Renascent Argentina," Isidoro Cheresky traces the emergence and consolidation of what he defines as an "autonomous citizenry" in contemporary Argentina. Its main expressions are the emergence of new social actors; the vanishing of the "captive vote" held by parties, and veto power through protest mobilizations. This resurgence of citizenship should be viewed against the background of the country's corporatist tradition, established under Peronism, which had closed spaces for the development of autonomous civil society. The process of constitution of autonomous social actors began in the late 1970s with the opposition to the military regime and the development of the human rights movement. It continued in the 1980s and 1990s with large-scale shifts in voting preferences. Finally, it reached its climax in the massive protests of 2001 that culminated in the forced resignation of Fernando de la Rúa. The determining factors of this democratizing process were the weakening of corporatism, structural changes induced by economic liberalization, political instability, and the crisis of representation at the turn of the twenty-first century. This transformation harbors the potential to induce greater involvement of civil society in the workings of government and, in the end, produce greater accountability and transparency.

Manuel Mora y Araujo, in "Argentina After the Nineties: Changes in Social Structure and Political Behavior" argues that Argentina has witnessed a dramatic shift in power distribution preferences. In the 1980s, preferences for corporatism and classic statism were the first plurality, in the 1990s "neoliberal" preferences rose, whereas now in the beginning of the twenty-first century "noncorporatist" preferences dominate, with a bias in favor of state as opposed to private-market power. However, contrary to conventional wisdom, Mora y Araujo presents empirical evidence that popular confidence in democracy remains high, even as affection for or participation in parties decline. In inverse correlation, with mistrust in parties there is a growing acceptance of civic organizations. Historically, Argentina has not had a strong civil society, but there are indications that it is on its way to becoming one. Prevailing values are increasingly in favor of de-ideologization and positive results, as opposed to general values and broad conceptions of the world that, in the Latin American context, have often contributed to political polarization and authoritarian outcomes. In Argentina, Mora y Araujo finds that people with low competitive capabilities, the losers of the 1990s, still tend toward nationalism, protectionism, and old left-wing ideas. Among segments of the population more capable of competing in a globalizing economy one finds that "Jeffersonian" ideas are focused on more decentralized political structures, vocal citizenship, and results. The emerging alternative model, still conjectural, has these elements: a decline of parties, commitment to democracy, a growing number of civic organizations and NGOs, and a search for new forms of decentralized political participation.

Wendy Wolford, in "Sem Reforma Agraria, Não Ha Democracia: The Struggle over Access to Land and Deepening Democracy in Brazil," discusses the Movement of the Landless Rural Workers (MST) in Brazil. Since the mid-1980s, the MST has mobilized a previously excluded segment of society—the landless peasantry—that has grown to become one of the largest grassroot social movements in Brazilian history. The movement's struggles for land can be seen as part of the broader process of emergence of a contentious segment in society. She points out that the land seizures it has pursued have been increasingly accepted as legitimate forms of political action within Brazilian society. The MST has been one of the most vocal critics of economic and social policies in the past decade, but the strategic construction of an antistate oppositional identity has become problematic since the beginning of the administration of Luis Inacio "Lula" da Silva, the leader of the Workers' Party. Wolford shows that the MST is now at a turning point: after providing a space for expanding, if contentious, participation, it must now choose between critical support and opposition, the latter perhaps from a radical antiglobalization stance.

Finally, Daniel H. Levine in "Civil Society and Political Decay in Venezuela" makes the case that the Venezuelan democracy established in 1958 was not "exclusionary" but rather institutionalized popular representation that delivered basic social services and economic opportunity. However, this regime decayed as the result of the interaction of economic decline and the inability of institutions, notably established political parties, to adjust to the modernization of the society. This systemic decay opened the door to a wide range of movements claiming a voice as "civil society." These groups are linked to politics through government finance and, often, political affiliation. However, these new forms of social mobilization failed to establish enduring channels of contact or control in the political sphere. Meanwhile, the Chavez regime emerged as a classic "movement politics," tying the personal appeal of the leader to his alliance between the Left (both populist and orthodox) and the military. The opposition coalition consists of a loose alliance of remnants of the decayed political parties, the trade union movement, the Catholic Church and a broad range of the groups self-identified as "civil society." Levine contends that mobilizations such as these are difficult to sustain, a fact typical of "cycles of protest." Be it absent enduring organization or trusted political intermediaries and formal institutions or political parties, disillusionment will inevitably set in.

The State of the Debate

From different angles and theoretical perspectives, these chapters discuss a core issue: the relationship between civil society and democracy. They raise a series of issues of central significance for understanding the nature of civil society, its dynamics, and its effects on political institutions.

The first controversial theme is the relationship between historical trajectories and the emergence and strength of civil society. One of the classical theoretical issues has to do with the stark fact that strong civil societies have arisen only in some countries or types of country. The understanding of the institutional and cultural matrix that has produced these varied results is still in its infancy.[3] Is it a unique product of Western civilization, as Ernest Gellner (1994) has claimed, and as such not easily exportable to other environments? If this is the case, how Western are Latin American societies? If this proposition is not correct, what are the institutional and cultural prerequisites of civil society? Oxhorn raises the issue of whether the Western conception of civil society is applicable to Latin America, and argues for adding collectivistic components, which would be more appropriate to Latin American social structure and culture. Within Latin America, Avritzer shows how the institutional frameworks and cultures of different societies have produced different types of relationships between state and society. Waisman, in a similar vein, argues that a strong civil society presupposes citizens' capacity for citizenship, and thus its development will be uneven in strongly inegalitarian societies. Without falling into deterministic pessimism, it remains true that contemporary civil societies and the organizations that make them up spring from a path-dependent process, and that their structures, agendas, and forms of political action carry the weight of the institutional and cultural trajectories of their societies.

A second contested topic is the relationship between civil society and a market economy. There is a strand in the theory of civil society that argues that both are inseparable. In fact, Gellner considers that they are different aspects of the same phenomenon. By definition, a strong civil society would be incompatible with a statized economy, but whether some forms of still untried noncapitalist enterprise (such as market socialism) would be congruent with it is, of course, an open question. In any case, what we know is that all existing strong civil societies have developed within market economies. Most of Latin America, during the period of autarkic capitalism known in the region as "import-substituting industrialization," had a statized and overprotected form of capitalism, which generated capitalist classes and working classes dependent on the state. Recent economic liberalization, except in Chile, has been partial and not very effective, largely because it was not supported by the institutional infrastructure characteristic of advanced market economies. The main deficit in Latin America in this regard has to do with subordination to the rule of law, effective protection of property rights, an adequate level of transparency, and a state capable of extracting enough revenue to provide essential public goods and regulating markets effectively. When states of this type undertake large-scale reform, the danger is intense social and political polarization and the decay of democratic legitimacy. Therefore, the institutions of a market economy are imperfectly institutionalized in most countries in the region, and current attempts to strengthen them may delegitimate democracy.

Several of these chapters discuss different aspects of this troubling situation. Avritzer argues that there is a correlation between degrees of economic liberalization and the forms of reemergence of civil society, and Oxhorn claims that Latin American social structures are more collectivistic than those of advanced capitalist societies. Waisman points out that economic liberalization has dualized society into two poles—a civic pole, which is productive of civil society, and a marginal or disorganized pole, which is prone to passivity, clientelism, or non-institutionalized forms of behavior. Mora y Araujo shows, for the case of Argentina, the effects of this type of dualism on public opinion: While the "winners" of economic liberalization support markets, the "losers" espouse protectionism, nationalism, and antiglobalization. The landless movement discussed by Walford, which represents an economically and politically marginalized group, displays an ideology similar to this second segment of Argentine society, viewing the state as the oppressive instrument of economic elites and foreign capital, and perceiving market reforms as part of an offensive against its interests.

A third question is the relationship between civil society and political parties. There is nothing in Tocqueville's original argument or in its contemporary applications or extensions that implies that civil society is a more important determinant of a strong democracy than the party system, or that there is an inherent antagonism between civil society organizations and political parties. In fact, the proposition that a well-functioning democracy requires an effective party system is unquestioned in social science. The old distinction between articulation and aggregation of interests indicates the different functions of interest groups and parties, and the clear need for both. However, some critics of contemporary neo-Tocquevillean arguments have claimed that the new emphasis on civil society entails neglect of the party system.[4] Nevertheless, even if there is nothing of this sort at the theoretical or normative level, and established democracies have both, the empirical issue of the relative strength of the two institutions and the consequences of their imbalances calls for analysis.

Several of these chapters address this underexplored matter. Levine, Cheresky, and Mora y Araujo argue that the rise of civil society organizations in Venezuela and Argentina has taken place alongside the decay of political parties. For the two latter authors, the combination of a strong civil society and relatively weak parties has had positive effects on democracy in Argentina: the outcome seems to have been a revival of the practices and attitudes characteristic of citizenship that could help regenerate the political system. However, what happens to parties is still centrally important to the quality of democracy. Levine shows that Venezuelan civil society organizations, by themselves, are unable to institutionalize political representation. This is because civil society-based coalitions are transitory and usually have a narrow focus (in this case, the overthrow of Chavez). Moreover, it is difficult for civil society organizations to sustain high levels of political mobilization over time.

A fourth theme is a classical one in the study of Latin American politics: the question of state corporatism. This has been, in several countries in the region, a nondemocratic form of articulation between state and society, particularly between the government and labor (e.g., Argentina, Brazil, Mexico) and, in the Mexican case, with the peasantry as well. State corporatism implied extension of participation to these groups, contingent on government control. The mechanism involved was the direct oversight by the government of unions and other group associations (and, in some cases, the requirement of governmental permission for their formation). Linkages of this type were especially important in the post–World War II period. State corporatism declined in the following decades, for three main reasons: the growing autonomy of the subordinate sectors subject to it; the inability of the state and opposition from the capitalists to exchange economic and social benefits (sometimes provided by the capitalists) for organizational dependence; and changes in political culture. However, state corporatism has remained in the state's "tool box." Both Oxhorn (implicitly) and Waisman (explicitly) argue that some form of state corporatism could reappear in "weak civil society" situations. Deprived and dependent masses are susceptible to corporatist appeals, especially where nonstatist labor parties are ineffective or absent. Levine's description of Venezuela's Bolivarian movement shows that it has some traits of corporatism. Mora y Araujo's data indicate that there is a growing cultural rejection of corporatism in Argentina, but there could still be a propensity to some of its forms among the poorest sectors of the population. However, Cheresky's discussion of the movement of the unemployed in Argentina (*piqueteros*) is interesting in this regard: these organizations play the role of channels for distribution of social benefits, and thus produce autonomous alternatives to clientelism and corporatism.

A fifth and centrally important issue for the quality of democracy in contemporary Latin America are the consequences of political mobilization by social organizations. As pointed out above, in some countries associations representing important interests and values have interacted among themselves, with parties, and with the government within the institutional channels provided by democratic institutions, and thus they have behaved as what the Tocquevillean tradition would call a strong civil society. Even in contexts in which this is not the case, some strong social organizations have civic orientations. Both Levine and Mora y Araujo document the existence, in Venezuela and Argentina, of associations devoted to improving the quality of governmental organizations and processes, and Cheresky views the mobilization of civil society organizations at the turn of the twenty-first century in Argentina as being positive for democracy, for it constitutes a demand for representation and accountability.

In other cases, to which we have referred above, social mobilization has taken place outside institutional channels, and the product was the weakening of democracy. The overthrow of democratic governments by mass protests and the acceptance of this outcome by the society constitute clear indications of the absence of a strong civil society. Venezuela is an extreme case in Latin America today. Levine shows how social organizations have, along with the Chavez administration, been agents in the process of social and political polarization in this country. Wolford points out that the strategies followed by the MST, which included extralegal forms of collective action presented as struggles for democracy and citizenship, are in Brazil supported or justified by a majority public opinion that at the same time expresses distrust for democratic institutions. This volatile combination raises serious questions about the future quality of democracy in some of these societies.

Finally, we should not lose sight of the global context, a view requiring more rigorous study. Even though the key determinants of social mobilization in the region are domestic, external influences are significant at two levels. First, the most important social organizations are endogenous and locally controlled (except, of course, for the Catholic Church and other religious organizations), but many of the new civic ones have international linkages, as Levine and Mora y Araujo point out for Venezuela and Argentina. Second, international demonstration effects have been important sources of civil society activation. Agendas, discourses, and forms of political action travel across societies. Members of the intelligentsia and social and political activists are the agents of these processes of borrowing. Finally, governments in the industrial world and multilateral organizations have contributed to the formation and strengthening of some civil society organizations, particularly during the transitional period.

This volume brings into focus some of the gaps in our knowledge, and thus directs our attention to some of the issues that the research agenda on civil society and democracy in Latin America should address in the future. We simply need more comparative analyses, both in Western and non-Western contexts, about the institutional and cultural frameworks and historical trajectories that have produced different types of associational webs and civil societies of varying strength. Only in this way can the Western exceptionalism thesis be tested. Similarly, the question of the relationship between market and civil society calls for analyses of the relationship among state, economy, and society under different types of capitalism. Whether or not the relative weakness of civil society in most of Latin America is connected with the difficulties in institutionalizing a market economy in the region is an open question that can be addressed only after further empirical research. The matter of the relationship between civil society and political parties is a promising theme for theoretical innovation. We need a clearer understanding of the different patterns of connection between associations and parties in the context of the new Latin American democracies, and of the possible evolution of these relationships. The affinity for state corporatism in much of Latin America is one of the recurring themes in the study of the region. As these chapters make clear, the corporatist tradition matters. However, is state corporatism only a feature of Latin America's past? Could this form of relationship between state and society be somehow revived, especially in failing democracies? Finally, the study of just how civil society is influenced by international demonstration effects and cross-border linkages is still in its infancy. We need more case studies of these often subtle but potentially powerful processes.

Acknowledgments

This project originated in a conference on civil society and political transformations in Latin America, organized by the Center for Iberian and Latin American Studies at the University of California, San Diego (UCSD) on March 24–25, 2003. We thank the Division of Social Sciences and the Institute for International, Comparative and Area Studies at UCSD for their support.

La Jolla, California, June 2005

Notes

1. For a contemporary use of this criterion, see Adam Przeworski (1991).
2. This conception goes back to Machiavelli's concept of civic virtue. See J. G. A. Pockok (1975), which underlies Montesquieu's and Tocqueville's theories of democracy. Tocqueville's argument is, of course, presented in *Democracy in America* (1969). For a contemporary analysis, see Robert A. Putnam (2000).
3. For a contemporary analysis, see Ernest Gellner (1994).
4. See Michael W. Foley and Bob Edwards (1996), especially their critique of Robert Putnam's analysis of Italy (1993).

Bibliography

Dahl, R. A. (1971) *Polyarchy*, New Haven: Yale University Press.

Foley, M. W., and B. Edwards (1996) "The Paradox of Civil Society," *Journal of Democracy* 7, 3:38–52.

Gellner, E. (1994) *Conditions of Liberty*, London: Hamish Hamilton.

Pockok, J. G. A. (1975) *The Machiavellian Moment: Florentine Political Thought and the Atlantic Republican Tradition*, Princeton: Princeton University Press.

Przeworski, A. (1991) *Democracy and the Market*, New York: Cambridge University Press.

Putnam, R. D. (1993) *Making Democracy Work*, Princeton: Princeton University Press.

——. (2000) *Bowling Alone: The Collapse and Revival of American Community*, New York: Simon & Schuster.

Schumpeter, J. A. (1987) *Capitalism, Socialism, and Democracy*, London: Allen & Unwin.

Tocqueville, A. (1969) *Democracy in America*, New York: Anchor Books.

Part I

Theoretical And Comparative Perspectives

Chapter 2

Autonomy, Self-Regulation, and Democracy: Tocquevillean-Gellnerian Perspectives on Civil Society and the Bifurcated State in Latin America

Carlos H. Waisman

Civil society is a diffuse concept in the social sciences, and the fact that it has entered political discourse has limited further its applicability in academic research. In the first part of this chapter, I propose a conceptualization of civil society based on Alexis de Tocqueville's (1969)[1] analysis and what I consider is its contemporary operationalization by Ernest Gellner (1994). My focus will be the complicated issue of what constitutes a strong civil society. In part II, I will show that, when defined with some precision, this concept can help us understand central aspects of the relationship between state and society in contemporary Latin America. I conclude that the social dualization characteristic of most countries in the region that intensified during the recent period by economic liberalization has produced what I call regime bifurcation.

Conceptualizing Civil Society

Civil Society and Democracy

The specter of civil society is haunting the enemies of democracy and the market economy. But they should feel relieved: this specter's insubstantiality has rendered it quite harmless. Since the meaning of the term "civil society" is so fluid, the propositions derived from it, loosely inspired by superficial readings of Tocqueville, are hard to test empirically. Civil society is supposed to be the magic bullet against the old and the new enemies of democracy (Communism and authoritarianism in the past, jihadism in the present) and the market economy. More specifically (and problematically), civil society would be the midwife of democracy. However, these are little more than rhetorical images, due to the extreme fuzziness of the concept.

In the world of practical politics, the opponents of Communism in Central Europe in the 1980s, initially a small segment of the intelligentsia, seized on this term as a label. Since then, opponents of authoritarian and even populist regimes (e.g., the Chavez government in Venezuela) have done the same, whatever their level of civility. Governments and international organizations, both intergovernmental and NGOs, have also appropriated "civil society," and used it vaguely to refer to nongovernmental groups or institutions. Thus, a collection of speeches by an American secretary of state, dealing with variegated subjects such as freedom of the press, human rights, the recovery of Holocaust-era assets, democracy, refugees, and freedom of religion bears the title *Strengthening Civil Society and the Rule of Law*.

The Inter-American Development Bank points at more specific entities, and defines civil society as a "set of citizens' activities, either individual or associative, in the economic, social and political fields" (BID n.d.:7). This definition includes both private and public activities, and within the latter both informal and associational ones. This document classifies "civil society organizations" (CSO) as follows: civic participation and social interest promotion CSO, CSO that render social services, CSO that promote enterprises ". . . established under a social criterion of integration and solidarity . . .," and CSO engaged in developmental philantrophy (BID n.d.:18).

The International Monetary Fund, in a discussion paper about its relations with civil society, applies the term to international, development-oriented organizations based in the north and community and advocacy groups representing or favoring the poor and the underprivileged in the south (e.g., Oxfam, Friends of the Earth, Forum of African Voluntary Development Organizations, etc.) (Dawson and Bhatt 2001:6). An Oxfam publication on the subject defines its subject by arguing that civil society groups coalesce not on the basis of primordial attachments, such as ethnicity, language, or religion, but rather on "small issues" that cut across boundaries and bring people together in new coalitions, and cite credit schemes or health clubs as examples (Oxfams 2000:128).

The Johns Hopkins comparative nonprofit sector project is a good example of this approach. It claims that civil society is a ". . . major social force . . . throughout the world . . . (that is comprised of) thousands of private community groups, health clinics, schools, day care centers, environmental organizations, social clubs, development organizations, cultural institutions, professional associations, consumer groups, and similar entities . . ." (Salaman et al. 1999:xviii).

The term is used with greater specificity in academic discourse, in general connoting the realm of society that lies outside the state, but it still lacks conceptual rigor, and its operationalization is usually not very definite. Adam Seligman (1992:3, 5) calls civil society all that that lies within the public sphere and outside the state. Victor Perez Diaz (1993:3, 57) includes markets, voluntary associations, and the public sphere, as long as they are outside the control of the state. Jean Cohen and Andrew Arato subsume the private realm within civil society. They define the term as "a sphere of social interaction between economy and state, composed above all of the intimate sphere (especially the family), the sphere of associations (especially voluntary associations), social movements, and forms of public communication" (Cohen and Arato 1992:ix).

Robert D. Putnam focuses on civil and political associations. He argues that a civic community, the basis of democracy, is characterized by the values of participation, political equality, solidarity, trust, and tolerance, which are embodied, following Tocqueville, in civic and political organizations. "A dense network of secondary associations both embodies and contributes to effective social collaboration" (Putnam 1993:90).[2] Larry Diamond, finally, gives the term a definition closer to its Tocquevillean meaning, as we will see: "(T)he realm of social life that is open, voluntary, self-generating, at least partially self-supporting, autonomous from the state, and bound by a legal order or set of shared rules . . ." (Diamond 1999:221), excluding individual and family life, economic society (business firms) and political society (parties).

Beyond definitional differences (Seligman and Diamond focus on the public sphere and autonomy from the state, Perez Diaz and Cohen and Arato include markets or family life, Putnam does not distinguish between civil and political associations), it is imperative to specify systematically what constitutes a strong civil society, or what makes a society civil. This is essential for the testing of propositions linking civil society with democracy.

The reason is clear. The proposition that the mere presence of a civil society, or even of a vibrant one is a necessary or even sufficient cause of the generation or the maintenance of democracy makes little sense. Highly mobilized and organized societies could be very highly polarized, and thus inhospitable to democratic institutions. Weimar Germany, the Spanish II Republic, or Argentina and Chile in the 1970s are cases in point. Larry Diamond (1999:218–260) and Michael W. Foley and Bob Edwards (1996) have argued that a flourishing civil society could mobilize citizens to either strengthen or undermine democracy, and Sheri Berman (1997) has documented the nefarious role of Weimar's vigorous civil society.

What these arguments miss is that the independent variable, in the Tocquevillean and Gellnerian tradition is, as we will see later in this chapter, not just a civil society but also a strong one, and "strong" does not mean that only major and highly mobilized social organizations exist. Moreover, of course, the proposition would be that a strong civil society is a necessary but not sufficient condition of democracy: how could a major institutional complex have a single cause that is valid everywhere? Affirming the civil society hypothesis does not preclude the causal efficacy of the economic, political, and cultural determinants discussed since classical times, even though the hypothesis implies that these other determinants, from Seymour Martin Lipset's (1981:27–30) level of economic development to Putnam's (1993) civic political culture, are mediated by civil society.

The Tocquevillean-Gellnerian Position

As is well known, Tocqueville argued that the central political process of the contemporary world is the spread of equality of condition, or the democratization of society, by which he basically meant the abolition of ascriptive privilege. When he argued that the process of democratization is irresistible and necessary, he was referring to this sense of the term. He did not expect a democratic polity to be the necessary, or even a likely correlate of democratic society. In fact, his central point was that a democratic society would generate a strong tendency toward despotism. For Tocqueville, the state as an organization is inherently driven toward centralization. Unless societal forces check this tendency, a despotic regime would be the natural outcome.

He contended that equality of condition had two consequences: the disappearance of powers that had, in aristocratic societies, mediated between the state and the citizenry (Tocqueville 1995), and the citizens' growing willingness to surrender to the state. His argument in this regard represents an early use of an explanation based on mechanisms. Equalization of condition would lead to voluntary submission because of the operation of two mechanisms that facilitate the centralization of power: first, that of modern society that produced growing individualism; and second, the fact that people are more interested in equality than in liberty (Tocqueville, 1969:507–509, 503–506). As a consequence, citizens end up acquiescing to the expansion of state control.

The task of preserving political democracy, then, consists in creating countervailing forces not controlled by the state, which would involve citizens in the public sphere and block centralization of power. He was interested in studying the American polity because, from the standpoint of his theory, it appeared as a deviant case, a democratic society whose polity had remained democratic. As is well known, he concluded that this was due to a combination of peculiar factors: mores, institutions, and physical circumstances, in descending order of causal efficacy (Tocqueville 1969:305). However, in the end his general argument (i.e., what is generalizable from the American case) turned out to be more institutional than cultural. He focused on variables such as the existence of a strong web of independent voluntary associations, the separation of church and state, the existence of administrative decentralization, and strong local government, the jury system, an independent press, etcetera.

His well-known conclusion was, of course, "Tocqueville's Law": "Among laws controlling human societies, there is one more precise and clearer . . . than all others. If men are to remain civilized or become civilized, the art of association must develop and improve among them at the same speed as equality of condition spreads" (Tocqueville 1969:517).

Gellner's analysis represents, in my view, the most encompassing and systematic application of the Tocquevillean concept to contemporary societies. As John Hall (1995:15) has pointed out, his focus was on understanding civil society as the self-organization of strong and autonomous voluntary groups that balance the state. Civil society is autonomous in the sense that its constituent units are self-governed, but it is still linked to the state, and it operates within its institutional channels. Gellner (1994:5) defined civil society as "that set of diverse non-governmental institutions which is strong enough to counterbalance the state and, while not preventing the state from fulfilling its role of keeper of the peace and arbitrator between major interests, can nevertheless prevent it from dominating and atomizing the rest of society."

As Tocqueville before him, Gellner has argued that a strong civil society is inherently connected with democracy, to the extent that the two are different labels for the same type of society (and part of a broader institutional package involving the decentralization of economics and culture). "Without these institutional pre-conditions, 'democracy' has little clear meaning or feasibility" (Gellner 1994:189). However, separating analytically the system of voluntary associations from political and governmental institutions allows us to return to Tocqueville's original question, and look into the relationship between civil society and democracy. If we make the distinction, Gellner's response in this regard would be consistent with Tocqueville's: a strong civil society is a necessary foundation for democracy.

Operationalizing a Strong Civil Society

I will now attempt to operationalize the term, in the sense most consistent with Tocqueville and Gellner's arguments, for the purpose of examining the relationship between the characteristics of civil society and the existence and quality of democracy. Civil society is a slice of society, whose core is the web of voluntary associations that articulate interests and values, and their system of interaction, as long as these units are not under the control of the state. Though it may contain communities and, though eventually civil society as a whole may generate a strong community, it does consists of (relatively independent) associative units. In Weberian terms, civil society may subsume affectual collectivities, or *Gemeinschaften*; but it is constituted by *Gesselschaften*, driven by instrumental or value-based interests. This slice of society, for Tocqueville, is different from political society, and thus from the party system. Of course, this conception of civil society also excludes economic society, and the family and other institutions in the private sphere.

This definition has an important implication. In the tradition inherited from classical theory, *pace* international agencies, and NGOs, civil society includes associations representing both the underprivileged and the privileged, the excluded and the included (and also the excluders), the poor and the rich; in sum, the "good" and some of the "bad" people as well.

We can now address the operationalization of civil society strength. For this purpose, it is useful to consider that there are three analytically distinguishable dimensions—density, autonomy and self-regulation—that constitute civil society.

Density refers to the extent to which all the major interest and value communities existing in the society are organized and mobilized. Elites usually are, so the issue is the extent to which nonelite social forces too are organized and mobilized. Autonomy implies self-rule, rather than absolute independence from the state. Of course, there is no reason to assume that civil society organizations will always have an antigovernmental orientation or will refuse to participate in governmental activities. Self-regulation means that the units of the associational web, in representing the interests and values of their constituencies, function within the institutional channels of the democratic state. They may form coalitions and engage in conflict, but they act within the boundaries of the constitution and the laws.

These dimensions are relative, of course: in the most democratic of societies, some significant interest or value groups are not organized, associational autonomy is formally constrained by the laws and, formally and informally, limited by the government, and self-regulation is always bound by the legal, administrative, and political framework of the society.

Based on these dimensions, we can formulate four ideal types of society:

(i) Density is Low. In this kind of situation, few or no autonomous groups exist, because of either nonmobilization or exclusion/repression. The latter is the simplest mechanism available to the state for reducing or blocking the autonomy of society. Russia in the Tsarist period is an example.

(ii) Autonomy is Low. A situation in which there is a dense web of associations representing interests and values, but the web is heteronomous. State corporatism is a second, and more sophisticated, mechanism for the control of society by the state. If density is high, this is the pattern of relationship between the state and the associations, characteristic of totalitarian and some populist regimes. The Soviet Union is an extreme case, Mexico under the PRI (Institutional Revolutionary Party), a more partial one.

(iii) Self-Regulation is Low. Whenever this happens in a society in which the web is dense and its constituent units are highly autonomous and yet there are intense cleavages, then high polarization ensues. Weimar Germany, Lebanon today, and Argentina or Chile in the 1970s are instances of this situation.

(iv) All the Variables are High. Only when the associational web is dense, autonomous, and has a high capacity for self-regulation, that is, for conflict resolution within the institutional channels of democracy, will the civil society be strong. For this to happen, Tocqueville's "art of association" should be supplemented by the "art of negotiation."

Therefore, what the Tocquevillean-Gellnerian proposition asserts is that the type iv society is a necessary, albeit not sufficient, condition for the generation and maintenance of a high-quality democracy. This latter criterion implies that the dependent variable itself also requires conceptualization. Indeed, it is possible to have a democracy, and a stable one, without a strong civil society. However, it is likely to be what Juan Linz and Alfred Stepan (1996) have called a low-quality democracy, varieties of which are Guillermo O'Donnell's (1994) delegative democracy (a democracy with deficient accountability), Fareed Zakaria's (1997) more extreme illiberal democracy (i.e., a democracy in which the rule of law and civil rights have a low level of institutionalization), and Diamond's[3] (1999) pseudodemocracy (an authoritarian regime with electoral façade). In fact, there are at least three different types of democracy, with ascending levels of quality. These are the basic electoral or Schumpeterian kind; the Dahlian or liberal one (characterized by high levels of inclusiveness and contestation, and strong institutionalization of civil and political rights), and the republican type, which includes, in addition to the institutions of liberal democracy, a highly active and organized citizenry (Schumpeter 1987:250–283; Dahl 1971).

Based on this conceptualization, I will now examine the emerging relationship between state and society in contemporary Latin America.

STATE AND SOCIETY IN CONTEMPORARY LATIN AMERICAN DEMOCRACIES

The Articulation between Society and the State in Latin America

There is a rich tradition of associational life in Latin America. Since the reestablishment of democracy old organizations, such as trade unions, professional associations, entrepreneurial groups, churches, community organizations of all kinds, sports clubs, etcetera, have sustained a vigorous internal life and a very visible public presence. New organizations representing the poor and the excluded, many of them the victims of recent processes of economic liberalization, have come into being in the recent period (e.g., the landless movement in Brazil, the organizations of the unemployed, or *piqueteros*, in Argentina, etc.), and some of them have displayed a high capacity for mobilization. Finally, organizations based on ascriptive identities (gender, sexuality, race, and ethnicity), akin to their counterparts in advanced industrial societies, have mushroomed. However, this intense associational landscape is not indicative of a strong civil society, at least in the sense discussed above. Large segments of the society are not organized, and some of the organized ones are neither very autonomous nor very civic.

Social and economic dualism has been a central, and enduring, characteristic of most Latin American societies.[4] For most of the twentieth century, only Argentina and Uruguay, the region's most developed countries, which had eliminated their peasantries in earlier periods and whose population consisted largely of European immigrants, had avoided this trait. Dualism has intensified in the past two decades, this time in all countries, because of intense economic liberalization and most states' limited capacity to implement effective compensatory policies. Throughout the region, social polarization (and in at least one case, Venezuela, political polarization as well) has increased. Dualism has major implications for civil society, state–society relations in general, and the quality of the new democracies.

The reason is that these changes are taking place in polities whose institutions, in most cases, differ substantially from those advocated by the classical liberal model and from the norms and practices that prevail in the established democracies of Western Europe and North America. These differences appear in three layers: the preservation of authoritarian residuals, the weakness of the rule of law, and the articulation between state and society. I will focus on the third.

The first layer consists of the preservation of authoritarian residuals (e.g., Chile, where the Senate has been packed with "institutional representatives," mostly of state agencies that were the core of the previous military regime; or Argentina, where presidents routinely circumvent Congress by abusing decree powers). The second is the fact that the rule of law has a low level of institutionalization in most of these polities: governments make an instrumental use of constitutions and laws, the judiciary is ineffective, dependent, or even venal, and substantial corruption exists.

Finally, there is the third layer. Clientelism has been pervasive in Latin America, state corporatism was an important feature of the institutional structure of some of its larger societies (Brazil, Mexico, Argentina) during the period of intense urbanization and industrialization that followed World War II, and almost all the countries in the region have experienced protracted authoritarian regimes, some of them quite coercive. These three institutional frameworks represent varieties of a state–society relationship in which government is the principal and citizens the agent: the exact reverse of the relationship presupposed by the ideal model of liberal democracy. An interesting peculiarity of Latin American states is that, while in most cases being weak vis-à-vis their elites and major powers, they have nevertheless developed these relationships of vertical control with their societies.

State corporatism became unviable once the newly urbanized and industrialized societies outgrew its straightjacket. Authoritarian regimes succumbed to legitimacy vacuums, the mobilization of their societies, effects of international demonstration, and the withdrawal of major powers' support. However, clientelistic tendencies persist, and mark the new democracies as fundamentally different phenomena from their counterparts in advanced industrial societies. As we will see, dualism and clientelism are inherently related and persistent, to the extent that they could be considered the "deep structure" of Latin American societies. The overall effect is partial democracy, or what I will call the bifurcated state.

I hasten to point out that "old" or established democracies have also been characterized by considerable dualism and some clientelism in the past (and some residues are still around), but the difference between them and the new Latin American democracies is substantial enough to produce a different relationship between state and society as a whole.

Dualism, Economic Liberalization, and the Bifurcated State

My argument can be summarized in three propositions: First, that economic liberalization intensifies traditional dualism, and has a contradictory effect on civil society. Second, that a dualized society generates affinity with what I call a bifacial state, one that engages the two emerging poles of society based on different sets of rules. Third, that the dynamics of democracy tend to reinforce dualism. The evidence is as follows.

Economic Liberalization Intensifies Traditional Dualism, and Has a Contradictory Effect on Civil Society

The liberalization of previously semiclosed economies (privatization, deregulation, and the opening-up of the economy) is governed by the logic of differentiation.[5] The first effect of economic liberalization is the increase in both vertical and horizontal differentiation. Polarization between the affluent and the deprived widens, but there are "winners" and "losers" within most social classes, sectors of the economy, and regions, be they rich or poor. As some industries expand, either because they are internationally competitive or because they serve an expanding local demand, the fortunes of the social classes connected with them and the regions where they are located improve. Conversely, as industries shrink because of their inability to withstand foreign competition or because they serve markets hurt by economic liberalization, their owners and workers suffer, and so do the areas in which they operate.

The experience of advanced countries indicates that the very dynamics of capitalism (and, in some cases, policy) reduce the overall level of differentiation in a second stage (even though the development of capitalism keeps producing differentiation, both at the micro and the macro levels). However, this happens when effective market institutions and states are in place, something that does not exist in most Latin American countries. Thus, one can break the eggs and in the end fail to make the omelet. This may be the outcome of economic liberalization in some parts of the region. In medium and large Latin American countries in the 1990s, the period of large-scale liberalization, income inequality, measured by Gini indices, has been substantially reduced only in Chile and stabilized in Mexico. It has grown in most other countries, spectacularly in Argentina (World Bank 2004:8). Whether and when this second stage will occur in Latin America is still an open question.

The consequences of this economic transformation on civil society have been contradictory. On the one hand, the strengthening of market mechanisms has produced the social dislocation discussed above; on the other, it has reduced the state's control of its society, and solidified autonomous associations in some areas of society within the class segments and regions that can be considered "winners" in the process of economic differentiation. As I noted above, these "winners" are located in all social classes: if the Brazilian automobile industry is internationally competitive, the companies producing cars benefit, and so do the unions, the firms related to this industry via forward and backward linkages, and the regions in which the plants are located. The ensuing social environment has been conducive to the generation and strengthening of associations within these groups and the establishment of "civic" relations among different interest constituencies and between them and the government. An open market economy contributes to the emergence and consolidation of a bargaining culture among interest groups. This facilitates the spread of mechanisms for the management of social conflict that do not involve the state as a decision maker (a situation compatible, of course, with a governmental role as a regulator or last-instance adjudicator). This is the institutional environment in which societal self-regulation is likely to grow. Also among the "winners," relations with the government have tended to be the ones characteristic of democracy: demand making, offering of contingent support, etcetera. Overall, these are the traits of what we have called above a strong civil society.

The other side of the picture is the weakening of civil society among the "losers." If the Argentine textile industry is not competitive, its firms disappear, its workers become unemployed, and the areas housing the mills turn into rust belts. The logic of differentiation has intensified preexisting economic and regional cleavages, and the outcome is the polarization of society into a "civic" pole, characterized by strong associations and capacity for self-regulation, and a "disorganized" or marginalized pole, with a low level of autonomous group organization, and a low capacity for sustained, organized, independent mobilization.

A gulf in this regard exists in all democracies, to the extent that Ralf Dahrendorf (1988) has argued that the cleavage between the "organized" and the "disorganized" sectors is becoming the central one in advanced capitalist countries. However, the level of deprivation and inequality in the United States or Western Europe is incomparable with that of Latin America: World Bank income distribution tables for the former contain empty cells in the column "Population under $2 a day," but for the latter the proportions were 43 percent in Brazil and 40 percent in Mexico at the turn of this century (World Bank 1999:196–197). The ratio of income received by the tenth to the first deciles of the population was, at that time, seventeen in the United States and fourteen in Italy, versus fifty-four in Brazil and forty-five in Mexico (World Bank 2004:2).

The extent to which cleavages are cumulative is especially important for political institutions. Where the spatial organization of the economy into cores and peripheries produces a territorial concentration of civic and disorganized fragments, more or less like it is in the Italy described by Putnam (1993), and real or imagined cultural differences between the areas in question exist, there is a potential for serious state crises. Such a situation could lead to the development of centrifugal forces in "rich" regions, or the breakdown of state control in the poor ones.

Thus, the effect of this fragmented society on democratic institutions is complex. There is no automatic link between a rich associational life and a high-quality democracy. The civic pole generates an involved citizenry that, in the process of advancing or protecting its interests and values, cooperates with or opposes the government and, at the same time, limits or balances it. However, the mere existence of a large disorganized pole invites governments and parties to relate to it through one of the several nondemocratic linkages institutionalized in Latin America's recent historical trajectory.

A Dualized Society Generates Affinity with a Bifacial State

A setting of this type generates a propensity for a bifurcated state. This is due to two facts: the forms of political action to which the two poles of society are prone, and politicians' incentives.

First, it should be obvious that the two poles generate very different kinds of social input into politics. The civic pole produces citizens and citizen groups; that is, forms of political action characterized by the making of demands and the offer of supports, in which individuals and the associations they form view themselves as principals and the politicians as agents. The disorganized pole, on the other hand, is more likely to generate apathy, perhaps punctuated by short-lived mobilization, or the dependent participation characteristic of clientelistic or corporatist arrangements. People living below the poverty line, who are either unemployed or employed informally or intermittently, and who in some cases live in environments characterized by social disorganization, lack the resources for or the inclination to the sustained exercise of citizenship. Moreover, their deprivation renders them the ideal candidates for clientelistic or corporatist co-optation. Instances of independent mobilization are likely to be short-lived, often noninstitutional and, in some cases, violent. Since redemocratization started, instances of urban or rural disorder have occurred in several Latin American countries (Argentina, Bolivia, Ecuador).

Politicians' incentives together, especially in a democratic setting, form the other factor. Politicians and governments respond to demands, and marginal sectors and regions are unlikely to sustain high rates of social and political participation, and manage resources convertible into political influence. Political parties and government agencies will be more likely to interact with and engage with the civic segment, and to deal with it based on the rules of citizenship. Therefore, democracy may become the game the winners play, or at least a game whose most permanent players are the organizations and groups within the civic pole.

Parties and governments may build constituencies within marginalized groups and regions, of course, and these constituencies may jump to the center of the political stage in some situations (especially when they display noninstitutionalized forms of behavior). However, the relationship between them and government and parties are likely to be clientelistic or state-corporatist, and thus not conducive to the strengthening of civil society. Finally, if sectors of the marginal pole resort to violent forms of collective action, coercion may become the standard state response. Hence the bifacial state: liberal democratic vis-à-vis the civic pole, and clientelistic, corporatist or coercive vis-à-vis the disorganized one.

The Dynamics of Democracy Tends to Reinforce Dualism

It could be expected that democratic institutions, whose dynamics depends on citizens' preferences, will generate, unlike the authoritarian regimes that preceded them, incentives among politicians to focus their agendas on the reduction of the gulf between the two poles of society. The fact that, in many of these societies, almost half the electorate lives under the poverty line should be the focus of democratic politicians' minds.

It is not so obvious that this will be the case. In societies whose economic performance is not impressive and whose governments' ability to extract revenue is limited, shifting resources to the poor and the excluded would imply withdrawing them from other groups, elite or nonelite, but still part of the civic pole. This does not mean, of course, that redistributive policies are impossible in the absence of sustained economic growth, but they are unlikely. Governments undertaking this road in times of fiscal stringency so common in Latin America would collide with segments most able to deploy political resources in all but the lowest social strata.

In fact, the norm seems to be that for democratic governments, even those on the Left, law and order and macroeconomic stability; that is, the "winner's" agenda, seem to loom larger than redistributive policies, which are consigned to the realm of political rhetoric and token social programs, or some effective but narrowly targeted ones. Even in the face of massive poverty and dislocation, attempts to reduce subsidies and dysfunctional entitlements to the non-poor have been sparse and limited. This in societies where, in many cases, the affluent profit from credits, specifically targeted tax benefits, and toleration for large-scale tax evasion; and the middle classes also enjoy the latter, plus generous pensions for high government officials and free higher education. Likewise, the privileged segment of the working class, those who participate in the formal economy, is assisted with public-sector featherbedding and rigid labor markets.

As we can see, the relationship between civil society and democracy is very complex in Latin America. What are the prospects for these partial democracies? The desirable outcome, the emphasis on policies designed to reduce inequality, and its consequence, the strengthening of civil society and the expansion of citizenship, presupposes a strong state. This road is easier for countries with effective economic institutions or those locked into expanding trade areas, such as Chile or Mexico. However, the very establishment and maintenance of these institutions implies a high level of state capacity: in order to have a sustained high-level performance, an open market economy requires a state capable of delivering rule of law, manageable levels of corruption, effective regulation of markets, adequate levels of revenue, etcetera. This presupposes a government relatively insulated from distributional coalitions, and a Weberian state apparatus (albeit a modest one). These are in short supply in Latin America.

The alternative is not the centralization scenario predicted by Tocqueville for situations in which societal barriers fail to prevent state expansion, since both civil society and the state are weak in most of Latin America. Rather, the alternative is the further decay of democracy and its transformation into a mere façade. This would happen if this Janus-like state articulated by the large civic and marginal political cultures that exist at the two poles of the society is institutionalized. This would amount to a return to the past: the renaissance, under a new guise, of the "liberal" limited democracy regimes that existed in much of the region before industrialization.

NOTES

1. See especially vol. 1, parts I and II.
2. See also pages 86 to 91.
3. See chapters 1 to 3.
4. For a survey of inequality in Latin America, see World Bank (2004).
5. For a discussion of this process, see Carlos H. Waisman (1998), and Arend Lijphart and Carlos H. Waisman (eds.) (1997:235–237).

BIBLIOGRAPHY

Albright, M. K. (2000) Excerpts of Testimony, Speeches, and Remarks on Strengthening Civil society and the Rule of Law, Public Information Series, United States Department of State, Bureau of Public Affairs, Document # S 1.2: F68/Civil.

Banco Interamericano de Desarrollo (n.d.) Modernización del Estado y Fortalecimiento de la Sociedad Civil, Washington, DC: Banco Interamericano de Desarrollo.

Berman, S. (1997) "Civil Society and the Collapse of the Weimar Republic," *World Politics* 49, 3:401–429.

Cohen, J. L., and A. Arato (1992) *Civil Society and Political Theory*, Cambridge: MIT Press.

Dahl, R. A. (1971) *Polyarchy*, New Haven: Yale University Press.

Dahrendorf, R. (1988) *The Modern Social Conflict: An Essay on the Politics of Liberty*, Berkeley: University of California Press.

Dawson, T. C., and G. Bhatt (2001) "The IMF and Civil Society Organizations: Striking a Balance," Washington, DC: International Monetary Fund.

Diamond, L. (1999) *Developing Democracy: Toward Consolidation*, Baltimore: Johns Hopkins University Press.

Foley, M. W., and B. Edwards (1996) "The Paradox of Civil Society," *Journal of Democracy* 7, 3:38–52.

Gellner, E. (1994) *Conditions of Liberty*, London: Hamish Hamilton.

Hall, J. A. (ed.) (1995) *Civil Society: Theory, History, Comparison*, Cambridge: Polity Press.

Lijphart, A., and C. H. Waisman (eds.) (1997) *Institutional Design in New Democracies*, Boulder: Westview Press.

Linz, J., and A. Stepan (1996) *Problems of Democratic Transition and Consolidation*, Baltimore: Johns Hopkins University Press.

Lipset, S. M. (1981) *Political Man*, Baltimore: Johns Hopkins University Press.

O'Donnell, G. (1994) "Delegative Democracy," *Journal of Democracy* 5:55–69.

Oxfam (2000) *Development, NGOs and Civil Society: Selected Essays from Development in Practice*, Oxford: Oxfam.

Perez Diaz, V. (1993) *The Return of Civil Society*, Cambridge: Harvard University Press.

Putnam, R. D. (1993) *Making Democracy Work*, Princeton: Princeton University Press.

Salamon, L. et al. (1999) *Global Civil Society: Dimensions of the Non-Profit Sector*, Baltimore: Johns Hopkins Center for Civil Society Studies.

Schumpeter, J. A. (1987) *Capitalism, Socialism, and Democracy*, London: Allen & Unwin.

Seligman, A. (1992) *The Idea of Civil Society*, New York: Free Press.

Tocqueville, A. de (1969) *Democracy in America*, New York: Anchor Books.

———. (1955) *The Old Regime and the French Revolution*, New York: Doubleday.

Waisman, C. H. (1998) "Civil Society, State Capacity, and the Conflicting Logics of Economic and Political Change," Philip Oxhorn and Pamela Starr (eds.), *Market or Democracy?*, Boulder: Lynne Rienner.

World Bank (1999) *World Development Report 1998/99*, New York: Oxford University Press.

———. (2004) *Inequality in Latin America: Breaking with History?*, Washington, DC: World Bank.

Zakaria, F. (1997) "The Rise of Illiberal Democracy," *Foreign Affairs* 76, 6:22–43.

Chapter 3

Civil Society in Latin America in the Twenty-First Century: Between Democratic Deepening, Social Fragmentation, and State Crisis

Leonardo Avritzer

Civil society is a concept that was bound to the West until the beginning of the third wave of democratization (Cohen and Arato 1992; Keane 1988). The concept of civil society emerged in the nineteenth century, around 1820 (Riedel 1984:132), as a dualist concept capable of expressing two changes brought about by Western modernity: the differentiation between the family and the economic sphere caused by the abolition of bondage and the differentiation between state and society. In this context, social differentiation meant that ". . . the state is not the state if it always merges with civil society and that the latter is not society when it is political society or the state" (Riedel 1984:133). In its first formulation civil society is a dualist concept which expresses the beginning of a process of state and society differentiation in the West. It has also found at least two other formulations in the nineteenth century: the Scottish enlightenment formulation and the Tocquevellean. In the former, civil society is linked to the development of a market economy and the market is deemed as fulfilling a civilizing mission. Civil society in this version is linked to the pacification of social spaces and the introduction of new habits fostered by a market economy (Ferguson 1995). Last but not least, civil society assumed a collective action dimension with Tocqueville. For him, ". . . the most democratic country in the world now is that in which men have in our time carried to the highest perfection the art of pursuing in common the objects of common desires and have applied this new technique to the greatest number of purposes" (Tocqueville 1969:514).

During the nineteenth century the concept of civil society could not make its way out of the West because the social processes it expressed belonged exclusively to the West. In the case of Latin American societies, their colonization led to a different model. Due to its specific form of colonization, the early-modern differentiation between the household economy and the private sphere did not take place in Latin America until early twentieth century. In the context of nation-building, this resulted in a disproportionately large private sphere and the always open possibility of extending personal relations to the political realm. Franco (1974) shows how in postcolonial Brazil the public activities of free men took place in the private space of the big landowners. Guerra demonstrates a similar phenomenon in Mexico, where the large haciendas "constituted more important centers than the small villages. For those who inhabited their centers as well as for those who inhabited their peripheries . . . they represented the centers for the exercise of worship, festivals, etc . . ." (Guerra 1988:134). Thus, the kind of society built in Latin America during its 300 years of colonization was a society with a strong private space that personalized formal relations, establishing some sort of hierarchy between all free members of society. In this social structure there was no space for civil society for two reasons: first because an holistic and hierarchical society, like the one which existed in Peru or Mexico (Fisher 1966), could not have led to a society of equals; second because the fusion between the private and the state could not have led to any process of differentiation. Thus, the idea and the concept of civil society remained alien to the Latin American political and social scenes until the twentieth century.

The concept of civil society reemerged in the late twentieth-century political and social scene that was in two strong ways different from its nineteenth-century meaning: it involved a tripartite meaning according to which civil society is differentiated from both the market and the state and as a concept which sought to explain social processes taking place in the West, the East, and Latin American societies (Cohen and Arato 1992; Habermas 1995; Keane 1998). The tripartite meaning of the concept of civil society is linked to the late twentieth-century differentiation between market and society. It has received different formulations in the literature. Cohen and Arato in their seminal work on civil society differentiated it from ". . . the steering mechanisms that coordinate action in the economy (money) or in formally organized bureaucratically structured organizations (power)." They traced civil society to "the institutional level of a lifeworld socially integrated and hermeneutically accessible" (Cohen and Arato 1992:429). This is one of the roots of a tripartite model of civil society that may also be traced to other traditions of social thought, among them the differentiation between civil society, political society, and the state in Gramsci (Bobbio 1988; Oxhorn 1995) or to a neo-Tocquevillean or neo-Durkheimian tradition (Shils 1997; Roniger 1994; Waisman in this volume), a tradition that links civil society with the transition from corporatist to horizontal forms of social interaction. According to this perspective ". . . the core of civil society is the web of voluntary associations of all kinds which stands between the economy and the family/community structure, on the one hand, and the state, on the other. The relationship between civil society and the state is best understood on the basis of two dimensions: autonomy and capacity for self-regulation" (Waisman in this volume). In all three cases, civil society acquired the meaning of a concept whose revival went beyond nineteenth-century dualist models of state and society differentiation.

Civil society emerged in Latin America as a concept linked to its new tripartite form. Civil society expressed the new tripartite conceptualization in its own particular way: it linked the emergence of the concept to the process of reconstitution of social ties by the Latin American poor (Alvarez, Dagnino and Escobar 1998; Avritzer 1998; Oxhorn 1995) and middle class sectors (Aguayo 1996; Cheresky in this volume; Olvera 1997; Peruzzotti 2002; Stepan 1988; Weffort 1989) in a situation in which social actors were under the pressure of an authoritarian regime. Civil society was also employed to establish a watershed between the actions of an authoritarian regime and its political opposition (Weffort 1989). In this latter dimension, civil society involved human rights groups (Jelin 1996), electoral monitoring (Aguayo 1996), and all the activities related to the restoration of civil and political spaces. Both dimensions of civil society involve its understanding as a concept capable of demarcating the newly emerging social and political actors from both the market, understood as the private economic interests associated with the authoritarian regime, and the authoritarian state.

Yet, two major caveats remained in the use of the concept of civil society as democratization took place in Latin America: the first one was that different forms of connection between civil society and the state emerged in Brazil, Chile, and Mexico and there were no conceptual tools to understand these new emerging situations. Some authors argued in the direction of a new corporatism whereas others stressed the neopluralist dimension (Avritzer 1998). In all cases there was a need for theorizing the new democratic practices in which Latin American civil societies became involved. In second place, the cases were not equal and no clear attempt at differentiation among them emerged. At least three different models of state and civil society emerged: the first one grounded on the Southern Cone countries in which the previous presence of an organized civil society and the complete outlawing of political society constituted the major explanatory device (Oxhorn 1995); the second case, involving Brazil and also perhaps Mexico, in which civil society was understood as a reaction to a process of economic modernization against social actors and in which civil society actors expressed demands for a more radical form of citizenship and democracy (Dagnino 1994; Avritzer 1994, 1998; Alvarez, Escobar and Dagnino 1998; Olvera 2002; Dagnino 2002). Last, but not least, was the Andean case in which countries such as Colombia never experienced a breakdown of democracy and in which civil society expressed a form of social organization related to the satisfaction of very basic needs that resulted from the process of state disintegration (Colombia) or extreme state weakness (Peru) (Panficci 2002). Thus, although the tripartite model explains most of the characteristics of the different cases, there is still no common ground to explain what civil society is in Latin America, and, more importantly, what role it might play in the process of deepening democratic practices in the new democracies.

This article has two parts: in the first, I will examine the different cases of emergence of civil society throughout Latin America in the 1970s and 1980s. The main variables employed to differentiate the cases will be: type of authoritarian regime; relationship between authoritarianism and economic liberalization; previous political tradition, and level of renewal of social actors. The different combinations of these characteristics led to the emergence of four cases, namely, the Brazilian, the Southern Cone (Argentina and Chile), the Mexican, and the Andean.

In the second part of the article, I will show that there are at least three models of civil society in contemporary Latin America. I call the first, which involves Argentina and Chile, the liberal democratic model of civil society. In this model, civil society reorganizes itself after authoritarianism in order to make the political system more accountable. Liberal democratic civil societies do not seek to redefine the boundaries between themselves, the political system, and the state. The second model of civil society in Latin America is the Andean model. The main characteristic is that civil society acts with a non-pacified political space in which the state suffers a severe systemic crisis. I call these cases, the preliberal cases. Finally, there is a third case, which involves Brazil, and also perhaps Mexico. These are cases in which civil society organizations broaden the design of local institutions in order to incorporate more participation. I call it the civic-participatory case.

CIVIL SOCIETY IN LATIN AMERICA: EXPLAINING THE EMERGENCE OF THE CONCEPT

The emergence of civil society in Latin America was a consequence of several processes: the antisocietal form that authoritarianism in the Southern Cone (Argentina, Chile, and Brazil) assumed; the technocratic characteristics of the process of economic modernization in most Latin American countries (Brazil and Mexico); the opposition of liberal and middle-class sectors to the lack of rules and accountability in the political process (Mexico) and the impact of the process of economic liberalization on social ties. The latter feature, though present in all cases, expressed itself at very different moments. In Chile and Argentina, authoritarianism led to economic crisis and sharp liberalization that had an impact on the need for self-help among the poor (Oxhorn 1995; Auyero 2001). In Brazil and Peru, liberalization was part of the economic strategy of democratically elected presidents, Fujimori and Cardoso, and was only introduced during the 1990s. Thus, although these features are common to most cases, their combination is not. The specific characteristics assumed by these features in each case vary a lot. In this part of the article, I would like to differentiate four models of formation of civil society in Latin America: the Brazilian model, the Southern cone model (Argentina and Chile), the Mexican, and the Andean cases.

In the countries of the Southern Cone of Latin America, civil society emerged during the authoritarian period. Stepan (1988) was the first one to characterize the process. For him, civil society is the arena in which ". . . manifold social movements (such as neighborhood associations, women's groups, religious groupings, and intellectual currents) and civic organizations of all classes (such as lawyers, journalists, trade-unions and entrepreneurs) attempt to constitute themselves in an ensemble of arrangements so that they can express themselves and advance their interests" (Stepan 1988:3–4). Stepan also links civil society to a specific moment of the liberalization process of authoritarian regimes. For him, "liberalization refers fundamentally to civil society" whereas democratization refers fundamentally to political society. This position was later assumed by Diamond (1994) and Linz and Stepan (1996). For them ". . . at best, civil society can destroy a non-democratic regime. However, a full democratic transition and, specially, democratic consolidation must involve political society" (Linz and Stepan 1996:8). Linz and Stepan's remarks, which are correct at a more general level, do not solve the problem of an emerging conflict between civil and political society caused by different traditions and forms of articulation between civil society and the state.

The different models of emergence of civil society in Latin America need to be distinguished according to their moment of constitution, the degree of authoritarian influence that existed in the postdemocratization period, and the type of legal traditions that existed in each country before authoritarianism. In each one of the cases, the combination of these elements is different. Civil society in Brazil was an institution of the process of liberalization. Before that, it only existed in a fragmentary and semidemocratic form. The emergence of civil society in Brazil involved the following characteristics: first of all, the entrance of new social actors on the political scene and the change in the relation between middle-class actors and the authoritarian state (Sader 1988; Alvarez 1990). This was the moment in which a change in the pattern of association, particularly at the urban level, took place. Neighborhood associations in Brazil blossomed in the early 1980s (Boschi 1987; Avritzer 2000): in this period, lawyers, doctors, and economists broke their long-term association with the authoritarian regime (Avritzer 1998). A new discourse on rights also emerged linked to the attempt to extend the scope of citizenship within democratic politics (Dagnino 1994). Thus, the Brazilian case offers a first path for the conceptualization of civil society. It must be characterized by three elements:

1. a weak legal tradition and an authoritarian regime that was able to use semilegal devices to control society entered into crisis. "More than an economic miracle, the years of terror produced a real political miracle by undermining traditional ideas on the relations between state and society" (Weffort 1989:345).

2. An authoritarian regime that took the initiative of liberalizing, lost control. The emergence of civil society associations and forms of occupation of the public sphere radicalized the process of transition and brought up the issue of an autonomous agenda sponsored by civil society actors.
3. A conservative leadership within political society that defended an elitist political conception and alienated important sectors of civil society showed it was unable to act as a social mediator. Since the process of civil society emergence has led to social renewal and, given the inability of the major political parties in Brazil during the 1980s (PMDB and PFL) to act as social mediators, Brazilian civil society kept a large degree of autonomy after the completion of the process of transition and became an active player in the new Brazilian democracy.

Oxhorn (1995) characterized the emergence of civil society in Chile with a theory different from the one advanced by Stepan and Linz. For him, it is the repression carried out by authoritarian regimes, a repression that targets political society, which explains the emergence of civil society in the Southern Cone. "Rather than eliminating self-organized and autonomously defined political space, repression can have the effect of shifting the locus of political activity to non-party arenas by effectively proscribing traditional political party activity" (Oxhorn 1995:7). This characteristic of the process of emergence of civil society is also valid for the Argentinean case. In both cases, unlike that of Brazil and Mexico, authoritarianism effectively outlawed political society and transformed civil society into the only available place for political activity. There is a second characteristic that marked the emergence of civil society in Chile: the need for society's self-organization in order to resist the process of economic liberalization. Again, Oxhorn described this feature of the Chilean case very well. For him, "the social costs associated with these neo-conservative policies are typically reflected in a prolonged period of urban unemployment rates characteristic of an economic depression, a substantial fall in real wages, the weakening of organized labor and a regressive redistribution of national income. They may leave the popular sectors with few alternatives to the creation of self-help organizations . . ." (Oxhorn 1995:9). This characteristic is also shared by the Argentinean case in which liberalization policies were also introduced by the authoritarian regime (Smith 1989). And there is still a third important characteristic that explains the reemergence of grassroots activity that played a strong role in Chile, which was a preauthoritarian heritage.

This feature further differentiates cases, such as the Chilean, from the Brazilian. In Chile, there was a well-established tradition of the rule of law and a tradition of political parties acting as social mediators. The outlawing of political society opened a space for civil associations to substitute the social role previously played by political parties, particularly in the poor neighborhoods. Thus, the main characteristics of the emergence of civil society in Chile were: (1) the way authoritarianism targeted political society, (2) the way authoritarianism was associated with economic liberalization, and (3) the existence of a pre-authoritarian democratic tradition that could be recovered. The two former characteristics are shared by Argentina though the third is not: Chile had a much stronger and continuous democratic tradition than Argentina.

There is a third case of emergence of civil society that should be analyzed—the Mexican case. It is different from all the Southern Cone cases, first of all, because of the nature of Mexican authoritarianism, which was not introduced by the military and did not have the component of outlawing political society (Middlebrook 1985:124). In the Mexican case, the emergence of civil society in the early 1980s is linked to three factors: "first, at the systemic level, the turn towards neo-liberalism . . . deepened the processes of differentiation of the state, economy and society . . . Second, for the first time since the revolution of 1917, a consolidated party system and democracy appeared as a potential means for a regime change. Third, several civic-cultural movements spread across the country, creating a civil society centered on the struggle for political rights, democracy and the rule of law" (Olvera 1997:111–112). Thus, in the Mexican case, economic liberalization preceded the crisis of an authoritarian regime making it a case completely different from the Brazilian but sharing, at the economic level, some characteristics with the Chilean and Argentinean cases. However, at the political level, the Mexican case is different from all the Southern Cone cases, mostly because the Mexican authoritarian regime was deeply ingrained at the societal level and had succeeded for a long time in introducing corporatist forms of societal co-optation (Camin 1988). In second place, Mexico experienced lower forms of social repression than Brazil, Argentina, and Chile, which meant that the problem of organizing civil society did not imply coping with grassroot repression but rather with the corporatist regime strategies of co-optation. Finally, civil society in Mexico involved a more classical, almost Tocquevillean dimension: a dispute between the political system and societal actors regarding the organization of the political process (Foweraker and Craig 1990; Aguayo 1995).

Thus, in the Mexican case, the process of formation of civil society had two main characteristics: (1) the dispute with the authoritarian regime regarding the rules of the political game, in particular, the determination of electoral rules, and (2) the dispute with the regime regarding the forms of social organization and state and society mediation.

There is still a fourth case, which is the case of the Andean countries. This case should, first of all, be differentiated from the authoritarian experiences of the Southern Cone and Mexico in terms of the fragility of its state structures. Colombia, together with Venezuela, was the only Latin American country that did not experience an authoritarian breakdown in the 1960s and 1970s; the utilization of the structures of a formally democratic state to repress social movements created a fracture in the process of state-building (Uprimy and Garcia-Villegas 2002). In the case of Peru, which did not share the characteristics of the other Southern Cone experiences, the country passed through a brief authoritarian experience: it involved agrarian reform and a late attempt of import substitution (Kahatt 2002). Yet, after the collapse of the Peruvian authoritarian regime, a process of state disintegration with a strong guerilla movement also took place. The path of civil society formation in the Andean region is different from all other cases: in the case of Colombia it involved the reaction of sections of the population to the authoritarian actions of a democratic state and the attempt to create a pacified political space (Romero 2002; Uribe 2002) and in the case of Peru it involved the deep economic crisis of the Alan Garcia years and the movement of self-help of the displaced population, which flew to the outskirts of Lima during the war against Sendero Luminoso. In both cases, the problem of the systemic crisis of the state is at the root of the process of formation of civil society. Civil society emerged as a reaction to a weak and fractured democratic state that allowed the dissemination of violence in its interior and lacked minimal systemic capacities to perform compensatory social policies.

The main characteristics of the emergence of civil society help differentiate between cases: in Brazil, authoritarianism in its first phase (1964–1974) targeted civic organization more than the political society. On the one hand, authoritarianism in Brazil involved a legal political opposition around the PMDB (Kinzo 1988) but it precluded independent unions or strong civil society organizations (Avritzer 1998). The organization of civil society was considered a challenge to the authoritarian state. In Chile and Argentina, authoritarianism targeted political society more than they targeted civic organizations leaving more space for autonomous social organizations and, thus, it was almost natural that the opposition would concentrate at the civil society level. In Chile, Argentina, and Mexico the emergence of civil society is de facto linked with the introduction of neoliberalism and its disaggregation effect on the societal level. Yet, there are also important differences between the Mexican and the Southern Cone cases: neoliberalism in the Southern Cone involved effective deindustrialization as a response to labor organization whereas neoliberalism in Mexico was a form of integration with the U.S. economy. And finally, the Brazilian authoritarian regime did not make any serious attempt to implement neoliberal economic policies (Maxwell and Schneider 1997), a fact that makes Brazil a different case in this respect. Neoliberal policies in Brazil were associated with democratic regimes and only at that time did they involve the reaction of civil society actors.

It is also possible to see some overlapping phenomena: in all the cases, there is an authoritarian regime involved in the process of formation of civil society, perhaps with the possible exception of Colombia whose democratic state behaves very similarly to the other authoritarian states (Uprimy and Garcia-Villegas 2002). Yet, the way the authoritarian state targeted political society or social actors was strictly linked to the historical processes specific to each country. Thus, in Brazil and Mexico, the possibility of maintaining some form of electoral competition throughout the authoritarian period led to a lower level of repression of political society. In Chile and Argentina the center of authoritarianism was outlawing political society, in particular, the left-wing Peronist groups in Argentina and the communists and the socialists in Chile. There is a second common element between all the cases discussed, that is the emergence of neoliberal economic policies. The reaction to neoliberalism involved, from the very beginning, the organization of civil society in Chile and Mexico. Though the emergence of neoliberalism in Brazil took place much later, it also played a role not in the emergence but in the occupation of alternative spaces by civil society (Dagnino 2002). The last overlapping aspect between all the cases is the role the civic associations played both in the transition process and the reaction to neoliberalism: in Brazil, Chile, and Mexico, civil society involved the entrance of new actors on the political stage (Avritzer 1998; Ramirez 1990; Tarres 1992; Oxhorn 1995) and an increase in associative patterns. Neighborhood associations, environmental groups, human rights groups, and movements for the improvement of health conditions were all formed in Brazil as a reaction to the authoritarian regime's policies (Avritzer 2002). In Mexico, urban social movements, movements for electoral monitoring, and some gender initiatives in Guadalajara were also formed as a reaction to authoritarianism (Olvera 2002). Again there are variations vis-à-vis previous traditions. In Brazil associational life before authoritarianism was low (Avritzer 2000). In Mexico, there was a huge number of associations but these were traditionally linked to the state. In Chile and Argentina there were associations but these were traditionally linked to political parties. In all the cases, there was the move to more autonomous forms of associations, in many cases linked to new actors. Thus, in spite of the differences between the cases there is common ground, the same phenomenon, to speak about and it is possible to point out why the tripartite model was so important: in all the cases, civil society was a reaction to an authoritarian regime and, in most cases, civil society was also a response to a process of further differentiating market and society, brought about by neoliberal social policies. In all the cases, civil society survived the process of democratization and remained autonomous vis-a-vis political society.

Civil Society and Democracy in Latin America

Latin American civil societies were acting in an overwhelmingly democratic setting in the 1990s. The cases of democratization differed in the Latin American context: in Argentina the authoritarian regime collapsed and the new political system had very little continuity with authoritarianism (Linz and Stepan 1996); in Chile the authoritarian regime did not collapse and was capable of designing most of the institutions of the postauthoritarian political scene; Brazil is an intermediate case, with an organized withdrawal of the military to the barracks while their civilian counterparts were able to have a very strong influence on the political scene (Avritzer 1998). Mexico is a case in which the withdrawal of the authoritarian powerholders from the political scene will (or will not) take place depending on the capacity of the PRI to win elections after its July 2000 historic defeat. In most of the cases there has been a continuity between authoritarianism and democratization and, in the Argentinean case, in which there has been no continuity, the military used rebellion to press their agenda upon the new democracy.

Argentina and Chile seem to be more classical cases of return to democracy. Though the two cases of transition to democracy are completely different—in Argentina a transition through the collapse of the authoritarian regime and in Chile through an organized withdrawal—their postdemocratization setting also shares many important aspects. In both cases, there seems to be a return to a classic democratic elitist political design and a return to a system of party mediation between social action and state action. The main activities of civil society are concentrated at the level of social accountability (Peruzzotti 2002). In this model, human rights social movements and NGOs seem to be the main organizers of social action (Saba 2002). The main actions of Argentinean and Chilean civil societies involve challenging the state, the judiciary, and the legislative branches in relation to basic acts of social accountability. In the Argentinean case, civil society organizations focused ". . . on problems such as the inefficiency of the courts for solving citizens' legal problems, corruption in the government as a new form of abuse of power and the need to develop a civic culture as the only way to hold officials accountable and make democratic institutions work . . ." (Saba 2001:30). In the case of Chile, a similar scenario can be traced: one in which the role of political parties as mediators and the identification of democracy with the political system has been higher (Valenzuela 1986). In this situation, civic organizations and NGOs stay on the sidelines of the political order bringing up new issues to be processed by the political system and the state. The postauthoritarian setting is one of weakness of collective and communitarian social ties (Maza 2002:28).

The first case of civil society action in democratized settings in Latin America could be described as a more liberal form of civil society organization. This case has the following characteristics: first, civil society represents a cultural innovation in a liberal order that has been ambiguous in relation to democracy and the rule of law: civil society organizations target the courts and the executive in order to make them more accountable to citizens. Yet, civil society organizations do not seek to redefine the boundaries between civil society, political society, and the state. They do not innovate in terms of the articulation between the state and civil society; in particular, they do not seek the introduction of forms of participatory democracy. They act within a liberal tradition using its main tool: the presentation of their demands in public when political institutions do not perform their traditional role of accountability and responsiveness in these new democracies.

All other cases in Latin America imply some redefinition of the boundaries between civil society, political society, and the state. Peru and the Andean case in general is a case in which civil society acts in order to create a self-help structure to offset the impoverishment caused by neoliberal policies and the process of state disintegration.

It is difficult to establish precisely which of the phenomena causes the other. What could, for sure, be pointed out is that the process of hyperinflation at the end of Alan Garcia's government—the strongest attempt in Latin America to break with IMF-sponsored politics—sharply reduced the state's capacity and, thus, its role as a systemic actor. A parallel and nonformal economy has grown since then, reducing state tax collection capacity. At the same time, between 1980 and 1993 the Peruvian civil war led to 27,000 deaths and the displacement of 570,000 people (Kahatt 2002:10–11). In this situation of conflict between civil and noncivil political actors, the traditional form of political and social mediation vanished. Peruvian civil society is the result of society's need to produce two primary "public goods" usually provided by the state: security (or self-defense) and self-help. Civil society organizations in Peru encompass self-defense committees (more than 5,000 of them existed by 1994) and self-help organizations such as community soup-kitchens, committees for the distribution of milk, and associations of mothers (Sunborn and Cueva 1999).

Colombia does not seem to be a very different case in spite of a previous liberal tradition. Also plagued by civil war, Colombia has seen the rise of incivility and the attempt by civil society to create peace zones (Romero 2002; Uribe 2002). One of the most important civil society movements in Colombia in the last few years was the attempt to create peace communities in the middle of the war region. San Jose Apartado's experience with the Peace Marches in Bogotá in these attempts involved communities, local and international NGOs, and the Catholic Church. The problem in Colombia is the disintegration of traditional forms of mediation, in particular the weakness of traditional political parties, coupled with the inability of civil society initiatives to generate new stable forms of political mediation. Both in the case of Peru and Colombia there are strong forms of collective action that lack effective forms of political mediation. Civil society in this case, is a preliberal institution because its actions do not take place within a fully pacified political space. Civil society in these cases lacks the connection with a tradition of rights and the rule of law that could provide the background for their actions within a pacified political space. I call these cases preliberal.

Brazil seems to be a second case in which there has been an increase in the activities of civil society after democratization. Dagnino explains the increase in the activities of civil society by pointing out some long-term characteristics of the Brazilian party system, namely the fact that ". . . parties in Brazil have historically been inclined in the direction of the state . . . limiting their search for representation in civil society to electoral periods and to mechanisms seen as most effective at these moments: patronage, exchange of favors, personalism, etc." (Dagnino 2002:3). I would add to that the fact that civil society associations in Brazil took advantage of the redesign of the country's constitution and proposed many new forms of political participation for individuals and for associations. Article 14 of the new constitution guaranteed "popular initiative" in the exercise of peoples' sovereignty. Article 29 on the organization of cities required "the cooperation of representative associations in the process of city planning." Article 194 of the Brazilian 1988 constitution on the organization of social security assures ". . . the democratic and decentralized character of the social security administration through the participation of labor representatives, social security employees, retirees and the government in its administration." Article 204 on the organization of social assistance requires ". . . the participation of the population, through its representative institutions in the formulation of policies and in the control of state actions." Article 227 on children's care forecasts that ". . . the state will organize the assistance of children and teenagers and the participation of NGOs will be admitted" (Brazil 1988). In all these cases, the legislation enacted latter, the so-called organic laws on the organization of health (LOS) and social assistance (LOAS) and the Statute on Children and Teenagers Rights incorporated into ordinary law the Constitution's plea for participation. The acknowledgement of the importance of voluntary associations and the attempt to incorporate them into the process of decision making in the cases of city planning and social policies was one of the major gains made by civil society in the Brazilian Constituent process. Some of the most important cases of civic participation in Brazil in the 1990s, such as the policies council, drew on this newly acquired institutional format (Tabagiba 2002). In other important cases, such as participatory budgeting, it was the presence of previously existing practices and a negotiation between civil society—in this case represented by neighborhood associations—and the state that explains the emergence of new participatory policies. Thus, the Brazilian case seems to be a case in which civil society associations took advantage of a tradition of weak forms of political mediation between society and the state and established forms of participation that became political hybrids constituted by both civil society and state actors. These hybrids significantly changed the political landscape of democratic Brazil. The main issue posed by this form of social action is the formation of new public spaces sponsored by civil society participation. These new hybrid spaces helped to create a new democratic culture in Brazil. "The very existence of these spaces confronts . . . the elitist conceptions of democracy as well as technocratic and authoritarian conceptions of the nature of decision-making inside the state" (Dagnino 2002:21). Thus, Brazil can be nominated as a third case that may be called civic-participatory. In this case, civil society articulation with the state leads to enhanced forms of participation and hybrid institutions.

Mexico is a different case from all the ones analyzed above. The formation of civil society in Mexico involved two different phases: a first one, as early as the 1980s, was similar to other Latin American cases and involved the formation of urban social movements in the struggle for the legalization of urban tenure (Ramirez 1990). This phase had mixed results leading, on the one hand, to the emergence of forms of social action independent from the state, and on the other, to the attempt at incorporation of social leaderships by the state. Mexican civil society in the 1990s pursued a different form of social action linked to challenging the process of generalized election fraud that took place in 1988 and to the attempt to constitute a civic movement for monitoring elections. Following the acknowledgment of the importance of fair elections, several civic organizations began to monitor local and state elections. In December 1993, seven NGOs with different origins, backgrounds, memberships, and aims—the Mexican Academy of Human Rights; the National Accord for Democracy; the Council for Democracy; the Convergence of Civil Organizations for Democracy; the Arturo Rosenblueth Foundation; the Higher Institute for Democratic Culture; and the Citizens' Movement for Democracy—started to meet with the aim of promoting free elections. They initiated a project of comprehensive observation which involved taking polls, advocating electoral reform, and inquiring into cases of vote buying and coercion. This movement led eventually to negotiations between civic associations, political parties, and the PRI government on a comprehensive electoral change.

The path of civil society development in Mexico in the 1990s is different from all the above cases due to the role civil society played in the reestablishment of fair rules for political competition. Mexican authoritarianism did not resemble the Southern Cone cases in which the involvement of civil society in political activity was a result of the closing of all spaces in political society. In the Mexican case, the involvement of civil society in political negotiations assumed a different form due to the role played by corporatism and electoral fraud in support of the authoritarian regime. In addition to that, the fact that the authoritarian regime party occupied the center of the political spectrum, flanked both on the right (PAN) and on the left (PRD) by opposition parties made both the Mexican transition and the formation of civil society in the country specific processes. Electoral competition has been possible for so long without leading to regime collapse precisely because of the PRI's centrist position. Civil society in Mexico also assumed a particular shape due to the forms of civil society organization that placed themselves on the right and on the left of the political spectrum. In the case of Guadalajara, conservative groups up to the early 1990s supported the PRI government. Yet, an urban tragedy, the explosion of a sewage pipe due to gas infiltration, led to the conservative groups' perception of a basic dimension of liberal-democratic society: corruption, irresponsibility, and a general lack of accountability (Olvera 2002). As a follow-up to the Guadalajara disaster, a conservative group of active women started organizing themselves and campaigned for the PAN candidate who won the Jalisco governorship. The women's group proposed a new standard of accountability for public officials and was incorporated neither by conservative politicians nor entrepreneurs. It shows a liberal democratic dimension of democratization of a kind similar to that already analyzed in the Argentinean and Chilean cases.

Yet, the formation of civil society in Mexico also shows a second dimension, take the case of the emergence of forms of citizen participation in Mexico City. Mexico City has been the center of forms of social mobilization in the 1980s, particularly, after the conflicts caused by the 1985 earthquake. In the aftermath of the quake, in order to oppose the government plans to remove the poor population to the outskirts of Mexico City, several neighborhood associations were organized and these were able to fight relocation (Ramirez 1990; Avritzer 2002). The tradition of neighborhood associations independent of the state and able to represent different Mexico City constituents was already in place when the negotiations for democratization resulted in the lifting of the PRI veto and the first free election of a D.F. governor. During the electoral campaign, the PRD was able to retrieve the tradition of citizen participation in the process of decision making on the distribution of public goods. Cardenas's victory in the 1997 elections for governor of the D.F. pointed in the direction of overcoming old corporatist arrangements and opening new venues for citizen participation (Olvera 2002). A new law on citizen participation was approved. The 1988 law on citizen participation instituted a horizontal form of representation in Mexico City's 1,270 neighborhoods. A total of 572,000 people participated in the election of 8,410 representatives, who are now members of Mexico City neighborhood committees, introducing a more horizontal form of claiming material goods and negotiating their delivery with local authorities (San Juan Victoria 2001). Thus, what seems to be taking place in Mexico is the creation of a second path of connection between civil and political society, which is a more participatory venue. Mexico represents a case in which two forms of connection between civil and political society are posed on the agenda, a more classical liberal model of participatory accountability and a more participatory model based on the transfer of decision-making prerogatives from the state to civil society associations.

It is possible to see that there is a wide range of models of civil society development. These models are based on a combination of the model of democratic formation existing before the authoritarian period, the model of opposition against authoritarianism, the type of civil society associations that emerged during the authoritarian period and the specific form taken by the shift from a state-oriented to a market-oriented economy.

Models of Civil Society in Latin America in the Twenty-First Century

The above discussion points in the direction of three main models of civil society organization in Latin America: the preliberal model, the liberal-democratic model and the civic-participatory one. I will now develop the main characteristics of each one.

The first model of civil society organization in Latin America is what I call the preliberal model. It is characterized by three elements: the first is a weak state that cannot guarantee, at the national level, the structure of rights that constitute a precondition for the existence of civil society. Civil society in this situation constituted itself without the guarantees that are part of the pacification of the political space. In addition to that, the second element of the uncivil case is that the market economy appears mostly as a form of imposition of privatized social relations without being able to expand a network of social ties. Civil society in this condition seeks to guarantee two dimensions: the dimension of a pacified political space and the dimension of minimal social needs. In both cases, the organization of the political does not seem to be connected with political society, either because political society does not exist (Peru) or because it is so fractured vis-à-vis the political system that it sees civil society as a danger (Colombia). Although I would argue that features of the preliberal model exist today in all Latin American countries (see, for instance the case of land conflicts in Brazil or the *Zapatista* uprising in Mexico), I would also argue that the Andean case is the one that comes closer to it as an ideal type. This is so because of the weak state structures that preceded democratization and the damage that civil war and a fractured political society caused in the region. The many forms of collective action that exist in the region are subordinated to the destructive dynamics of state politics. Yet, it should be clear that the state was not the only actor responsible for political involution. Economic actors also had a hand in this process that has deindustrialization as one of its components. The challenge of the Andean case is to find out whether civil society can produce civility and pacify the political space in spite of the state and the market.

The second model I call a liberal civil society model. The main element of the liberal model is a process of state construction that had been relatively successful at the systemic level before the authoritarian period. In addition to that there are party structures that exercise the mediation between society and the state. These structures acquired the capacity to exercise mediation, structures that at the end of the authoritarian period could be reconstructed. Civil society has a dynamic that is different from political society due to both the way it had been constituted throughout the authoritarian period and its internal dynamics in the democratization period. Civil society in these cases is related to the reconstruction of a rights structure and to forms of collective action aiming to secure accountability and the rule of law. Thus, civil society cannot be reduced to political society, even if the level of collective action in this case is usually low. This model is closer to a liberal model for three motives: because it builds on the structure of rights that are not placed at stake by either civil or political actors, because the actions of civil society in the democratized period do not seem to challenge the available structure of political mediation, and because civil society triggers structures of social action only if the political system fails to fulfill its roles within a liberal order. Thus, civil society plays the role of a structure capable of radicalizing the available forms of control of political society by the citizens, without assuming a deliberative or administrative role. This model, which might apply to many forms of civil society action in Latin America, seems to be closer to the Argentinean and the Chilean cases.

There is still a third model of civil society organization in Latin America that I will call the civic-participatory model. In this model the constitution of civil society also took place within the framework of an already consolidated process of state construction. Yet, civil society challenged a central aspect of the process of mediation between political society and the state by not only introducing alternative practices at the societal level but also by institutionalizing these practices at both the constitutional and the legal levels. The case that most clearly expresses the civic participatory model is the Brazilian case. Today there are in Brazil many forms of participation at the public level that establish effective forms of mediation between citizens and the state. Forms of political participation such as participatory budgeting or the policy councils represented the opening of new venues of mediation at the local level between citizens and the state. They represented a radicalization of the participatory aspect in the new Brazilian democracy. It is still early to point out the direction in which the new Mexican democracy will evolve, but it is possible to suggest two alternatives: the first one points in the direction of the public participatory model present in Brazil and the other in the direction of an evolution towards a more liberal model, such as the one in Argentina and Chile.

Thus, civil society in Latin America at the same time, expresses, similar and different characteristics. The similar characteristics are related to the emergence of forms of collective action that express a shift from a tradition of homogeneous forms of mobilization to a tradition of social differentiation that seems to have taken place in all Latin American countries by the end of the 1970s as a reaction to authoritarianism. The different characteristics are related to the different possibilities of state, market, and society articulation. The three different temporalities of state construction in Latin America seem to have played a role in the models of civil society allowing us to differentiate between cases of consolidated state (Brazil, Mexico, Argentina, and Chile) and cases of unconsolidated states (Peru and Colombia). At the same time, different models of political society construction and different temporalities also seem to play a role in the construction of civil society. In this case, we can differentiate between countries in which political society has been able to establish itself as an effective form of mediation with the state both before and after the authoritarian experience (Argentina, Chile, and perhaps Mexico) and countries in which political society has not been able to become an effective form of mediation (Brazil, Peru, Colombia, and perhaps, Mexico). Last but not least, we should differentiate between countries where, faced with a lack of political mediation, civil society solved the lack of political mediation by providing a civic, public, and participatory response (Brazil, and perhaps Mexico) and countries in which civil society fulfilled the role of a provider for basic social needs (Peru) or an ephemeral form of mobilization (Chile and Argentina).

This typology not only helps us to understand the differentiation between the preliberal, liberal and civic-participatory models of civil society. It also helps us to see the kinds of roles civil society can fulfill in the near future: in the cases of the preliberal civil societies, their role should be to contribute to the pacification of the political process, which should involve the reduction of current levels of violence and the attempt to link civil society construction to the pacification of political disputes and the acknowledgment of rights. In the liberal cases, civil society should seek to broaden the scope of participation filling the voids created by the incompleteness of the forms of political mediation. In the public participatory cases, civil society should seek to extend the practice of participation to other sectors and to become able to reconstruct effective forms of political mediation. In all the cases, there is the risk of falling into the noncivil characteristics that persist in Latin American civil society. Yet, in all the cases, there is also the potential to move to a more civil, liberal, public, and participatory society.

BIBLIOGRAPHY

Aguayo, S. (1995) "A Mexican Milestone," *Journal of Democracy* 6, 2:157–167.

Alvarez, S. E. (1990) *Engendering Democracy in Brazil: Women's Movements in Transition Politics*, Princeton: Princeton University Press.

Alvarez, S. E., E. Dagnino et al. (1998) *Cultures of Politics, Politics of Cultures: Re-visioning Latin American Social Movements*, Boulder: Westview Press.

Auyero, J. (2001) *Poor People's Politics: Peronist Survival Networks and the Legacy of Evit*, Durham: Duke University Press.

Avritzer, L. (1994) *Sociedade Civil e Democratização*, Belo Horizonte: Del Rey.

——. (1998) "The conflict between civil and political societies in post-authoritarian Brazil: An analysis of the impeachment of Collor de Mello," *Corruption and Political Reform in Brazil*, K. Rosenn and R. Downs (eds.), Miami: North South Center, 119–138.

——. (2000) "Democratization and Changes in the Pattern of Association in Brazil," *Journal of Interamerican Studies and World Affairs* 42, 3.

——. (2002) *Democracy and the Public Space in Latin America*, Princeton: Princeton University Press.

Bobbio, N. (1988) *Gramsci and the Concept of Civil Society*, London: Macmillan.

Boschi, R. R. (1987) *A Arte da Associação*, Rio de Janeiro: Vértice.

Camin, A. (1988) *Despues del Milagro*, Mexico: Cal y Arena.

Cohen, J. L., and A. Arato (1992) *Civil Society and Political Theory*, Cambridge: MIT Press.

Dagnino, E. (1994) "Os movimentos sociais e a emergência de uma nova noção de cidadania," *Os nos 90: Política e Sociedade no Brasil*, E. Dagnino (ed.), São Paulo: Brasiliense.

——. (2002) *Sociedad Civil e Espaços Públicos no Brasil*, São Paulo: Paz e Terra.

Diamond, L. (1994) "Toward Democratic Consolidation," *Journal of Democracy* 5, 3:4–17.

Ferguson, A., and F. Oz-Salzberger (1995) *An Essay on the History of Civil Society*, Cambridge, NY: Cambridge University Press.

Fisher, L. E. (1966) *The Last Inca Revolt, 1780–1783*, Norman: University of Oklahoma Press.

Foweraker, J., and A. L. Craig (1990) *Popular Movements and Political Change in Mexico*, Boulder: L. Rienner Publishers.

Guerra, X. F. (1988) *Mexico: Del Antiguo Régimen a la Revolución*. Mexico: Fondo de Cultura.

Habermas, J. (1995) *Between Facts and Norms*, Cambridge: MIT Press.

Jelin, E., and E. Hershberg (1996) *Constructing Democracy: Human Rights, Citizenship and Society in Latin America*, Boulder: Westview Press.

Kahatt, F. (2002) "Sociedad civil y governabilidad democratica en el Peru," *Sociedad Civil y Gobernabilidad Democrática en los Andes y en el Cono Sur*, A. Panfichi (ed.), Mexico: Fondo de Cultura Económica.

Keane, J. (1988) *Democracy and Civil Society: On the Predicaments of European Socialism, the Prospects for Democracy, and the Problem of Controlling Social and Political Power*, London, New York: Verso.

——. (1998) *Civil Society: Old Images, New Visions*, Stanford: Stanford University Press.

Kinzo, M. D. A. G. (1988) *Legal Opposition Politics under Authoritarian Rule in Brazil*, New York: St. Martin's Press.

Linz, J., and A. Stepan (1996) *Problems of Democratic Transition and Consolidation*, Baltimore: John Hopkins University Press.

Maxwell, S., and B. R. Schneider (1997) *Business and State in Developing Countries*, Ithaca: Cornell University Press.

Maza, G. D. L. (2002) "Sociedad civil y democracia en Chile," *Sociedad Civil y Gobernabilidad Democrática en los Andes y en el Cono Sur*, A. Panficci (ed.), Mexico: Fondo de Cultura Económica.

Middlebrook, K. J. (1985) *Political Liberalization in an Authoritarian Regime: The Case of Mexico*, La Jolla: Center for U.S.–Mexican Studies.

Olvera, A. (1997) "Civil Society and Political Transition in Mexico," *Constellations* 4, 1:94–104.

——. (2002) *Sociedad Civil, Espacios Publicos y Democratización en Mexico: Los Contornos de un Proyecto*, Mexico: Fondo de Cultura Económica.

Oxhorn, P. (1995) *Organizing Civil Society: The Popular Sectors and the Struggle for Democracy in Chile*, University Park: Pennsylvania State University Press.

Panfichi, A. (2002) *Sociedad Civil y Gobernabilidad Democrática en los Andes y en el Cono Sur*, Mexico: Fondo de Cultura Económica.

Peruzzotti, E. (2002) "Emergencia, desarrollo y reconstruccion de la sociedad civil Argentina," *Sociedad Civil y Gobernabilidad Democrática en los Andes y en el Cono Sur*, A. Panfici (ed.), Mexico: Fondo de Cultura Económica.

Ramirez, J. M. (1990) "Urban Struggles and their Political Consequences," *Popular Movements and Political Change in Mexico*, J. Foweraker and A. Craig (eds.), Boulder: Lynn Rienner Publishers.

Riedel, M. (1984) *Between Tradition and Revolution*, Cambridge: Cambridge University Press.

Romero, M. (2002) "Sociedad civil, cooperacion y mobilizacion por la paz en Colombia," *Sociedad Civil y Gobernabilidad Democrática en los Andes y en el Cono Sur*, A. Panfichi (ed.), Mexico: Fondo de Cultura Económica.

Roniger, L., and A. Gunes-Ayata (1994) *Democracy, Clientelism, and Civil Society*, Boulder, Colorado: Lynn Rienner Publishers.

Saba, R. (2002) "The Human Rights Movement, Citizen Participation Organizations and the process of building civil society and rule of law in Argentina," *Sociedad Civil y Gobernabilidad Democrática en los Andes y en el Cono Sur*, A. Panfici (ed.), Mexico: Fondo de Cultura Económica.

Sader, E. (1988) *Quando Novos Personagens Entraram em Cena*, São Paulo: Paz e Terra.

Sanborn, C., and H. Cueva (1999) "Entre el Estado y el Mercado: La Importancia del Tercer Sector para el Desarrollo Humano," paper presented at the conference Social Policies for Human Development, organized by UNICEF, PNUD and Universidad del Pacifico, Lima, Peru, November 23.

San Juan Victoria, C. (2001) Ciudad de México, Instituciones y Sociedad Civil: Experiencias de una Ciudad en Transición, Xalapa, Veracruz, Mexico: Universidad Veracruzana.

Shils, E. (1997) *The Virtue of Civility: Selected Essays on Liberalism, Tradition and Civil Society*, Chicago: Liberty Fund.

Smith, W. C. (1989) *Authoritarianism and the Crisis of the Argentine Political Economy*, Stanford: Stanford University Press.

Stepan, A. (1988) *Rethinking Military Politics*, Princeton: Princeton University Press.

Tabagiba, L. (2002) "Os conselhos gestores e a democratização das políticas públicas no Brasil," *Sociedade Civil e Espaços Públicos no Brasil*, E. Dagnino (ed.), São Paulo: Paz e Terra.

Tarres, M. L. (1992) *La Voluntad de Ser*, Mexico: El Colegio de Mexico.

Tocqueville, A. d., J. P. Mayer et al. (1966) *Democracy in America*, New York: Harper & Row.

Uprimy, R., and M. Garcia-Villegas (2002) "Tribunal constitucional e emancipação social na Colômbia," *Democratizar a Democracia*, B. d. S. Santos, Rio de Janeiro: Civilização Brasileira.

Uribe, M. T. (2002) "Emancipação social em um contexto de guerra prolongada," *Democratizar a Democracia*, B. d. Sousa Santos (ed.), Rio de Janeiro, Civilização Brasileira.

Valenzuela, J. S., and A. Valenzuela (1986) *Military Rule in Chile: Dictatorship and Oppositions*, Baltimore: Johns Hopkins University Press.

Weffort, F. (1989) "Why Democracy," *Democratizing Brazil*, A. Stepan (ed.), New York: Oxford University Press.

CHAPTER 4

CONCEPTUALIZING CIVIL SOCIETY FROM THE BOTTOM UP: A POLITICAL ECONOMY PERSPECTIVE

Philip Oxhorn

The idea of "civil society" has increasingly become a central topic in research on democratization since the 1980s, when it was rediscovered in the social mobilization against Communist regimes in Eastern Europe that literally captured the imagination of the world, not to mention social scientists. Although the literature on democratic transitions in Southern Europe and Latin America had emphasized the role played by civil society in bringing an end to authoritarian governments (O'Donnell and Schmitter 1986), the literature's focus on elite-led processes and outcomes often overshadowed this dimension in its conclusions. The sudden collapse of Soviet-style communism further fed a growing optimism that resurgent civil societies would carry this new "revolution" toward the inevitable end of free-market economies and consolidated political democracies. As Carlos Waisman (in this volume) has shown, this "double transition" has proven far more problematic for civil society than initially anticipated.

Regardless of how civil society is actually defined, the *idea* of civil society has been approached in a variety of ways. Most recently, it represents a goal for newly democratizing countries, one that the established liberal democracies of Western Europe and North America have achieved. Historically, however, the approach was more empirical and descriptive (although certainly not without normative overtones), and civil society was "discovered" rather than predicted or sought after (Black 1984; Ferguson 1966; Tocqueville 1969). Either way, this goal is often a normative one, suggesting that "civil society" is the product of a unique Western cultural heritage that, *grosso modo*, is essentially liberal in nature (Seligman 1992). This is one reason why the concept was both slow to be applied to Latin America and had to be transformed in the process (Avritzer, this volume).

Surprisingly, even though political democracy (which similarly has a strong liberal normative heritage and has been most durable in Western Europe and in some of Western Europe's former colonies) appears to have few competing alternatives today, "civil society" is much more contentious, at times even polemical. Focusing on its normative dimensions, some have argued that it is of limited relevance outside of the relatively few Western societies where civil societies seem to have more or less thrived. Others have dealt with this normative question by attempting to elaborate distinct normative models of civil society stemming from a variety of philosophical, cultural, and religious traditions (Chambers and Kymlicka 2002). The effect of both reactions to the alleged normative biases in the literature has been to reduce the idea of civil society to an essentially normative ideal (albeit with competing normative systems or models). At the same time, some have even argued that a strong, robust civil society can even undermine democracy under certain circumstances, suggesting that too much of a "good thing" can be as problematic for democracy as its absence.

If there is anything that seems to unify the now quite large literature on civil society, it is the notion that civil society (whatever it may actually be) involves people at that point in which they first enter the "public" or "political" realm outside their immediate families (the so-called private sphere). This might imply that the idea of conceptualizing "civil society," the epitome of mass participation, "from the bottom up" is redundant at best, and unoriginal at worst. Albeit unintentionally, I argue that predominant theories of civil society offer an elitist view of civil society that not only marginalizes a majority of Latin Americans from its purview, but also places democratic stability at risk by misunderstanding the problematic nature of Latin American civil societies. In particular, an excessively individualistic perspective and a focus on what I call a "thick" consensual basis for civil society divert attention from the need to build stronger collective organizations and identities. As a consequence, I argue we need to rethink civil society from a more collectivist perspective that emphasizes the need for the state to both nurture and work with these collectivities in order to confront the most pressing problems facing Latin American societies today.

This chapter takes as its starting point three common problems in the way the literature tends to define "civil society" that have resulted in an elitist, often ethnocentric view that unnecessarily limits the concept's usefulness for comparative analysis. These are 1) a focus on the individual at the expense of the collective, 2) a normative (usually liberal) teleology, and 3) an excessively rigid state–civil society dichotomy. As an alternative, the next section of the chapter suggests the need for a political economy perspective that focuses attention on power relations and a "thin" notion of the consensual basis for civil society's emergence. To illustrate the usefulness of this approach, in the third section I focus on a paradox, arguing that civil society is most important when levels of societal trust are low and societal heterogeneity is high. This is demonstrated in a brief examination of the role civil society must play in resolving three key issues: transitions from authoritarian rule, establishing rule of law and basic civil rights, and securing a more effective use of educational resources. In the final section, I argue that the future of democracy in Latin America will to a large extent depend on the state working with civil society to overcome the principal challenges it faces. This, in turn, will require that the state play a more active role in nurturing civil society so that both the state and civil society are up to the task.

"CIVIL SOCIETY": AN ELITIST, ETHNOCENTRIC CONSTRUCT?

Modern conceptions of civil society reflect at least two distinct, if not mutually exclusive, intellectual traditions in Western political thought: a liberal or Lockean perspective and a collectivist perspective associated with the works of Montesquieu and, more recently, communitarians. Although this would imply that there are two competing models of civil society within Western political thought, the liberal model has become by far the predominant view. This reflects both a particular view of West European history and a confluence of factors beginning with the eclipse of Keynesian social welfare policies (and the developmentalist state in Latin America) by market-oriented neoliberal policies in the late 1970s and culminating with the end of the Cold War after the collapse of Soviet-style communism in the early 1990s. Although the specific elements of civil society that one perspective focuses on generally coexist to a greater or lesser degree with the elements emphasized in the other, each highlights different aspects of modern societies in ways that influence both the substance and conclusions of the comparative research they inspire.[1] More specifically, the dominance of a liberal perspective has contributed to a paradoxically elitist and arguably ethnocentric view of civil society that is fundamentally exclusionary in three ways: 1) it focuses on the individual at the expense of the collective, 2) it implies a normative (usually liberal) teleology, and 3) it creates an excessively rigid state–civil society dichotomy.

The Individual at the Expense of the Collective

The liberal perspective defines civil society in terms of individual rights and obligations. It is characterized as being coterminous with the spread of the market economy (Ferguson 1966). Rational individuals who decide to live together to further private, individual interests create civil society. Individual freedom is valued above all, and this requires the rule of law and respect for private property. Membership in any group becomes a function of interest maximization. Groups and group identities lose any sense of intrinsic value. Voluntarism and the absence of coercion, in turn, historically have justified unequal status by restricting citizenship rights for those who are defined as incompetent or dependent (such as women, youths, illiterates, the poor, and the working class).

Although the liberal perspective serves an important heuristic purpose in elucidating key aspects of how modern civil societies actually function, it also limits the usefulness of "civil society" as a comparative concept for understanding political processes in countries that only recently experienced transitions to democracy or are still governed by nondemocratic regimes. In focussing on voluntarism and an often idealistic view of the market, liberal definitions of civil society ignore the importance of marked inequalities of power among actors in determining social relations and political outcomes.[2] "Liberal" societies, principally the United Kingdom and the United States, come to represent the ideal of civil society (Seligman 1992).

This individual bias seriously limits the relevance of such a model to different historical contexts and regions of the world. Many societies simply do not recognize the centrality of the individual in the public or political realm, and instead emphasize the communities and larger social networks to which the individual belongs. In Latin America, this is particularly true of indigenous communities.

The liberal emphasis on individual rights also neglects the important collective dimension of rights in established democracies (Oxhorn 2003). On the one hand, rights are in effect granted to groups of people—women, the aged, illiterates, and so on—regardless of their legal and normative justification as individual rights of citizenship. On the other hand, such rights for disadvantaged groups are frequently the results of collective struggles reflecting the social construction of citizenship, just as people often must organize to ensure that the rights they are entitled to as individuals are respected by the state and other individuals in practice. Conversely, a principal threat to civil society itself may be the unrestrained pursuit by individuals of their own self-interests.

Civil Society's Normative Teleology

An important aspect of competing conceptualizations of civil society has revolved around the normative quality of the concept. Although the focus has shifted over the centuries, in recent years there has been a growing tendency to equate civil society with a very liberal normative framework that closely parallels the predominance of an exclusive focus on the individual as described above.[3] At the normative level, this tradition is heavily influenced by Alexis de Tocqueville. An important turning point came in the publication of Robert Putnam's influential book on democracy in Italy, which put the concept of social capital at the forefront of studies of civil society (Putnam 1993). But even earlier, important theorists of civil society were emphasizing its normative foundations in terms of norms of "civility" (Shils 1991), "civil spiritness" (Gellner 1991), and the broad set of liberal values of trust, associability, and the like associated with a liberal "civic culture" (Almond and Verba 1963).

While it is never very clear how such values become predominant, particularly the trust that is generally seen as pivotal in order for people to organize and form vibrant civil societies, at a minimum, their presence at the level of society is seen as a prerequisite for civil society's emergence.[4] But because of the lack of any intrinsic value attributed to group and organizational identities stemming from the focus on individuals associated with this perspective, an appropriate political culture in effect becomes synonymous with civil society itself.[5]

There is an implicit (and sometimes quite explicit) parallel with the teleology associated with modernization theories of the 1960s, which also focused attention on the importance of political culture to undergird democratic regimes in a way that more or less mirrors the idea of civil society as a strictly normative construct.[6] The source of civil society's normative foundation is ultimately seen as the outcome of historical processes going back centuries, though these historical processes often remain a black box in terms of what actually happened, thereby minimizing (and, in the case of early modernization theory, rejecting) the uniqueness of such processes as well as their inherently conflictual nature. Ironically, given the ideally secular nature of "modern" liberal politics and the threat that religious and other forms of identity politics are now seen to pose for civil society's continued existence (Hall 1995), this foundation is generally located in religious traditions, the early emergence of national identities and other social factors that are seen to have contributed to a high level of social homogeneity and consensus in the now established democracies of Western Europe, North America, and Japan.[7]

From this perspective, the requisites for a highly organized, vibrant civil society are quite high. It is consistent with the historical fact that such civil societies have been relatively rare, and have been most closely associated with the development of Western (and now democratic) countries. The problem is not that the "bar" for entering what is a rather exclusive club is high, but the way in which that bar appears to be set. This perspective deliberately posits a *thick* notion of the consensual basis for civil society's emergence that tends to be equated with a narrow set of Western values and unique cultural experiences. For societies that do not share (or necessarily want to share) those values and history, such as most Latin American countries where, for example, the level of societal trust is notoriously low (Lagos 1997), such a conception of civil society is extremely alienating. As Chris Hann (1996:1) notes,

> There is something inherently unsatisfactory about the international propagation by western scholars of an ideal of social organization that seems to bear little relation to the current realities of their own countries; an ideal which, furthermore, developed in historical conditions that cannot be replicated in any other part of the world today.

As I will be arguing in this chapter, the problem is that the level of consensus required for civil society's emergence is actually much lower. Moreover, the specific norms that it might represent, beyond a *thin* notion of societal consensus, are actually the result of a very political and conflictual process that is, paradoxically, most important to understand precisely when societies are marked by low levels of trust and high levels of social heterogeneity. Civil society is still quite difficult to achieve, but the reasons have less to do with culture and the absence or presence of liberal norms than the kinds of power relations between distinct segments of a society and the state. Before explaining why this is so, it is important to first look at the third problem in civil society literature.

AN EXCESSIVELY RIGID STATE-CIVIL SOCIETY DICHOTOMY

With some notable exceptions (Migdal, Kholi, and Shue 1994; Skocpol 1996; Waltzer 1999), protecting the necessary autonomy of civil society is generally seen to require a virtually impermeable barrier between the state and civil society. In many ways, this is an important legacy of Hegel's sharp delineation between the private sphere, civil society, and the state. It has been reinforced (if not reified) by the prominent role civil society played in opposing the state during recent transitions to democracy. Cooperation was obviously ruled out (at least for most civil society actors since compromises often were reached among political elites in the so-called pacted democracies). This sharp separation between civil society and the state was further accentuated by the shift to a new market-oriented development paradigm beginning in the late 1970s, which resulted in a markedly reduced role for the state in society and the economy. Civil society has concomitantly been called on to play a much more important role, particularly in the provision of social services and, in Latin America at least, in helping people cope with the economic dislocations and instability the shift in development models has entailed.

There are several problems with this. First, it ignores how the nature of the state and political regime fundamentally shape civil society. The nature of state institutions in general creates incentives and opportunities for distinct kinds of social mobilization and organization. For example, a state which has institutional mechanisms for interacting with civil society actors is likely to encourage their emergence indirectly, and most established democracies directly aid civil society's emergence through subsidies, both in kind and in material terms. Even in the United States, the epitome of a liberal civil society, the state plays an important role in facilitating the emergence of civil society actors through a variety of mechanisms, including the provision of tax exemptions for such organizations and for citizens who make financial contributions to these organizations. Authoritarian regimes similarly condition the nature of civil society's reaction to them through the nature and extent of repression, as well as the economic development model they attempt to implement. This is one important reason why civil society often seems to demobilize after transitions: incentives and opportunities to mobilize change radically. Conversely, the nature of state institutions can determine the role that civil society might play in undermining democratic regimes.[8]

Fundamentally, states play a role in directly creating and/or strengthening civil society actors. This has been historically the case in the United States (Skocpol 1996) and a hallmark of corporatist modes of interest intermediation both in developed and developing countries. The basic rights necessary for civil society to flourish (among other key demands of civil society in opposing authoritarian regimes) can be guaranteed only by the state. Such rights (freedom of association, of the press and speech, basic civil rights, among others) are a principal reason why strong civil societies are associated with established democracies: strong civil societies demand them and the strength of these civil societies is reflected in state policies intended to grant such rights. More importantly, the effectiveness of such rights (if not their *de jure* existence in formal laws and constitutions) will generally depend on the ability of civil society to demand their enforcement when such rights are transgressed by the state and/or non-state actors.[9]

Second, this rigid separation of the state and civil society ignores the fact that many civil society actors, including social movements, business groups, and organized labor, directly target the state in order to secure the passage of laws and regulations favorable to their interests. Whether it is an environmental movement or an antiabortion movement, for example, the state is seen as the central locus for ensuring that their goals are achieved, at the same time that they may work at the level of civil society to reinforce complementary norms (a "green" style of living or a respect for what is framed as the right to life of the unborn). More generally, the division between the public realm defined as the legitimate jurisdiction for the exercise of state authority and the realm outside of direct state intervention, where civil society (and individuals!) pursues its interests autonomous of state intervention is quite fluid in practice and often one of the principal axes for political debate in modern democracies (Maier 1987).

Perhaps most importantly, the state and civil society frequently must work together to achieve important outcomes or *synergy* (Evans 1997). I will return to this point later, but here it is important to emphasize that the state and civil society are not in competition with one another, suggesting that important development outcomes might actually require their close cooperation. The rigid dichotomy of the state versus civil society would seem to rule this out, even though reality suggests that some of the most important achievements of the Western European welfare states, for example, would have been impossible without the close cooperation between organized business interests, labor movements, and the state (Goldthorpe 1984).

Together, these three problems in the literature on civil society contribute to an elitist and ethnocentric perspective. Aside from the inherently elitist nature of any normative arguments that stress the inherently positive characteristic of certain cultures and societies in comparison to others that lack those same qualities, civil society from this perspective comes to play a paradoxically exclusionary role within many Latin American societies. On the one hand, the importance of individual self-interest and the market inevitably favors business and elite economic interests over more materially disadvantaged groups. This is not to suggest that organized business interests are not a legitimate part of civil society, but to stress the unbalanced, unequal nature of civil society in much of the region today. On the other hand, disadvantaged groups are the most affected by the retreat of the state, both in terms of the state's social welfare function and the enforcement of basic civil rights (Waisman, this volume). Similarly, it is often the disadvantaged groups that have the most to gain through a synergistic relationship between civil society and the state.

It is important to emphasize that the elitism associated with the dominant conception of civil society also goes beyond economic relations. It ignores or downplays the societal costs and coercion involved, for example, in achieving a high level of social homogeneity in West European countries in terms of language, ethnicity, religion, and race. Persistent gender inequality and other forms of identity-based discrimination can easily fall outside the immediate purview of this concept of civil society. This is particularly true for indigenous populations in Latin America, whose communitarian cultures are often at odds both with the individualism associated with this perspective on civil society and its focus on "modern," "rational" forms of organization and participation. Fundamental issues relating to "difference" are thus obscured.

Civil Society and the Social Construction of Citizenship[10]

An alternative view of civil society begins from a collectivist perspective that stresses the importance of organization and struggle. Civil society is defined here as "the social fabric formed by a multiplicity of self-constituted territorially and functionally based units [excluding families and business firms][11] which peacefully coexist and collectively *resist subordination* to the state, at the same time that they *demand inclusion* into national political structures" (Oxhorn 1995a). "Inclusion" is defined much more broadly than electoral inclusion and the existence of electoral or political rights, although this is an integral part of inclusion (Oxhorn 2003). It reflects the limits of political democracy in much of Latin America (what Waisman in this volume refers to as the marginalized pole in most Latin American democracies today). It also reflects historical problems of inequality that continue to condition the development of civil society throughout the region (Avritzer, this volume). But this ideal of inclusion is not limited to new democracies; the so-called new social movements that emerged throughout Western Europe, Canada, and the United States starting in the 1960s reflect the same dynamic, albeit in less dramatic circumstances associated with consolidated political democracies and modern welfare states.[12]

From this perspective, the normative content of civil society is deliberately ambiguous. It is in large part a function of the historical specificities of a given society, which in turn is a reflection of which groups are organized within civil society and which are not. The social construction of citizenship involves struggle, negotiation, and compromise, and the state is the locus of this process. It is therefore of paramount importance to understand who is and who is not participating in this process of social construction, particularly given the high stakes implied by Latin America's extremes of inequality. The organization of, first, workers, then women and, more recently, other groups including indigenous groups in Latin America is reflected in the gradual expansion of citizenship rights. The autonomy of such groups is reflected in their ability to define and defend their own interests in their interactions with other actors, including the state. Civil society itself becomes a realm of conflict and compromise, not (at least initially and certainly not on all issues relevant to a given polity) consensus. The boundaries between the state and civil society are also necessarily more fluid as a result of this process.

This dual dynamic of demanding inclusion and resisting subordination to the state may be latent or so routinized in established democracies that it is taken for granted. But even in these cases, critical turning points in national histories reflect the emergence of new groups within civil society trying to effect change through demands for inclusion and/or resistance to what are perceived as unacceptably intrusive state policies. In the United States, for example, this was the case with the civil rights and women's movements in the 1960s, as well as the antiwar movement during the Vietnam era. In Western Europe, in addition to the rise of the women's movements, environmental and antinuclear/peace movements have had important impacts on both the state and society, to give just a few examples. In Latin America, where social inequalities are far greater, the importance of this dual dynamic is similarly more critical, first to the establishment of democratic political regimes and later to their subsequent deepening. The weakness of civil societies throughout the region is consequently reflected, both historically and in the current period, in the limited scope of citizenship rights enjoyed by most Latin Americans and, until recently, the high levels of democratic instability.

This dual dynamic of resistance and inclusion characteristic of civil societies also implies that strong civil societies reflect a relative dispersion of political power throughout entire polities. The terms "power" and "power resources" are used to refer principally to economic resources and the organizational capacity to autonomously define and defend collective group interests. The latter can be based on a strong sense of collective identity, an ideology and/or organizational skill. It can also derive from the availability of selective incentives for members. Coercive power is not relevant here because it is generally used for ends that are antithetical to development of civil societies. It is important to note that the emphasis here on both power relations and the way power is defined stand in stark contrast to more predominant (and liberal) views on civil society that tend to downplay these factors.

The focus on social construction and power relations raises important questions about social cohesion and the level of "difference" a society can tolerate before centrifugal forces tear it apart. This is equally important to a more individual or liberal perspective, but the thick normative census that this perspective presumes tends to obscure it. The reality in much of Latin America (and, historically at least, many of the now established democracies) is that such a consensus is either utopian or masks forms of exclusion that are inherently undemocratic by their nature and frequently quite coercive. Following the seminal work of Dankwart Rustow (1970), a *thin* notion of the consensual basis for civil society's emergence consists of a shared sense of national identity. This may be the basis for a thick notion of societal consensus, but it can also reflect societal stalemate and/or the practical infeasibility of secessionist alternatives. In other words, just as democracy was seen by Rustow as a "second best alternative," so too might the acceptance of belonging to a given national community on the part of different actors in civil society. On this thin consensual basis, the process of the social construction of citizenship can begin. It necessarily requires that civil society actors be self-limiting in terms of their demands and expectations so as to be able to coexist (even reluctantly) with other civil society actors. More specifically, demands for "inclusion" cannot have as their objective the taking of institutional power to the permanent exclusion of other actors, ruling out both revolutionary movements on the Left and reactionary movements on the Right, as well as fundamentalist movements and other groups whose objectives are not readily classifiable on a Left–Right spectrum.[13] The ideal that this represents is that the different actors in civil society ultimately "bond together in difference" (Taylor 1998) or, to take the example of religious (and moral) difference, provide "a space for continuous dialogue among religious traditions and between the religious and the secular" (Nandy 1997). But this is an ideal that only strong civil societies can aspire to, not a prerequisite for their existence, and even in Western countries it often remains an elusive goal.[14] For similar reasons, the precise content and extent of the moral consensus that is the reflection of a strong civil society is necessarily a contingent outcome. In other words, it matters which groups do (and do not) participate in the social construction of that consensus.

It is important to emphasize that the achievement of this ideal is often a tremendous challenge. The violence of ethnic nationalism—including Irish nationalism in the other paragon of liberal civil society after the United States, the United Kingdom—shows how difficult it can be to achieve if ethnic nationalism escapes the bounds of civil society. The experience of indigenous mobilization in Latin America is an important, albeit so far limited, example of the importance of such self-limiting goals. Similarly, the difficulties that revolutionary movements throughout Latin America have faced in trying to integrate themselves into democratic politics can be understood in these terms as reflecting the challenge of immersing themselves in civil society after years of being excluded from it. Conversely, it becomes even more apparent why movements such as Peru's *Sendero Luminoso* would deliberately target organizations that would fall within the realm of civil society as defined here: they represent alternative, mutually exclusive forms of organization in relation to insurrectionary movements. Indeed, the strength of civil society organizations can help mitigate the centrifugal forces of diversity and inequality, and successful revolutionary movements tend to reflect the weakness of civil society as understood here in that they represent the only alternative available after prolonged periods of coerced exclusion by the state.

From this collectivist perspective, it is also important to emphasize that civil society cannot be understood independent of the state. Much of the political activity and bargaining characteristic of civil society does not—and should not—take place directly in relation to the state (Waisman, this volume). This is one of the reasons why civil society often complements the state by allowing common interests to develop and by providing an opportunity to resolve conflict without resorting to state institutions.

At the same time, the state conditions civil society in fundamental ways. As part of the competition among social organizations within civil society, these organizations also compete amongst themselves to influence state policy. Their relationship with the state may be fluid and mutually reinforcing, as is the case in established liberal democratic regimes. But it can also be more selective, with preference given only to certain groups, as is the case with many Latin American democracies (also see Waisman and Avritzer's contributions to this volume). It can even be openly antagonistic in countries where civil society is engaged in ongoing struggles against authoritarian regimes. From the perspective offered here, civil society may be stronger or weaker, but it is still understood in the same terms as specified in the definition, independent of its specific relationship to the state. In other words, we cannot have two definitions of civil society, one applicable to nondemocratic situations and another applicable to democratic ones. Can there be too much of a good thing? Is there a "paradox of civil society" in which the same civil society associated with recent transitions to democracy can be turned against democratic governments (Foley and Edwards 1996; Rueschemeyer, Stephens and Stephens 1992)? From the collectivist perspective offered here, the answer is no. Although social mobilization can threaten a democratic regime, such mobilization is really antithetical to civil society and is more likely to reflect civil society's weakness, not its strength. The impressive, sustained mobilizations against Hugo Chávez in Venezuela is a case in point. On the one hand, virtually all of organized society seems to be against his continued rule, while on the other the unorganized, disadvantaged masses are among his most fervent supporters. Yet it is impossible to understand the level of support for Chávez among Venezuala's poor without recognizing the privileged, often corrupt nature of the same organizations typically associated with political democracy. Indeed, it is the weakness of civil society as defined here and the exclusionary nature of Venezuela's pacted democracy that largely propelled Chávez to power, as he campaigned *against* the increasingly delegitimized institutions of one of the region's oldest democratic regimes. While Venezuelan society can be characterized as a "strong one" (and the ongoing political stalemate would seem to justify such a conclusion), it is far from a strong civil society in the fundamental sense of a rich social fabric of autonomous, self-constituted organizations demanding political inclusion and resisting subordination to the state (also see Levine's contribution to this volume).

The Challenge of Civil Society

To illustrate the usefulness of this alternative approach, perhaps the toughest test is to examine civil society's potential role in resolving problems when the basic assumptions of the dominant approach do not hold. In what follows, I will briefly examine three such problems: transitions from authoritarian rule, establishing the rule of law and basic civil rights, and securing a more effective use of educational resources. In all these three issue areas, civil society's relationship to the state is central. Moreover, these are contexts that cannot be characterized by the existence of high levels of societal trust. In the latter two issue areas, civil society's role is necessary to compensate for extremes of inequality, problems associated with the privatization (de facto and *de jure*) of basic state functions and generally weak state institutions. Moreover, all three problems are (or were in the case of transitions) high priorities for most Latin Americans.

Civil Society and Democratic Transitions

The uncertainty and associated risks for actors in recent democratic transitions, at best, imply that little trust existed among them. This was a principal reason why pact making among elites was often so important in order to protect their principal interests in any transition. In fact, for many, the repression and corresponding fear this generated among political activists and the participants in social organizations opposed to the regime was an important stimulus to autonomous organizational activity (Oxhorn 1995b). While a certain level of trust was necessary for maintaining any semblance of organizational activity, distrust and fear still penetrated many popular organizations, and whatever level of trust that could be established within an organization often did not get transferred to other organizations and actors.

During this tumultuous period, the relative moderation or self-limiting quality of mobilization, what O'Donnell and Schmitter (1986) called the "popular upsurge," stands out. Despite O'Donnell and

Schmitter's caution regarding the ability of civil society to limit its demands, and in spite of the expectations of many of their critics that much more radical outcomes from such mobilization were possible (MacEwan 1988; Petras and Vieux 1994), the fact is that these "uncertain" transitions all ended with the instauration of reasonably stable (by regional historical standards at least) political democracies. Serious threats of reversal in the relatively few cases where such threats emerged would come only years after the transition. In sharp contrast to the Weimar Republic, where an extensive network of civil society organizations may have served as a focal point for the collapse of democracy and the rise of Hitler due to the weak, unresponsive nature of the state institutions and political parties (Berman 1997), in Latin America, civil society networks were actually strengthened as part of the struggle to replace unresponsive, repressive regimes with more democratic ones.[15]

The last point highlights an important aspect of the argument being presented here: not all social organizations should be considered part of civil society, no matter how strong or inclusive they may be. The "paradox of civil society" (Foley and Edwards 1996) really is not a paradox at all. Instead, the possibility of social mobilization turning against a democratic government would in reality reflect the breakdown of civil society in the context of unresponsive state and political party institutions—very similar to the situation Berman found in Weimar Germany. The fact that this has tended not to happen in Latin America in recent decades provides further evidence of changes in democratic norms within Latin American civil societies that could bode well for their future development (Avritzer 2002). The two most notable exceptions, Venezuela under Chávez and Peru under Alberto Fujimori's in the first half of the 1990s, also tend to support my basic point in that they reflect the massive deligitimation of unresponsive, corrupt, and ineffective state institutions and political parties.[16] Conversely, this approach helps explain why obviously strong and well-organized guerrilla movements like the *Frente Farabundo Martí para la Liberación Nacional* (FMLN) in El Salvador would find the process of integrating themselves into civil society to be so problematic.

Establishing Rule of the Law and Basic Civil Rights[17]

One of the unanticipated occurrences after the recent transitions to democracy in Latin America has been the dramatic increase in crime. This, in turn, has led to a qualitative change in state violence. As levels of political violence and systematic human rights violations on the part of the state have declined, they have been largely displaced by a different kind of state violence directed against the poor as opposed to the political opposition. This is reflected by the increasingly draconian policies to deal with crime that have the effect in many cases of criminalizing poverty.

Several factors are behind this trend. On the one hand, it reflects a growing fear of crime, particularly among the poor who are its principal victims.[18] On the other hand, state legal institutions suffer from very low levels of legitimacy caused by the abuse of the legal system by elites and a widespread perception that officials enjoy a level of impunity regardless of what they do. This reflects not only the continued distrust of state institutions caused by high levels of abuse under authoritarian regimes, but also the fact that such practices often do not end even after a transition to democracy. Laws and personnel are held over from the authoritarian regime and are difficult to change. People become accustomed to seeking extralegal redressal of their grievances. Moreover, elected officials have contributed to the pervasive lack of confidence in judicial institutions through their own political intervention in the courts. At the same time, "middle class and elite crimes," including corruption, fraud, tax evasion, and the exploitation of child or slave labor are ignored by judicial systems which focus on crimes committed by the poor. As a result, people are reluctant to cooperate with law enforcement agencies, even to the extent of reporting crimes. This, in turn, can create a vicious circle as the lack of citizen cooperation leaves few alternatives to applying more violence to fight crimes because effective law enforcement and crime prevention are dependent upon community involvement. Repressive police measures ultimately do little to improve the image of law enforcement agencies. Instead, there is a real danger that the situation will only be exacerbated as local communities withdraw further away from the legal community.

From a collectivist civil society perspective, this kind of situation reflects a fundamental inequality that favors privileged groups at the cost of denying large segments of the population basic civil rights. Alarmingly, the resultant vacuum created by ineffective and corrupt institutions is increasingly being filled by the military throughout the region, which only bodes for ever more violence.

The solution similarly can be found at the level of civil society. The vast human rights networks established as part of opposition movements to authoritarian rule have an important role to play in gathering information, struggling to ensure accountability, and representing the rights of the poor—a role not too different from the one they played before the transition to democracy, but one that will now require more active cooperation with democratic state institutions that are, at least ideally, supposed to be more responsive.[19]

In a similar vein, it is important that communities organize themselves to get involved in community policing initiatives. Important examples of this can be found in a number of countries, particularly in South Africa but also in Latin America (Findlay and Zvekiæ 1993; Roche 2002). In this way, civil society can help compensate for weak, corrupt state institutions in securing basic rights that are an essential cornerstone of democratic governance. Through the active collective involvement of citizens, motivated by a certain degree of fear and lack of trust in legal institutions rather than a democratic civic culture as the liberal perspective on civil society would suggest, confidence and trust in legal institutions can ultimately be improved as these institutions become more responsive to people's pressing needs. The vacuum in the midst of rising crime rates and the state's inability to respond democratically with authoritarian alternatives might ideally be filled by a more effective and vibrant civil society.

Securing a More Effective Use of Educational Resources

Many of the problems underlying Latin America's poor economic performance in recent years compared to other areas of the world, as well as its abysmal record in limiting extremes in social inequality, are reflected in the region's problematic educational system (Inter-American Development Bank 1998). Teachers and administrators remain largely unaccountable to the communities they serve. Educational systems have become skewed in favor of imposing uniformity and rewarding mediocrity rather than encouraging innovation. In many countries, more than ninety percent of total educational budgets go toward salaries, even though average salary of teachers often remains notoriously low. This only reflects the continued strength (and elitist, self-serving nature) of many teachers' unions. The result is poor quality education at a relatively high cost. At the same time, economically privileged segments of the population can avoid these shortcomings through access to private education.

The poor quality of education, in turn, makes going to school a less attractive alternative to entering the labor market as far as young people from low income families are concerned. While school attendance during the early years of schooling is comparable to other regions in the world, Latin America stands out due to its high and earlier dropout rates among the poor. This creates highly stratified educational systems that "do not constitute a mechanism for social mobility, or for reducing income differences, as is true in other areas of the world" (Inter-American Development Bank 1998). This is in sharp contrast to the role that public education played in contributing to the upward social mobility of large segments of the population in the postwar period through the end of the 1970s (CEPAL 1989).

Education reform must be viewed as the principal long-term basis for greater inclusion. Quality education is even more central to achieving both individual social advancement and higher levels of national economic productivity in an era marked by growing levels of free trade and the need to base international competitiveness on productive, qualified labor rather than on low wages. Additional resources in many cases will be less important than ensuring that existing resources are used more effectively. To achieve this, educational reforms should focus on increasing the accountability of teachers and local school administrators to parents and local communities who have an interest in ensuring that children are well educated. Bolivia's recent program of educational reform, emphasizing increased community involvement and introducing a multiethnic dimension to the curriculum, offers a particularly useful model for improving educational quality and reducing dropout rates among the poor (Contreras 1998).

The Bolivian example also demonstrates the particular role that education can play in constructing stronger civil societies from the perspective presented here. Efforts must be systematically undertaken at the grassroots level to begin to empower people by helping them to be proud of who they are, regardless of their social class, gender, ethnicity, religion, and so on. Under these circumstances, trust is either clearly absent, or the absence of trust is masked by the apparent deference of disadvantaged groups. Curriculums that respect difference by integrating distinct cultural, ethnic, and linguistic traditions are fundamentally empowering for disadvantaged groups.

To be effective, policies aimed at helping to mediate differences, and overcome extremes of social heterogeneity must start with concerted efforts to affirm collective identities in positive ways. Rather than assume that collective identities have no intrinsic value, as is the tendency in much of the literature on civil society, these need to be recognized explicitly. In this way, the foundation for a rich social fabric that is the definitive expression of a strong civil society can be set. The dialogues among different groups that Charles Taylor and Ashis Nandy suggest are necessary because true pluralist social cohesion depend on this. Moreover, the precise normative and moral contours of a particular civil society and its political culture depend on the effective inclusion of different groups in their social construction. Otherwise, they may remain alienated from any presumed national normative consensus and, as a result, continue to be susceptible to more extreme forms of social mobilization that by their very nature would belie the existence of strong civil societies. Studies have already demonstrated the success of such efforts to overcome people's symbolic exclusion (Fleury 1998).

CONCLUSIONS

The issues raised here are important in ways that are existential as well as theoretical. Elements of both kinds of civil society—a liberal individualist and a collectivist—simultaneously coexist within most societies, in Latin America as well as elsewhere. In this sense, they are not mutually exclusive, and the elements of civil society highlighted in the two competing theoretical traditions in fact have important, often complementary roles to play in supporting and strengthening civil societies as the foundation for more inclusionary democratic governance.

At the same time, if our theoretical perspectives do not recognize this reality, the risks to Latin American democracy and political stability will likely grow. There is a real danger that a civil society perspective that is too "liberal" and individualist will misdiagnose many of the fundamental threats facing democracy in the region. In particular, the weaknesses of the collectivist dimension of most Latin American civil societies are reflected in some of the core challenges democracies in the region must overcome if democratic governance is to remain relevant for seeking redress for the most pressing needs of the majority (Oxhorn 2001). For a variety of reasons, including the advantages that privileged groups have in a liberal, individualist civil society, Latin America's democracies retain important exclusionary aspects. The crises in Argentina and Venezuela are only the most dramatic examples of this contradiction. At the same time, some of the most pressing problems faced by Latin America's popular sectors, including but not limited to civil rights and the quality of education for their children, can be addressed most effectively through a close cooperative relationship between civil society organizations and state institutions.

From the perspective offered here, it is also clear that civil society in many cases simply may not be up to the task. Although it was often quite effective in mobilizing against authoritarian regimes, civil society in many instances seems to be in retreat from a collectivist perspective. For the poor, in particular, and the segments of middle classe most hurt by the processes of economic liberalization and economic instability, the combination of ineffective (and in many cases overtly corrupt), unresponsive state institutions and a weakening of social organizations capable of (and interested in) demanding inclusion into political processes is extremely alienating. This will sharply constrain the future prospects for democratic governance in the region, unless such alienation is overcome through the development of stronger, more inclusive civil societies, as defined here, that can take better advantage of the political rights commensurate with political democracy.

The challenge, ultimately, is to create the kinds of civil society organizations that cannot only work with the state to find solutions to pressing problems, but also demand that the state be accountable and responsive in attempting to address growing problems of social inequity. In the past, under authoritarian regimes, the Catholic Church played a vital role in a number of countries in fostering exactly this kind of organizational activity. Its retreat from this role with the return to civilian rule is undoubtedly one important factor in the apparent weakening of civil society after transitions to democracy.

The example of the Church's role in supporting popular sector organizational activity further highlights the importance of understanding organizational autonomy in terms of the ability of organizations to define and defend their own interests. Disengagement from other actors is no guarantee of success in this regard, although it can contribute to frustration and even irrelevance as larger political and social processes pass such organizations by. The relationship was certainly not without tensions, yet in many instances the Church was able to nurture this kind of organizational autonomy, despite the fact that it is one of most hierarchical and patriarchal, as well as among the oldest, institutions in the world and that organizations affected had few alternatives.

Now that the Church is no longer willing or able to assume this role the way it did during periods of authoritarian rule, the state must fill the void. The Church's past relationship with civil society, however, still offers an important (and not too distant) model of how the state could better nurture the kind of partners in civil society that it can work with to resolve pressing problems. After all, if the Catholic Church could support a myriad of autonomous organizations in civil society in a repressive environment, surely the state could do the same in today's more democratic, Latin American context. Fears of state co-optation, while real, cannot be used as an excuse for inaction. At the level of civil society, the defense of organizational autonomy should not become a justification for the political isolation (and powerlessness) of those organizations.

While this pattern of state–society relations is admittedly the ideal, it is also a pattern typical of the relationship between the state and civil society in established democracies, even in the United States, although the dominant theories of civil society may not sufficiently appreciate this. The critique of liberal theories of civil society offered here is as relevant to the West, where such theories originated, as it is to Latin America. But the consequences of misunderstanding civil society in more established democracies may be far graver for the newly established democracies in Latin America, where the policies such misrepresentations inspire can have serious repercussions for the region's still fragile democratic regimes. Ultimately, a challenge to civil society is also a challenge to the state, and our theories of civil society must underscore this.

Notes

1. Indeed, the relative balance of liberal and collectivist elements are a defining characteristic of any particular civil society. For this same reason, many of the differences between the perspective expressed here and that found in the chapters by Avritzer and Waisman in this volume reflect our respective differences in emphasis within the same larger Western tradition.
2. Waisman's chapter in this volume is an important exception to this.
3. Interestingly, this is the opposite of much earlier theoretical traditions. The normative dimension of civil society was perhaps strongest in Montesquieu's civic republicanism. Adam Ferguson, the first to equate civil society with the spread of the market, actually lamented the destruction of these same collectivist values in the process! See Ferguson (1966).
4. It is important to note that although both Avritzer's and Waisman's contributions to this volume adhere to many of the liberal assumptions I am criticizing here, they do not adopt its explicit normative bias. Both also emphasize that the ideal liberal teleology is far from guaranteed in the Latin American context.
5. I will return to the intrinsic importance of organization for understanding civil society below.
6. Avritzer's chapter in this volume makes a similar point.
7. With hindsight at least, Christianity, Protestantism, and Confucianism are all now associated with social capital and civil society. See Fukuyama (2001).

8. It is important to note that these authors argue that the nature of the state can lead to situations in which strong civil societies actually undermine democratic governance. I will return to this point in the following section.
9. In his chapter in this volume, Avritzer associates this with a liberal model of civil society that is but one model of civil society in Latin America. I would argue this is a fundamental characteristic of any civil society, even if it is not a predominant aspect of its current activity. One reason this aspect of civil society may be less pronounced is undoubtedly a reflection of state capacity (Waisman, this volume). Only when the Executive and judicial institutions of the state are sufficiently strong will civil society organizations likely target them to find redress for their concerns and interests.
10. Many of these ideas are developed to a greater length in Oxhorn (2003). See also Oxhorn (2001).
11. Families are excluded because these epitomize the "private sphere." Business firms are purely economic organizations and as such are outside of the realm of civil society, although economic models condition civil society in important ways (Waisman, this volume). It is arguable whether or not political parties should be considered part of civil society since they uniquely compete for control over the state and, following Hegel, are often characterized as forming "political society." From the perspective offered here, political parties are more appropriately understood as part of civil society. The literature on parties, for example, measures the strength of parties in terms of their ties to civil society and their ability to represent important segments of it, as well as their organization. Conversely, weak political parties are disconnected from civil society. See Mainwaring and Scully (1995). It is also worth noting that civil society might compete democratically for control of the state, suggesting that even this traditional role of political parties does not necessarily set them apart from civil society. See Kiss (1992).
12. Admittedly, this also reflects a distinctly more Gramscian view of the concept of civil society. See Davis (1999).
13. This is similar to the "self-limiting radicalism" often associated with so-called new social movements, although I am explicitly applying it to all civil society actors. See Cohen (1985).
14. It is also an ideal that, as both Taylor and Nandy emphasize, entails an explicit collective dimension that is not compatible with the liberal concept of civil society as developed in this chapter. Indeed, this is precisely the kind of liberal perspective, often associated with "civic culture," that they are criticizing.
15. It is important to note that Berman's persuasive argument about the role of civil society in Hitler's seizure of power is itself predicated on the same individualistic, liberal perspective I am criticizing. From the collectivist perspective developed here, civil society can be seen to have grown increasingly weaker in at least three senses. First, the civil organizations increasingly lost their autonomy as they were captured

by activists from the National Socialist German Workers' Party. Second, there was a strong antidemocratic and authoritarian set of norms associated with many of the civil society organizations at the time, suggesting that their goals were at best ambiguously related to the dual dynamic and thin normative consensus characteristic of civil society referred to here. Finally, in many respects German society was undergoing an acute form of social disintegration that left increasingly large segments of the German population excluded and in a state of anomie. Hitler filled a unique vacuum, mobilizing these people in a populist fashion, albeit his actual rule could hardly be characterized as being a populist. See Lepsius (1978). The problem therefore was not too much or too strong a civil society, but the breakdown of civil society.

16. In the case of Peru, it is also important to note that the country was wracked by hyperinflation, massive unemployment and a growing civil war, as well as the collapse of organized labor and the political left that participated in electoral politics. In many ways, this is actually quite reminiscent of the Weimar Republic (see note 13).
17. This section draws on Holston and Caldeira (1998); Kincaid and Gamarra (1996); McSherry (1998); Mendez, O'Donnell and Pinheiro (1999); NACLA (1996), Neild (1999), Oxhorn (2001). Also see Waisman and Avritzer in this volume.
18. While it is true that the wealthy and more advantaged are also the objects of crime, particularly kidnapping for ransom in several countries, the proportion of these segments of the population that are directly affected is much lower. Such events are much more dramatic, in part because they still remain relatively isolated. Moreover, these potential victims have recourse to a variety of countermeasures, including closed communities and private guards, which are not available to the average person.
19. While they have not always been as successful as they would hope, perhaps the best example of how civil society can involve itself in policing can be found in the public response to police abuses in major U.S. cities. Public protests by a variety of organizations, ranging from Church groups and civil rights groups, to international human rights organizations such as Amnesty International and Human Rights Watch, as well as community activists, have been pivotal in placing these issues on the public agenda. At the same time, the race riots and violence that sometimes results from an unresponsive judiciary can only underscore the danger to civil society posed by perceptions of impunity and a lack of effective avenues for recourse.

BIBLIOGRAPHY

Almond, G. A., and S. Verba (1963) *The Civic Culture: Political Attitudes and Democracy in Five Nations*, Princeton: Princeton University Press.

Avritzer, L. (2002) *Democracy and the Public Space in Latin America*, Princeton: Princeton University Press.

Berman, S. (1997) "Civil Society and the Collapse of the Weimar Republic," *World Politics* 49, 3:401–429.

Black, Anthony (1984) *Guilds and Civil Society in European Political Thought from the Twelfth Century to the Present*, London: Methuen & Co.

CEPAL (1989) *Transformación Ocupacional y Crisis Social en América Latina*, Santiago: United Nations.

Chambers, S., and W. Kymlicka (eds.) (2002) *Alternative Conceptions of Civil Society*, Princeton: Princeton University Press.

Cohen, Jean (1985) "Strategy or Identity: New Theoretical Paradigms and Contemporary Social Movements," *Social Research* 52 (Winter):663–716.

Contreras, M. (1998) "La reforma educativa," *Las Reformas Estructurales en Bolivia*, J. C. Chávez Corrales (ed.), La Paz: Fundación Milenio.

Davis, D. E. (1999) "The Power of Distance: Re-theorizing Social Movements in Latin America," *Theory and Society* 28:583–638.

Evans, P. B. (ed.) (1997) *State–Society Synergy: Government and Social Capital in Development*, Berkeley: International Area Studies.

Ferguson, A. (1966) *An Essay on the History of Civil Society*, Edinburgh: University of Edinburgh Press.

Findlay, M., and U. Zvekiæ (eds.) (1993) *Alternative Policing Styles: Cross-Cultural Perspectives*, Deventer, The Netherlands: Kluwer Law and Taxation Publishers.

Fleury, S. (1998) "Política social, exclusión y equidad en América Latina en los años noventa," paper presented at Política Social, Exclusión y Equidad en Venezuela durante los años 90 Balance y Perspectiva, Caracas, Venezuela, May 1998.

Foley, M., and B. Edwards (1996) "The Paradox of Civil Society," *Journal of Democracy* 7, 3:38–52.

Fukuyama, F. (2001) "Social Capital, Civil Society, and Development," *Third World Quarterly* 22, 1:7–20.

Gellner, E. (1991) "Civil Society in Historical Context," *International Social Science Journal* 129:495–510.

Goldthorpe, J. (ed.) (1984) *Order and Conflict in Contemporary Capitalism*, Oxford: Clarendon Press.

Hall, J. (1995) "In Search of Civil Society," *Civil Society, Theory, History and Comparison*, J. Hall (ed.), Cambridge: Polity Press.

Holston, J., and T. Caldeira (1998), "Democracy, Law, and Violence: Disjunctions of Brazilian democracy," *Fault Lines of Democracy in Post-Transition Latin America*, F. Aguero and J. Stark (eds.), Coral Gables, FL: North–South Center Press at the University of Miami.

Inter-American Development Bank (1998) "Facing Up to Inequality in Latin America: Economic and Social Progress in Latin America," 1998–1999 Report. Washington, DC: Inter-American Development Bank.

Kincaid, D. A., and E. A. Gamarra (1996) "Disorderly Democracy: Redefining Public Security in Latin America," *Latin America in the*

World-Economy, R. P. Koreniewsicz and W. C. Smith (eds.), Westport, CT: Praeger.

Kiss, E. (1992) "Democracy Without Parties? 'Civil Society' in East-Central Europe," *Dissent* 39 (Spring):226–231.

Lagos, M. (1997) "Latin America's Smiling Mask," *Journal of Democracy* 8:125–138.

Lepsius, M. R. (1978) "From Fragmented Party Democracy to Government by Emergency Decree and National Socialist Takeover: Germany," *The Breakdown of Democratic Regimes: Europe*, Linz, J. J., and A. Stepan (eds.) (1978), Baltimore: The John Hopkins University Press.

MacEwan, A. (1988) "Transitions from Authoritarian Rule," *Latin American Perspectives* 15:115–130.

Maier, C. S. (ed.) (1987) *Changing Boundaries of the Political: Essays on the Evolving Balance Between the State and Society, Public and Private in Europe*. Cambridge: Cambridge University Press.

Mainwaring, S., and T. Scully (eds.) (1995) *Building Democratic Institutions: Party Systems in Latin America*, Stanford: Stanford University Press.

McSherry, P. J. (1998) "The Emergence of Guardian Democracy," *NACLA Report on the Americas* 32:16–24.

Méndez, J. E., G. O'Donnell, and P. S. Pinheiro (1999) *The (Un)rule of Law and the Underprivileged in Latin America*, Notre Dame, IN: University of Notre Dame Press.

Migdal, J. S., A. Kholi, and V. Shue (1994) *State Power and Social Forces: Domination and Transformation in the Third World*, Cambridge: Cambridge University Press.

NACLA (1996) "Report on Crime and Impunity," *NACLA Report on the Americas* 30:17–43.

Nandy, A. (1997) "A Critique of Modernist Secularism," *Politics in India*, S. Kaviraj (ed.), Delhi: Oxford University Press.

Neild, R. (1999) "From National Security to Citizen Security: Civil Society and the Evolution of Public Order Debates," *Mimeo.*

O'Donnell, G., and P. C. Schmitter (1986) *Transitions from Authoritarian Rule: Tentative Conclusions about Uncertain Democracies*, Baltimore: The Johns Hopkins University Press.

Oxhorn, P. (1995a) "From Controlled Inclusion to Coerced Marginalization: The Struggle for Civil Society in Latin America," *Civil Society: Theory, History and Comparison*, J. Hall (ed.), Cambridge: Polity Press.

——. (1995b) *Organizing Civil Society: The Popular Sectors and the Struggle for Democracy in Chile*, University Park, Pennsylvania: Pennsylvania State University Press.

——. (2001) "When Democracy isn't All That Democratic: Social Exclusion and the Limits of the Public Sphere in Latin America," *North–South Agenda Paper* 44, Coral Gables, FL: North–South Center, University of Miami.

——. (2003) "Social Inequality, Civil Society and the Limits of Citizenship in Latin America," *In What Justice? Whose Justice? Fighting for Fairness in*

Latin America, edited by S. Eckstein and T. Wickham-Crawley. Berkeley: University of California, 35–63.

Petras, J., and S. Vieux (1994) "The Transition to Authoritarian Electoral Regimes in Latin America," *Latin American Perspectives* 21:5–20.

Putnam, R. (1993) *Making Democracy Work: Civic Traditions in Modern Italy*, Princeton, NJ: Princeton University Press.

Roche, D. (2002) "Restorative Justice and the Regulatory State in South African Townships," *British Journal of Criminology* 42:514–533.

Rueschemeyer, D., E. Stephens and J. D. Stephens (1992) *Capitalist Development and Democracy*, Chicago: University of Chicago Press.

Rustow, D. (1970) "Transitions to Democracy: Toward a Dynamic Model," *Comparative Politics* 2:337–363.

Seligman, A. (1992) *The Idea of Civil Society*, New York: Free Press.

Shils, E. (1991) "The Virtue of Civil Society," *Government and Opposition* 26:3–20.

Skocpol, T. (1996) "Unravelling from Above," *American Prospect* 25 (March–April): 20–25.

Taylor, C. (1998) "The Dynamics of Democratic Exclusion," *Journal of Democracy* 9:143–156.

Tocqueville, Alexis de. 1969. Democracy in America, edited by J. P. Mayer. Garden City, NY: Anchor Books.

Waltzer, M. (1999) "Rescuing Civil Society," *Dissent* 46 (Winter): 62–67.

Part II

Country Case Studies

Chapter 5

Citizenship and Civil Society in Renascent Argentina

Isidoro Cheresky

The presence of citizens and popular sectors is a crucial component of Argentina's public and political life. This statement may seem irrelevant since all democratic societies are based on a pronouncement by their citizens. However, Argentina, a country with a populist tradition that has experienced recurrent mass mobilization, presents significant innovations today: newly appeared actors who cannot be identified by previous paradigms and who develop to the detriment of traditional institutions, in particular political parties and trade unions.

Caceroleros[1] and *piqueteros*[2] are terms that were coined to identify those new actors in public life: groupings of individuals that are constituted in the public sphere itself, some of which enjoy a brief presence, others a sustained one. The very names used to designate them reveal the existence of a new generation of collective actors. They are distinguished not by a common social condition, but by the features and resources they use to protest: some use domestic utensils to noisily express their discontent; others, short-term or prolonged road blocks. These actors became visible through their acts of protest and tried to gain influence in public life by expressing their claims or their discontent; they have no institutional representatives and if in some cases they have leaders, these are not recognized by all the members of the group.

Caceroleros and *piqueteros* have recently emerged to public life and although they are distinct, sharply differentiated groups, both illustrate a deep transformation that has taken place in collective identities. They are united by the common distance from the traditional actors now displaced from center stage. Unions and traditional political parties, together with other corporative actors, have retreated as far as claims and protest are concerned; moreover, some of these more established actors appear to be decidedly weakened. Not only presence in the streets but also the agenda of recognized grievances are embodied in the new expressions.

It can be argued that although the new actors seemed to question institutional political representation with their expansion, in the 2003 presidential and legislative elections, legitimate political leaderships were formed and ratified despite the fact that comprehensive political renewal has not taken place and that successful candidates have little or no relation with the social movements in question. However, the links of political representation continue to be questioned. Although the clanging of pots and pans was an eruption that left behind a meager organizational structure, the tension between citizens and leadership continues and with it, fluctuating preferences. The president and the government chosen in the 2003 presidential elections were supported by postelectoral public opinion that allowed them to overcome institutional resistance and improve their position in this area. The fact that a presumably weak government could become stronger by direct relations with citizens illustrates a shift in legitimacy that makes political life depends on the renewal of public credit to a much greater degree than it did in the past. In this sense it could be said that the sound of clanging pots and pans has quietened down, but its possible reemergence looms over the actions of the representatives.

The *piqueteros*'s actions and the dilemmas their demands and transgressions create continue to occupy a central place in public debate. Can this new situation be only a product of circumstances? Is it a consequence of the exceptional debacle that started to develop in the last years of the 1990s that later exploded in December 2001 bringing about a break in the economic model and the externalization of the crisis of representation?

It is possible to point out the limits of social and political protest. The rallying cry, "*Que se vayan todos*" (All of them must leave) that presided over citizen mobilization at the beginning of 2001 has not yielded explicit results in terms of political renewal. But, on the other hand, would a voluntarist and possibly post-Peronist government that came to power conditioned by civic discontent, have been imaginable without the great convulsion created by the emergence of an independent citizenry?

The *piqueteros* have not created a political alternative unlike what the leadership of their revolutionary wing would like to claim, and even the moderate leaders who have sought elected office have not been successful. This fact confirms the presumption that the movements of the unemployed possess different characteristics from previous mass movements. Their significance in political life, nevertheless, is considerable: they display before society the current limitations inherent in the condition of citizenry. This is not a marginal phenomenon like those present in other contemporary societies; rather, it is a particular situation in which the threat of nonsurvival hangs over almost two-thirds of the population and constitutes, therefore, a powerful incitement to political disaffection.

Undoubtedly, the collapse at the end of 2001 had effects on the formation and reinforcement of these actors and collective dispositions. That moment marked the culmination of a process that expelled many individuals from their normal circumstances and their provisions for the future. But the process of social deinstitutionalization that has become evident is conditioned by some factors presumed to be contingent—such as unemployment, although analysts do not think it will be overcome in the short run—and other factors that will probably be permanent, such as the fall of industrial employment, the general insecurity of employment, the growth of informality through the outsourcing of tasks, etcetera. These factors indicate, in Argentina as in the rest of the world, that the sociological base on which traditional social and political actors rested has become weak or is disappearing. Indeed, individuals' activities and their regularity, are as important as the legal and political relationships that channel them and these have experienced important transformations. One salient feature is the withdrawal of the system of guarantees and rights provided by the state and other public institutions, a system that had been in force in Argentina, albeit idiosyncratically. This reduction in social protection that expanded the extent to which individuals are left to their own decisions and resources has been called the passage from citizen individualism to patrimonial individualism (Orléan 1999).

Thus, the possibility that the present tendency of an expanding, fluid, public space with diverse actors, some of which are constituted in that *very* space, may become a permanent feature should be considered.

In the past, different forms of sociability were developed in Argentina stimulated by the diversity of the waves of immigration, which lead to the proliferation of rural cooperatives, community groups, clubs, associations with mutual aid or cultural purposes, community libraries, etcetera (Romero 1994). Since the 1930s, however, political instability and—when Peronism came to power—the pervasive corporatist organization in particular of the workers, and the encouragement of mass demonstrations and organizations that could be broken down only into functional divisions, reduced the sphere of voluntary associations for public purposes (Tocqueville 1988; Habermas 1996). The renewed political instability caused by the authoritarian interruptions of the constitutional order since the fall of Peron until the mid-1970s, created a public atmosphere dominated by national emergencies: accusations and repression of the opposition, military declarations, resistance to the ban on Peronism for eighteen years, and military governments that suspended political and civic rights. Strong, all-embracing and exclusionary political identities on the one hand, and military governments little disposed to the free expression of citizens on the other, formed the context of the following paradox: a society inclined to mobilization and political commitment but, due to the highly confrontational nature of the alignments in which it was involved, little disposed to deliberation and forming associations.

As in other countries, the core of civil society was forged by protest and resistance to an unprecedented kind of dictatorship. It was under the banner of human rights that the impetus for creating associations oriented towards the public sphere came back to life. However, only a meager legacy from that blossoming of civic initiatives seems to have survived to the present.

From People to Citizenship

The first half of the 1940s, known as the origins of Peronism, saw the reconfiguration of the social and political scene and placed the "populist people" center stage. Clearly, Peronism was the dominant identity. This was a *movimientista* identity, of a scope so far-reaching that it sought to coincide with the people as a whole, with hazy ideological contours and without formal procedures to work out the competition in its midst. Peronism's continuity was provided by the figure of its leader and the charismatic support he generated. The relationship between the leader and the mass structured the movement and the masses were the source of legitimacy that did not, however, exclude the electoral act, although the latter was considered formal and lackluster. Organizations (such as trade unions and the political party) that acted as intermediaries were also developed. This format took away a democratic meaning since it was entangled with the banner of social rights and the participation of the poorest sectors in public life. This "entrance of the masses in history," however, was disconnected from a wider institutionalization of liberties and individual freedoms.

During the years that preceded the fall of Peron in 1955, the corporatist constituency involved most of the workers, but these were organizations closely associated with the structure of the state. At the same time, there were severe restrictions on civil liberties. Besides, the trade unions had to have legal status, that is, recognition by the state, to bargain collectively with employers. The workers paid dues automatically to the unions, which provided them with social and recreational services that varied in quality according to the industry the union belonged to. But it is doubtful that this dense network of support could be considered part of civil society in contrast to the active, although incipient resistance that emerged in Peronism after it was ousted from power by a coup in 1955.

The "organized community" that expanded together with the Peronist state can be compared and contrasted to the abovementioned capacity for forming associations that had blossomed in Argentina during the first decades of the century under the effect of the influx of immigrants. This capacity for association was shown by the existence of plural trade unionism, independent of the state if not repressed by it, and even a large number of associations that resisted and critiqued the social order, some of which gravitated towards violence. It also included clubs that preserved the cultural identities of immigrants and other forms of sociability with a public purpose. In the second half of the twentieth century, all these organizations tended to fall back to middle-class spaces, less captured by Argentine mass-society.

Conversely, the typical figure of the Peronist people was the multitude gathered in *Plaza de Mayo*[3] around the leader and head of state, either in ritual celebrations or expressly summoned. They were a people who assented and celebrated the leader, participating without deliberating, they spoke through his voice. But they were also a people who developed an identity based on conflict and demands in the realm of trade union's activity that endured well beyond Peronism's fall from power and that legated a plebeian and therefore ambivalent popular disposition: resistant to domination but disinclined to follow formal institutional structures.

At that moment (the Peronist period), society was divided into two fields: one that defined its identity on the basis of the enjoyment of social advancements that were not yet rights—if by this term we understand formulated and sanctioned in a context of deliberation in which plural claims and interpretations of general principles prevail and decisions are taken through mechanisms of democratic representation. The other field perceived a loss of civil liberty in the rise of these social advancements. After the fall of Peron, the separation between social rights and liberties persisted but was reversed and now Peronists were deprived of their political and even civil rights during a long period in which, forbidden by law, they turned to be the "resistance"; that is, a clandestine or semiclandestine associational life completely geared to secure the return of the leader and the reestablishment of the Peronist state.

Obviously, political stability and the military dictatorships put in place due to the Peronism–anti-Peronism fracture, which weakened the legitimacy of the elected governments, contributed to depress associational life or to give it a character closely aligned to the change of political regime. In sum, since the 1930s the public space for creating associations was marked by political instability and recurring crises.

However, certain events that took place in the 1970s originated social movements that had never existed before. Although the sharp distinction between Peronism and anti-Peronism did not disappear, society was split by new cleavages and an increase in violence. Militarist revolutionary organizations captured and suppressed the mobilizational dimensions of the anticapitalist critique that expanded in the late 1970s at the incitement of a new, rebellious trade unionism and the confrontational student movement. In turn, these organizations grew, contributing to suffocate the social movement. In one way or another throughout the 1960s and 1970s the kind of associations that prospered and included many layers of society, in some cases, produced political critique and in others, militarization.

The militarization of the public sphere lead to unease and uncertainty in society, a situation favorable to establishing order at any price. Because of this, the military dictatorship was initially received with acquiescence and sometimes supported as a reaction to the previous atmosphere of chaos. But again, an environment of pacification without deliberation nor freedom of opinion prevailed in which the majority turned deaf ears to the sounds that rose from the catacombs (Cheresky 1997, 1998).

Like in other countries, an unusual dictatorship that referred to a future democratic order while at the same time resembling a totalitarian regime by building a machine of appropriation that transformed individuals into mere bodies, finally generated a resistance unheard of. A new kind of associational life developed that had to seek protection in semiclandestine existence in order to preserve its public appearances, because its politico-humanistic claims undermined the regime, contributing to its downfall. The movement did not aspire to rule nor to organize a violent opposition that would confront the military government in terms of power. What it did was to create civic resistance that could not be contained by the regime because it demanded basic rights and rule of law without attempting to constitute an alternative to the political regime.

Thus, an experience of social power took shape, which, through its effectiveness, disqualified discourses of violence as a way of presenting demands and as a path for social change. The human rights movement is, in this sense, an exemplary sign of the emergence of civil society. The point of departure was the chance encounter of family members in the places where they hoped to receive some news about the whereabouts of their absent loved ones, however, a few individuals with some previous political experience did play a facilitating role. The meaning of the demands and the struggle emerged from the very experience of confrontation with the authorities, but was considerably helped by international human rights networks, international personalities and institutions, and foreign governments. In fact, in the name of universal principles, this international action made the scope of national sovereignty relative, and in that sense constituted a precedent of the judicial and political globalization currently taking place. It was a society-based movement, born on the margins and against the current dominance of support or tolerance for the military regime. It was also a movement that emerged outside political parties that held a prudent, if not complacent, dialogue with the martial power and that expressly avoided referring to "the disappearance of persons" for years.

For the political parties and the traditional leadership that, towards the end of the military regime, acquired semilegitimate status, it was one more dictatorship with which to negotiate the terms of a controlled transition when it started to collapse. It was the movement of human rights which by persevering and gaining audience showed that the political regime of those years could not be compared to the classical dictatorships of the past.

The fact that a movement with marginal origins expanded through society and developed in spite of the indifference and hostility of the political parties and the institutional system, and confronted authority in the name of rights, constituted a new experience of social power that would leave its mark for the future. The figures of the Mothers of *Plaza de Mayo* in their rounds of mute interrogation of the regime about the fate of "the disappeared," are considered paradigmatic. On the same *Plaza* where the masses with their presence validated the leader-enunciator[4] who embodied the people, new figures (the Mothers of *Plaza de Mayo*) took the place of the old ones. The Mothers spoke through their voice or their silence. From their identity as citizens, they invoked principles (the right to life) inherent in the human condition before a regime—even if a "de facto" one—that was considered responsible for the fate of individuals and therefore required to inform and be accountable for what had occurred.

This appeal, at first repressed and isolated, contained the seeds of an autonomous citizenship, constructed on the basis of a peaceful challenge to those who controlled state power. The idea of rights, the basis of citizen autonomy, appeared precisely when the voices in the *Plaza* are raised, invoking universal principles that should be respected in equal measure; by those governing and those governed principles that can be invoked and subjected to public interpretation by each citizen. Confronted, on the one hand, by the authoritarian invocation of "reasons of state" by military who considered themselves the natural defenders of the nation and therefore did not intend to be held accountable for their acts, and on the other hand, by the populist tradition of a leader who embodied the interests of the people, unquestionable in themselves, "given," the idea of rights bursts on the scene as the critical discourse that will allow a more reflexive and eventually deliberative citizenry to emerge.

The victory of the Radical candidate in the 1983 presidential elections that marked the retreat of the military to their barracks and the beginning of their separation from a political role, was to a large extent the first entrance of the citizenry onto the center of the political stage. For the first time, the captive Peronist vote proved to be insufficient to win free elections and plunged this political force into an unprecedented crisis: the claim to represent "the people" and to act as if the political competitors could not aspire to the same position, was no longer enough to win elections. The defeat acted as a strong stimulant for the secularization of Peronism; that is, for its transformation into a party that had to win over the electorate to succeed in elections and within which several leaders aspiring to renew the tradition emerged.

The renewal of Radicalism also occurred on the basis of an extraordinary citizen mobilization. A massive influx of new adherents, strangers to the party tradition, enabled Raul Alfonsín—the leader of the internal current sector *Renovación y Cambio* (the "radical left")—to win office. He achieved this on the basis of unusual arguments and promises that indicated the incipient change in citizen culture: he condemned a military–trade union pact that his Peronist opponents had allegedly signed, and he repeatedly invoked the national Constitution and claimed to be better qualified than his opponents in assigning responsibilities for the events of the recent dictatorship. At that moment, this new central role played by the citizenry was expressed in the mobilization for the demands for human rights and justice. The unconventional political agenda was imposed on a political leadership that, as has been pointed out, generally lagged behind society. The new Radical leader who arrived at the president's office embodied those demands in his approach. However, the expansion of an independent citizenry that would erode the traditional workings of mass political parties would not be immediately evident since the repoliticization of the "democratic spring" seemed to follow the traditional channels of political street mobilization. Millions of Argentines rejoined the traditional parties and many of them participated in the campaign events too. But these events were no longer only ritualistic affairs, since citizens were closely following political debates and could, according to the circumstances, change their vote.

The consistence that the 1983 refoundation of democracy progressively acquired, was based in good part on this citizenry autonomy that would become more solid with time. Its expansion, as it went eroding the parties' captive votes, made political competition more credible and forced candidates to pay more attention to the expectations of the so-called "independent voters." In the 1983 electoral campaign, street mobilization was still important as a measure of organizational capacity and an expression of the correlation of forces but it was clear that politicians were increasingly aware that electoral activity was centered on elections and that these depended on a public space that the traditional political parties and trade union organizations no longer dominated.

During the 1980s the logic of corporative power coexisted with the above-mentioned logic of citizenry. At the same time, the perceived persistence of a military threat acted as a destabilizing factor. The trade unions were bent upon playing a salient political role in accordance with previous traditions but by the end of the decade, corporatism had become increasingly impotent and publicly discredited. Soon politicians realized that the ballot box was the only legal means to win office, which undermined the traditional connivance with corporatist politics. And yet, while these processes were developing, the first democratic government was beleaguered by the military, the trade unionists, and the business sector.

The experiences that reinforced citizen independence and led organizations and political leaders to permanently reformulate their "political supply" and recreate the link of representation, continued in the 1990s but now they were associated with social transformations that altered conditions of the citizenry. In particular, the changes that occurred under the government of Carlos Menem accelerated the demise of traditional identities. On one hand, the hyperinflationary outbreak that lasted for several months in 1989, allowed the government to deploy a conservative modernization strategy in the economy and the state, in spite of the populist atmosphere of the electoral campaign. The experience produced an interpretation of this kind of personalist and innovative leadership in terms of "delegative democracy" (O'Donnell 1992); that is, an increase in the decisionist capacities of a president who, claiming a direct link with the electorate, governs by "decree of necessity and urgency," forcing Congress to either acquiesce or take the initiative to gather opposing forces.

Although Menem's government was perceived as a social alliance between the poorest Peronist sectors and the world of finance and business, his policies reformed Argentine capitalism and generated a sector favored by "the model." In fact, his government relied on a heterogeneous base of support that cut across the traditional social structure, formed by his own political initiative and the interests generated by the new policies.

The referred citizen autonomy entails the end of captive political constituencies although not necessarily the capacity to create independent political alternatives. The support Menem received, in spite of the fact that his government program contradicted his electoral promises, stemmed from the hope that his stabilization program would extricate the country from hyperinflation and improve the efficiency of the state, in particular the provision of basic goods. So, the "transgressive" president was able to gain legitimacy by responding creditably to citizen expectations within an international context dominated by the doctrine of neoliberal solutions. Indeed, since the beginning of the 1990s, the implementation of promarket policy reforms such as deregulation and fiscal austerity, the privatization of service-providing public companies, and the pension system altered individual habits. The ideological change fuelled by diminishing expectations and the discontent with state services encouraged the hope that a sustainable order could be established accepting the necessary sacrifices.

The progressively more autonomous citizenry with its heterogeneous opinions and the privatizing, promarket tendencies that prevailed at the time changed at the end of the Menemist cycle. What favored the prevalence of more extreme variants of neoliberal doctrine than in other countries in the early 1990s was the relative weakness of the public sphere in which there was little real debate, and in which the new ideas easily prevailed over statist positions that had fallen into grave disrepute.

Within this context, the Olivos Pact[5] and its consequence, the constitutional reform implemented in 1994 to enable President Menem to run for a third term, revealed once again the capacity of those in power to configure a new political scenario and, in this case, the presidential ability to mask the detrimental effects on the Constitution and the institutions by the strength of his willpower, the efficacy of his government, and his power of extortion (Cheresky 1999a). However, early on, some sectors of citizens sensitive to the defense of the institutional order, resisted the president's hegemonic tendencies—this in the Argentine political tradition constituted an unprecedented event. A decisionist style of rule and a way of exercising power that encouraged corruption and was associated with the image of governing authorities closely linked to economic power, was beginning to fail.

For reasons that I will examine later in this chapter, although the initial reactions to presidential decisionism were individual rather than collective, they encouraged the emergence of new representations. The political party *Frente Grande*, later *Frepaso*, grew rapidly in the 1994 election for constitutional delegates as a reaction against the Olivos Pact that made possible a constitutional reform expressly destined to facilitate the president's reelection.

The emergence of this third political force, which had a strong influence on political life for the rest of the decade and had been associated with the alternation in power before it disappeared, was the first evidence that a new party with substantial support could develop on the basis of its action in the public sphere and appeal directly to the citizenry.[6] As previously indicated, it was one among several signals that would mark a change of direction in the formation of political identities and relations of representation.

In 2003, the post-breakdown political reorganization was also carried out by political institutionalization from above, similar to the way Menem built relations of representation for the conservative modernization process. But in the former case the circumstances were different. President Néstor Kirchner was elected accidentally as a result of circumstances[7] and seemed condemned to impotence due to the weakness of his original electoral legitimacy and his dependence on the party apparatuses that supported him. His voluntarist performance in office, however, absorbed the anti-Menemist wave of sentiment that had pervaded the campaign and gave it an energy that went far beyond the expectations of a disillusioned citizenry.

Nevertheless, in both Menem and Kirchner's cases of support building, citizens' disposition was defined by negativity; that is, by the rejection of a previous political experience (in one case hyperinflation, in the other the consequences of conservative modernization and a corrupt and decisionist style of rule). That negative state created an opportunity for a political force or leader to give it a positive meaning. The foregoing reinforces the idea that creating a link of representation requires political initiative and decision and that these are not limited to reflecting a state or set of preexisting demands. Of course, if they aspire to succeed, neither can the instituting leader or political force ignore certain citizen dispositions that determine, or rather limit, the situation.

As far as the 1990s are concerned, as has been pointed out, the emergence of an important third force that could affect the traditional bipartism was a symptom of diverse transformations. In first place, identities were no longer formed as they were traditionally within a social movement (the mobilization for political rights in the case of radicalism, and for social rights in the case of Peronism). Rather, the linkage became more mediated and contingent: the citizens' answer to the call of a popular leader who makes use of the media, above all television, to sustain his linkage to political representation.

The new party rapidly channeled its aspirations for political renewal, coming in second in the 1995 presidential elections. It codirected the opposing coalition that won the legislative elections in 1997 and, two years later, the presidential election removing a Peronist president from power for the first time. Other similar but less important experiences took place at local and national level, reinforcing the possibility of building popular support in the public sphere but also revealing its fragility.

The second half of the 1990s was characterized by the political fluidity that resulted from the expansion of an independent citizenry. In the 1995 presidential elections, the alternatives to Menem's modernizing and decisionist style were not considered consistent by the majority. What prevailed were two expectations: on the one hand, to ensure governability through the reelection of the president—although a wave of criticism was in the making, forged in an expanded public sphere in which journalists and mass media played a significant role (Waisbord 2001)—and on the other hand, the incipient renewal of the party system.

The alliance between Radicals and *Frepasistas* was built on those bases and possessed more public than organizational support. At that moment, the paradox of political forces—or a coalition in this case—that would become slaves of public opinion was formed. A popular leadership who apparently is in a representative relationship that allows innovation due to its plasticity can, however, lead to conformism. Thus, the coalitional experience of *Frepasistas* and Radicals evolved from the vigor of the negative convergence against Menemist power to immobility when candidates had to be chosen and the government program defined.

Clearly, citizen autonomy was eroding the traditional patterns of political captivity. Besides, in terms of vote, fluctuation and volatility encouraged dissidence within the party structures. Although this citizen autonomy was more rooted in Buenos Aires and the big cities, the logic of autonomy vis-à-vis party and corporatist structures gradually expanded and reached the traditional structures all over the country. One particularly significant moment was Menem's attempt to run for the third time. Although in the early stages it seemed that the issue would be resolved at the institutional and party level, when the initiative became publicly known, it moved from the interior of Peronism and the state to a wider stage that placed the citizenry as the ultimate arbitrators. The defeat of Menem's endeavor illustrated for the first time in a democratic context, that citizen opinion—as public opinion, or as citizen vote—counted more than institutional apparatuses. The latter finally bowed to the state of public opinion.

It is in this context that the new questions about the relation between institutions and quality of democracy are posed. From the dawn of the reconstruction of democracy, it has been impossible to establish strong institutions and respect for the law, though this ideal appeared in the literature on the subject (Mainwaring and Scully 1995). The fact is that the continuity of Argentine democracy has been fuelled by crises and, in particular, by processes of deinstitutionalization that made renewals possible. In some cases these generated political enthusiasm and in others the reestablishment of political authority and public trust, as in the recent process after the breakdown at the end of 2001. In that context of crisis, the existence of a sometimes active and generally vigilant and demanding citizenry has been the main factor of political monitoring. Indeed, the terms in which the dispute was formulated in the late 1990s could evoke a simple polarization in which one of the terms would be the virtuous people. In fact, however, increasing citizen autonomy produced a more demanding and vigilant institutional context but nothing was assured regarding future developments. In short, this circumstance did not exempt political leadership from their responsibilities in the constitution of politics.

Nevertheless, the defeat of the *Alianza*[8] undertaking led to a general questioning of the entire political leadership and produced disappointment with popular leaders, which, however, proved to be temporary. This transformation of the party system would go further since the historical parties had exhausted their traditional cohesive resources and started to break up under citizen demand for satisfactory representation. The increase of citizen autonomy entailed a crisis of representation that questioned the identity and the very existence of the traditional political forces. The successive political experiences of the governments of Menem and Fernando De la Rúa fueled that reaction of exhaustion that was expressed in the famous rallying cry: "They must all go." The reaction, however, seems to be part of a lasting change in the relationship between politicians and citizens that is leading to the formation of contingent identities that, although ideological dimensions are not absent, do not tend to adopt the forms of the traditional global and systematic antagonisms. Political antagonisms seem to be characterized by negativity more than by substantive identities, as seen in the past.

Finally, in the legislative elections of October 14, 2001, a true crisis of representation became evident. It was unexpectedly vented in the social explosion named the *cacerolazo* that led to the resignation of President De la Rúa. At that moment, voting became the opportunity to question political representation although not the representative system as such. The number of abstainers grew but most significant was the willingness to vote against the alternatives offered. Another expression of this protest, although less significant, was the vote for new political groups.

The strongest indicator of the ongoing crisis in the party system itself was the disintegration of the governing coalition manifested by the disaffection with the president expressed by official candidates during the electoral campaign. Just a few months later, the presidential mandate was interrupted by his resignation. When new authorities took office in a context of crisis, they adopted measures that radically altered the existing economic model. The declaration of default on the debt froze the credit and the financial links with the world and created doubts about the future of the country. At the same time of the country's breakdown, a considerable transformation of the sociopolitical scene was taking place.

CITIZENSHIP, *CACEROLEROS*, AND *PIQUETEROS*

Argentina's sociopolitical scene has experienced a significant transformation. In a short time, *caceroleros* and *piqueteros* replaced the traditional mobilizations of political parties and trade unions. The latter has not completely disappeared, but even in electoral periods their activity appears conditioned by a new public situation that, in contrast to the past, is beyond their control.

Deciphering the nature of the new actors and the new real and virtual linkages is a task that calls for new concepts and analytical instruments. In particular, the public constitution of new collective actors as citizens, different from the social conditionings that were characteristic of actors in the past, is a good point of departure for the intelligibility sought in this article.

The *cacerolazo*

From December 19, 2001 and for some months there after, the saucepans were resounding in the most varied contexts to express citizen discontent that at the time seemed boundless. Generally, from that date onwards, every Friday they rang out in the evening from balconies and street corners, their owners converged on neighborhood squares and then walked to *Plaza de Mayo*. They also sounded during the day in front of banks, certain public buildings, and the Courts in repudiation of the Supreme Court. But on that day, December 19, for the first time the saucepans were the instrument of a colossal protest that extended from the city to the greater Buenos Aires and to some cities in the littoral provinces. It led to the immediate resignation of the questioned minister of Economy and, hours later, of the president himself. It was an authentically spontaneous outburst the initial conducive condition for which was, in part, urban proximity that facilitates behavior contagion and, even more, television (and later, no longer spontaneous stages, the networks of Internet), which helped to disseminate information on the first demonstrations. No intervention of civic, corporatist, or political organizations was registered in the beginning of the social activation.

Argentina has a long history of street politics, a corporatist or party resource often used by power holders. The tradition of popular mobilization has always entailed organization from above: in particular, organized crowds walk to gathering points where political meetings take place, ritual affirmations of collective allegiances that leave little room for the individual, independent participant.

From this perspective, the outburst of December 19 possessed unusual characteristics. The tidal wave of demonstrators began in balconies and the doors of houses and buildings, some of them gathered at street corners and in squares and cut the traffic along some principal streets, accompanied by the sounding of car horns. This occurred for hours, at the end of which some demonstrators in groups started out on a long walk towards the traditional centers of power: the Pink House, the Congress, the president's residence in Olivos and their equivalents in the cities in the provinces. These demonstrators were at times citizens, at times neighbors. The symbol of the saucepan indicates the proximity of the domestic world, a continuum between the home and the public sphere that disturbs the traditional distinction between the private and the public realms. The participation of whole families emphasized this new, ambiguous condition.

The next day, December 20, in the *Plaza de Mayo* and the adjacent areas, clashes between demonstrators and the police produced several civilian deaths. This overstepping of authority together with the Peronist opposition's refusal to heed a last-minute appeal to form part of a government of national unity completed the scenario that produced the presidential resignation.

The vigor of this citizen plebiscite, the *cacerolazo*, triggered the resignation of two successive presidents—the successor of De la Rúa, Adolfo Rodríguez Saa who left amidst public protest and isolated by his own party—and loomed over by a third, Eduardo Duhalde, who had to shorten his mandate and advance the call for elections due to another violent repression of a popular demonstration that discredited him.

The power and critical potential of this social mobilization has run parallel to the weakness of the institutional system and the political parties. However, this street mobilization was different from its predecessors. Indeed, the strength of the *cacerolazo* outburst cannot be estimated in the same terms as traditional mobilization that took place in the customary places within a logic of force relations and whose success was measured by the number of people in attendance. In this case, the scope of the mobilization was decisive because it managed to shake the whole institutional system and yet, at the same time, was unmeasurable. The whole city seemed involved and everybody seemed to join the protest. Undoubtedly, the point was not the number of demonstrators in *Plaza de Mayo* but the extraordinary and immediate legitimacy effect (or, in this case, delegitimation).

The December 19 *cacerolazo* is paradigmatic of a social mobilization that is heterogeneous and irreducible to a single meaning. That day a new format of public intervention was inaugurated and its shining success was an invitation to incorporate within it all the demands and voice public discontent. The political activation was minimal, since it was sparked by the president's speech that evening, and perceived as unacceptable due to its divorce from reality and the plan to establish order limiting public freedoms by announcing a state of siege.

The citizens' protest, which broke out immediately after this extreme measure was announced, constituted, strictly speaking, an act of civic disobedience. At that moment the initial experience of a generic "veto" started to take shape, as a indication of citizen mobilization. They vetoed a government that showed a lack of sensitivity and authority. This was the minimum political meaning contained in the act of a whole society coming before its constituted authorities. The force of that expression could not be but negative: the heterogeneous convergence round a common rejection of the way political representation was exercised. This political negativity created a vacuum of representation and opened up all the possibilities of political renewal. The mobilized society identified with the national flag, with the cry "They must all go" and not much more. In the initial stages, the common noise of the pot and pans created the negative convergence, the unity before those who governed and the political leadership in general.

Since the movement expressed a veto and was generated by a "negative summons" on the part of the authorities, no unifying statements nor claims to replace the government were initially formulated. It was an action emanating from civil society that aimed to influence. No alternative order was envisioned and thus, the search for good representation constituted a reaffirmation of democracy. Accordingly, the extremely hostile character of the rejection of politicians was tempered by the persistently peaceful character of the protest.

The meaning of the protest was also closely linked to the context. It was about individual citizens beleaguered by a crisis. Many of those mobilized had never intervened in public life before. They just rushed out into the streets, overwhelmed by the government's lack of direction and the weakness of presidential authority, not because of any specific demands.

On the other hand, the social crisis had already erupted in Argentina, a few hours earlier, in a different guise. The citizen outburst was preceded by an explosion of poverty and exclusion, through looting driven by need but often accompanied by delinquency. Since the middle of December, demands for food and shop break-ins increased, in particular in Greater Buenos Aires. In the dawn of December 19, a wave of looting began that grew during the day. In the early afternoon, the rumor that a crowd of poor people was coming from beyond the city and that looting would occur in the very capital city, led most shopkeepers to close their establishments and many other people to return to their homes. De la Rúa's speech attempted to respond to this situation and these fears. Citizens in the city of Buenos Aires could have called for restrictions to ensure public order after the hours of fear they had experienced, but the unease and the discontent turned against the figure of the president, who was somehow considered responsible for what was occurring. This political meaning can be incorporated into the interpretation of the emergent mobilization. It was unexpected because it disproved the diagnosis of a citizen withdrawal from public life, at least in the form of active participation; although, with hindsight, the novelty of citizen activism was only partly contradicted, since it constituted an outburst, a presence limited in time.

The interpretations of the event varied considerably. Some considered it apolitical, the fact that it confronted the entire political leadership and the parties, the apparent negation of all representation and the prevalence of negativity with no positive pronouncements, gave credence to that interpretation. For others instead, because it was a movement "from below," foreign to parties and institutions, it embodied virtues that would regenerate public life. This position, which opposes the alleged inherent virtues of the people to the *natural* oppression of the leadership, had its moment of popularity within intellectual circles that hoped for a complete political change as a result of an immediate renewal. This grassroot illusion was blind to the future indetermination of the political situation. A fissure opened up between those governing and the governed and its resolution was uncertain.

But in spite of the fact that the development of the outburst depended on public actors' capabilities and not on a sense of just order inherent to the popular condition, citizen intervention incorporated the results of democratic learning of preceding years that lent it, even initially, a positive meaning. The citizen veto that triggered President De la Rúa's resignation unblocked the institutional impasse that institutional mechanisms could not. The president was discredited and did not have consistent parliamentary support. The future of his mandate generated strong skepticism at every level, but neither the opposition nor those in power dared initiate a motion of censure or impose an institutional settlement confronting the president. In this context, citizen intervention constituted an act of civic disobedience that interrupted institutional continuity but had a regulatory, clearing effect. It became possible to process the head of state's resignation through institutional channels that were acknowledged in spite of the discontent. The streets applied their veto power but did not claim decision-making power for themselves in the stead of legal institutions. The unblocking effect that De la Rúa's resignation brought about and the parallel activation of the public sphere produced relief, and not more fear than was already present.

According to De la Rúa's circle, the chaos that originated in the looting was encouraged by Peronist local bosses and government officials, in particular in Greater Buenos Aires. Indeed, there is abundant evidence that the looting was encouraged by certain actors; however, the main mobilization of the needy, a gesture of rebellion that spread through the country, was rooted in the urgencies of poverty, in inaction in the face of need and above all, in the discredit of the main political authority. All these factors fuelled an atmosphere of despair and impunity that different kinds of opportunists took advantage of. The claim that the mobilization was a conspiracy planned by the opposition was not believed by the Radicals least committed to the outgoing president (some of which formed part of the next Peronist president's cabinet, Duhalde) nor by the Radical and *Frepaso* deputies and senators who participated in a de facto parliamentary coalition with the new government.

What I call citizen "regulatory intervention" has been accepted as such and if different interpretations of the meaning of the *cacerolazo* exist, they do not emphasize the institutional discontinuity it produced. However, this acceptance has not been put into conceptual terms. It is probably feared that if the regulatory character of the intervention were recognized, it would imply justifying a plebiscitary development of democracy in which the opposition could repeatedly resort to activating street mobilizations against the institutions with the excuse that legitimacy was permanently at stake and that the legal renewal of mandates could be ignored. Indeed, this risk exists as recent experiences from other Latin American countries have shown, but it is perhaps inevitable if it is acknowledged that democracy constitutes, in essence, an unstable regime and that although institutions must be preserved, they are also subject to changes that originated outside themselves.

The inaugural *cacerolazo* on the evening of December 19 and the dawn of December 20, opened up a space and a time of protest that, as neighborhood assemblies multiplied, appeared to leave an institutional balance that invigorated civil society. In the city of Buenos Aires and the surrounding areas, weekly neighborhood meetings were held for a time, revealing the development of a stronger civil society. However, when the assemblies were about to progress to the next step by formulating general objectives and even public policies, the risks of divisiveness and progressive weakness became evident as a result of opposing political positions and the intervention of political militants who attempted to garner support for their projects. Could those neighborhood assemblies in which inexperienced individuals participated in the public sphere side by side with vanguard militants be transformed into spaces of pluralist deliberation? For some weeks, while efforts were concentrated on neighborhood activities, they were. In many cases the assemblies organized to carry out community work related to health, the dearth of buildings for public or recreational activities, the provision of cheap food, etcetera, but the tendency that prevailed attempted to keep up civic activity by promoting objectives that required permanent and spectacular activities on the part of the neighbors, thus evading a deeper but riskier deliberation for community life.

Frequently resorting to more aggressive actions, badly suited to the initial peaceful temper of the mobilization, led to a rapid reduction in the number of participants. Very soon the *escrache*[9] became an accepted practice. In fact, this term condenses forms of mobilization with different objectives: not only to cordon off banks and other public institutions but also to boycott of radio and TV programs, newspapers, and finally to protest, eventually including physical aggression at the domiciles of individuals, in particular politicians, government officials and judges. The clearest precedents of the public denouncements and calls for social sanctions against those who, suspected of crimes and misdemeanors, profited from judicial misfeasance could be found in the actions of human rights organizations that denounced torturers and kidnappers, and the heads of the military juntas in the 1970s who had evaded judicial action or been pardoned. In this case, the aim of the *escrache* was to indicate an unpaid debt to society that the public action attempted to settle, substituting for the inexistent or incomplete penal sanction. Likewise, the gatherings outside public buildings denounced the slowness of justice or suspicions of foul play.

But the spread of this kind of protest, pointing its finger at people in the private sphere who were frequently charged not with crimes but policies carried out while in public service, transformed the mobilized groups into lynch mobs. Thus, recourse to the law and procedures that could ensure that every person is judged under the protection of his legal right to a defense, was substituted by the subjective certainty or even the emotional outburst that calls for a scapegoat. This form of action that overrides social plurality contains the seeds of violent civil confrontation because each group defines its own law and its own victims and foregoes the framework of common norms and authorities.

The *cacerolazo* mainstream has fostered more specific consequences. The *ahorristas* (savers) whose deposits and investments were frozen in banks met to protest in the downtown area on some days and in the neighborhoods, on others. From January 2002, the accusations against the members of the Supreme Court and the request for their impeachment were channeled in meetings held every Thursday at midday in front of the Court buildings. In some cases, groups with opposing demands have mobilized, for example the debtors and the lenders, each one seeking to obtain rulings that would favor them.

The citizen outburst initiated a process of heterogeneous social activation, which, as pointed out above, is impossible to reduce to a single meaning. In order to understand the events, it is necessary to keep in mind the contextual circumstances mentioned above. Conceptually, the deep crisis of representation can be interpreted as promoting social destructuring or deinstitutionalization; however, this social activation reveals the imprint of the recent democratic experience. On the one hand, this social activation gave expression to the basic social impulse (the *okhlos*) and on the other, to the attempt to redefine the institution of political unity (the *demos*). Indeed, this social activity was discontinuous in respect to the subordinated politicization of the populist people, but it was also distinct from political conformism—that administration that confines individuals to a totally private state with no mediations between individual life plans and a state that guarantees the rule of law.

In its ideal form, the citizenship of the patrimonialist individual (Orleans 1999)—she who no longer depends on the state for public goods such as pensions, health care, and education—tends to a withdrawal from politics. Thus, representation is conceived as a functional relationship. The political class is exclusively in charge of public affairs that constitute the regulatory framework of an expanding private world. In this approach, to govern is to administrate and, consequently, an essentially technical task. The public role of citizens is to keep an eye on those who govern as when guiding a ship; that is, making sure the helmsmen keeps the ship sailing within the flow of the stream.

Towards the end of 2001, the crisis of representation reduced the features of patrimonialist individualism attributed to the citizens.

A transition took place from general consensus to general dissent, from the retreat to the private world to a certain blurring of frontiers between the private and the public spheres, and in any case, the occupation of public space. However, the sociological conditions of patrimonial individualism remain.

When society turned to public activity, its actual presence prevailed over the usual instruments for ascertaining public opinion: surveys and their interpretation by the media pundits of the state of opinion. Naturally, the media and the polls did not go away but were pushed aside by the emergence of a space of citizen enunciation and presence. The people were no longer the object of research and interpretation that referred to a latent other. They appeared in varied activities and acquired a productivity that was absent when produced by the survey of a market research agency, the tabloids or panels of the talking heads of the televised media.

A different public situation was shaped, at least provisionally, in which social mobilization exercised great influence over those institutions that it was at the same time calling into question. As indicated above, objectives of gaining office were not at stake, which is paradoxical given that the aim was to influence an institutional system with which all connection seemed broken. However, this kind of behavior showed a self-imposed restriction of mobilized society, which acted as a factor of containment in the face of possible greater violence or dangerous plans for political regime change.

To sum up, society was mobilized and it exercised its veto power against a government that was censured and suspect; that is, a very different phenomenon from a social movement characterized by mobilization for the defense or achievement of demands, or a change in rights or values.

It was also an individualist society, poorly organized and little disposed to establish associations with public purposes; a vigilant society that confronted representatives in which it placed limited trust and that expressed itself regularly as public opinion and occasionally through an outburst.

Piquetero Organizations and the Unemployed, between Revolutionary Utopia and Basic Needs

In appearance more traditional than the neighborhood mobilization, *piquetero* activity, however, possesses unusual features and challenges interpretation. *Piqueteros* both are and are not the expression of a social situation.

In Argentina, there has been a gradual but constant—and in the last years sharp—economic deterioration that has placed the majority of the population below the poverty line, and made a considerable proportion of them (one out of every three people) indigent. This rapid and pronounced downward path to poverty and unemployment has had profound social and political effects. From a social and political point of view, people have been deprived of social links since exclusion does not create identity linkages among those affected as having a job does. Besides the absence of a "spontaneous" collective linkage that could produce identity, in Argentina there was no social provision for unemployment subsidies that could create a network of state agencies at which to present claims. At first sight, then, independent of the number involved, to be unemployed becomes an individual situation that stimulates individual survival strategies. The growth of unemployment in the 1990s generated reactions of discontent of which the *piquete* was the most successful. Its initial, more spectacular expressions were associated to the *pueblada*.[10] But it was only in the year 2000 when this type of action became more frequent as a result of the simultaneous growth of unemployment and the reduction of the unemployment subsidies.

This is not simply a question of the unemployed who make demands; rather, it concerns an actor who is generated in the public action that reveals him as such. The road block is able to congregate individuals that seek public assistance because direct action pulls them out of passivity and impotence and imbues them with the feeling that they can do something to deal with their problems, or at least, make their presence felt before their fellow human beings. It is a demonstration of strength with concrete consequences: it interrupts the activities of others and obliges them to consider the existence of these protestors. And, above all, the picket occupies not only the sidewalk of the road it blocks, but also the public space in the media, in the news, and the debates and announcements that circulate within it.

The road block requires organizational activities before and after the event. Public action is at the center of this kind of social mobilization and within it the actors, the *piqueteros*, are constituted. This principle of direct action has invigorated the movement because it has proven effective: it has attracted public attention and produced an increase in social aid, in particular after the December 2001 breakdown.

The road block compulsively addresses those affected by it, although its principal aim is to get the government's attention and response. It usually marks the beginning of negotiations to obtain unemployment subsidies from government officials but sometimes the demands are purely political. The road block is a meeting place and different types of excluded groups attend it. The classic short- or long-term unemployed person is in a minority, the majority is composed of women, usually confined to the home, and young people who have never had a job, usually the most active when authorities are challenged (Svampa and Pereyra 2003).

But after the street action, road block or demonstrations are carried out and as far as the *piquetero* organizations become the distributors of a portion of public aid, a different social network is generated. These organizations are able to persist when they take over the tasks that the state has withdrawn from but as they fulfill that role they also become functional appendages. However, the *piquetero* organzations also produce changes in public welfare: they apply their own criteria to the distribution of goods. Thus, they become an alternative to Peronist clientelism and the state's attempts to apply universalist principles. These organizations which are—albeit virtually—representative of the world of the unemployed and excluded often foster subordinating and oppressive relationships.

It is necessary, however, to distinguish different types of action and organization. The *piquetero* movement is in fact formed by a constellation of dissimilar groups, generally the result of external intervention. The oldest were created by trade union sponsors: *Federación de Tierra y Vivienda (FTV)* (Federation of Land and Housing) and the *Corriente Clasista y Combativa (CCC)* (Classist and Combative Branch), although the latter is hegemonized by a revolutionary party of the left. The *Polo Obrero* and the *Bloque Piquetero Nacional* were founded towards the end of 2001, under the auspices of the Trotskyite, revolutionary left. The last two groups, based in the south of Greater Buenos Aires, are the ones that have grown most since then, taking pride in upholding an intransigent position before a government open to dialogue and expanding social policies. External intervention brought with it an influx of experienced cadres and the initial resources to set up the organization (Svampa and Pereyra 2003) besides ensuring leadership positions to those who took the initiative.

The constitutive traits of this collective identity have been the object of disputes between the different organizations. Since the national assemblies of *piqueteros* held in 2001, the characteristics of the road blocks have been debated and, more recently, so has their existence itself. The more reformist sectors, and even some of those who maintain long term revolutionary objectives, have chosen to organize road blocks that allow alternative crossings for vehicle traffic and have opposed the disturbing figure of the masked *piquetero*, armed with a club. In contrast, others have supported antiinstitutional actions and resisted the institutionalization of the subsidies, in particular state control of the funds. Nevertheless, the more radicalized sectors of the *piquetero* movement have tried to extend the direct-action methodology inspired in the road block to temporarily thwarting toll booth collections on the roads under private management and also subway entrances where they burst in, block the ticket booths and encourage users to travel without paying.

As far as the government, which took office on May 25, 2003, has addressed the issues of unemployment and the protest, the scope and radicalism of road blocks seem to have diminished while the differences between the *piquetero* organizations have increased. Neither have the attempts to spread civil disobedience among other citizens succeeded. The government's political response was based on the recognition of the legitimacy of the demands, and one of the consequences has been a widening of the margins of social tolerance to the protests. However, social attitudes vary since that same society desires order and security and watches the rise of direct action with unease and even rejection. It is well known that discontent with the protest methods has not affected the government's image. Tolerance has implied the acceptance of violations of the law, and the avoidance of repression and liability. This has meant ignoring the challenges in word and fact proffered by the more radicalized groups. The objective is to keep up the subsidies to the unemployed, redirecting them towards the market through small businesses, formal labor activities and training programs. Above all, and in strictly political terms, the aim is to show openness to dialogue, thus isolating the more radicalized *piqueteros*.

It must be kept in mind that the *piquetero* groups in the Greater Buenos Aires compete with the traditional clientelistic networks of the Peronist party machine in the area. As unemployment and poverty increased, political brokers and *manzaneras*[11] have been the main "problem solvers" in that field. Their relationship with the local municipalities is what makes possible the existence of informal networks that distribute resources of a varied nature. The term "networks" seems appropriate since the exchange does not only involve goods for political favors but also a wider sociability of belonging and recognition (Auyero, 2001). The accelerated increase in unemployment and poverty has produced a deluge of demands that exceed the existent channels.

Now that the political scope of the *piquetero* movement has been examined, the ambivalent nature of their representative function should be underscored. Although groups of the poor unemployed have entered the organizations, these most needy sectors are not the only ones that participate. In general terms, the organizations only incorporate a very low number of the unemployed. The significance of these organizations proceeds from their virtual representation rather than their real organizational capabilities. Probably, however, most of the unemployed that do not mobilize and those that do so only sporadically identify with the *piqueteros.*

In more general terms, as indicated above, society reflects an ambivalent attitude since it perceives in the *piqueteros* the expression of a social situation of need that concerns everybody. This has lead successive governments to be extremely prudent in the face of actions of protest that, although undoubtedly illegal, have been tolerated.

The *piquetero* actions do not seem destined to generate a permanent social movement. Unemployment and poverty will probably persist in time and, if they are to be reabsorbed, it will occur gradually. But if the tendency of recovery and economic growth continues, the current social policies should take on the core demands.

What is at stake, indeed, are the universalist and reincorporation policies that place the leaders who have embraced revolutionary or even autonomist strategies in a paradoxical position. Will these vanguards resign themselves to a process of institutionalization that would lead to stabilizing an ordinary associational life (community soup-kitchens, micro enterprises, neighborhood assemblies) that could, in turn, lead to either political indifference or a pluralist politicization like that of the rest of society, instead of cohesive structures based on an oppositional ideology or at least round leaders who are thus committed?

The 2003 electoral process has made evident that the political slogans of the *piquetero* leadership do not translate into votes. Even those who adopted a reformist position and proclaimed alliances with the government at the zenith of its popularity found little electoral support. As previously pointed out, the link between the organizers and the organized is problematic in itself. Various *piquetero* groups follow a logic in which they obtain public resources (unemployment subsidies and sometimes food) through mobilization and then distribute them according to meritocratic criteria of "those who struggle." But does this situation, often silenced due to mistaken principles of political correctness, disqualify the legitimacy of the *piquetero* movement?

The subject of "*piquetero* rights" is a complex one. Limiting protest to make it compatible with public order should be an inescapable government aim. The argument that restrictions on violence or judicial intervention in the case of crimes are untenable or unjust given the nature of the demands, is not admissible.

But the petition of not criminalizing social protest has its basis. The different *piquetero* groups can be critiqued by their fellow citizens but they cannot be censured for their ideological inclinations. Within the republican framework, only illegal acts are reprehensible. If the realm of the excluded is to be prevented from becoming fertile territory for the expansion of revolutionary organizations that question the democratic order, certain actions would be advisable. On the one hand, the presence of state agencies should be fostered in even the most removed areas in order to make the right to social aid effective without having to submit to any network, and the protection for all furnished by the rule of law should be promoted. On the other hand, the political options that represent and organize the excluded with a view to carrying out social reforms in a democratic framework should be strengthened.

To discriminate *piquetero* groups on the basis of their possible antidemocratic beliefs or in any way that would imply that opinions are punishable by law has no justification because only breaking the law should be penalized. Besides, it should be remembered that all links of representation establish institutions; that is, those represented cannot be considered individuals endowed with willpower or determined interests before the link of representation is instituted. However, there exist evident signs of divorce between the needs of the participants and the projects of the leadership; above all, the organizations' associational life seems to contain a degree of coercion alongside the voluntary components. The restitution of state networks would reestablish basic political liberty and provide a minimum of choice where it is scarce.

These observations on the social linkages established in *piquetero* organizations lead to questions about the emerging associational life. In the popular and marginal neighborhoods a communitarian kind of civil society has developed; that is, one based more on solving needs and on solidarity than on political liberties. This type of civil society, if it can be called that in spite of the distance from the classic ideal, emerges as a source of learning and empowerment that compensates for the situation of vulnerable individuals and corresponds partly to the classic ideal, in the sense that it associates individuals as they present demands to the government. Besides, as far as these demands do not simply seek firm legal guarantees, they are a form of struggle for rights.

SOCIAL AND POLITICAL IDENTITIES CONSTITUTED IN THE PUBLIC SPHERE

It would be of little use to attempt to unify conceptually the different tendencies that characterize Argentina's society today. Those who have slipped into a sphere of social exclusion that prevents so many Argentines from freely joining public life, and those who benefit from being citizens but are affected by the dissolution of traditional identities, simply coexist, or even overlap, but they are not articulated.

On the one hand, there is a growing citizen autonomy and a disposition to strong but changing political commitments; on other, a state of need and dependence on subsistence subsidies that do not yet work as rights. However, the manipulation of the subsidies could lead to political subordination more due to what remains of the traditional structures than to the new vanguard organizations, at least in reference to electoral manipulation.

Associational life presents a peculiar geography. The greatest political liberty seems to flourish where individualism and withdrawal from public life are highest, at least in traditional terms. ". . . an innumerable multitude of men, alike and equal, constantly circling around in pursuit of the petty and banal pleasures . . . ," for whom their fellow does not exist because "he exists in and for himself, and though he still may have a family, one can at least say that he has not got a fatherland," according to the famous description by A. de Tocqueville (1988:691–692) referring to the private individual who turns his back on public life. In order to question the pertinence of the French scholar's disqualification of the private individual, we should consider the possibility that in contemporary societies and also in Argentina, the relationship between individuals and public life could be understood in new and different terms: as an audience of the media that creates public opinion; that is, as an informed and passive citizenry through public opinion surveys, and yet this does not disqualify them as citizens involved in public affairs.

This citizenry is passive in relation to an effective mobilization but it is not indifferent nor is it subject to manipulation. Citizens' opinions are formed in a space inhabited not only by journalists, media pundits, and group leaders but also by small public action groups, far removed from the conformist consensus that tend to establish links of virtual representation with the citizenry. As seen above, citizen passivity can be interrupted by sudden mobilizations when the links of representation are deficient or emergency necessitates it.

In contrast, an associational life closer to the figure of civil society in its traditional format can emerge even in the most excluded popular sectors. The struggle for some and communitarism for others can constitute the vertebrae of sociability that pull individuals out of their loneliness, although its consequences on public life are still under study. Probably, the aftermath of the general collapse at the end of 2001 will give place to a different order that includes the renewal of the political system and associational life. But some parameters seem firmly established, citizen autonomy being one of them.

The present reformist government was consolidated on the basis of a direct relationship between the president and public opinion, which produced a certain disciplined convergence of parliamentary representatives and governors around his figure. It could be argued that the link with high popularity rates during the first months of government corresponds to an exceptional period of deep institutional reconstruction that favors an emergency consensus. However, it seems possible to forecast that future stabilization will be carried out within the frame of an active public sphere in which citizens will recognize themselves in conflictive and fluctuating social and political identities. Political parties and trade unions will continue to perform certain functions but will no longer be the main depositories of global identities.

Probably, leaders of opinion and associational groups of virtual representation will continue to play an important role in the political construction of a public sphere dominated by the media.

NOTES

1. Translator's Note (hereafter TN): *cacerola* means saucepan in Spanish, *caceroleros* are the people who clanged their pots and pans to express their protest.
2. TN: The term derives from "picketers," those who picket.
3. TN: *Plaza de Mayo* is the square in front of Government House, the Pink House.
4. TN: The author is referring to Juan D. Perón.
5. TN: A personalistic agreement between Menem and the opposition leader Raúl Alfonsín in November of 1993 to reform the Constitution.
6. The FREPASO (*Frente País Solidario*), and its predecessor the *Frente Grande*, were based on the growing notoriety of the dissident Peronist deputy, Carlos Alvarez. That is, a personalist political group was formed round a leader who became popular due to his parliamentary initiatives and, above all, his television appearances. This political force was formed on an organizational base of militants and small parties from

Peronism and the traditional Left, and militants from the human rights movements. However, the republican and anticorruption discourse, which made its leader, and emerging associated ones, popular, was poorly connected to and rooted in the relatively weak, grassroot organizational base. But the leadership or leaderships—for others such as G. Fernandez Meijide y A. Ibarra emerged—were very different from the spell of traditional populist leaderships. The new image and popularity of the leaders were not, indeed, the result of a frivolous construction by the media, as some interpretations could have it. On the contrary, their innovative aspects captured support with an agility that old party structures, with growing difficulties to innovate, did not possess. However, these representative linkages depend essentially on their reproduction in the public space; that is, they need to permanently renew their popularity. Of course, this fragility of new leaderships can be mitigated if they are institutionally reinforced.

7. TN: Kirchner obtained 22.24% of the vote in the first round of balloting but became president because the runner-up, Menem, withdrew from the run-off election.
8. TN: The *Alianza* refers to the coalition between the Radical Party and Frepaso Party.
9. TN: The term comes from *lumfardo* (Buenos Aires slang) and means "to uncover," "to denounce."
10. TN: In a *pueblada* the whole town rises to defend its survival, threatened, for example, by the privatization of an enterprise that provides jobs and income to the community.
11. In particular in Greater Buenos Aires, informal networks for the distribution of food and other domestic goods exist in a frontier area between the Peronist party structure and that of local municipalities. Local bosses receive demands from the neighbors and satisfy them through the public resources they have access to at a local level. Supposedly, the provision of goods is reciprocated by political loyalty from the beneficiaries to the local boss not only by voting Peronist but by being loyal to a certain internal party group and by attending rallies and demonstrations. The *manzaneras* is a structure for distributing food, in particular for children, created by Hilda Chiche Duhalde toward the end of the 1990s. This network is formed by women each of whom is in charge of satisfying the needs of the *manzana* (block) assigned to her. The *manzaneras* have also served as a resource for political mobilization by Peronism and, in particular, by Duhalde.

BIBLIOGRAPHY

Adrogué, G., and M. Armesto (2001) "Aun con vida. Los partidos políticos argentinos en la década del noventa," *Desarrollo Económico* 160, Buenos Aires.

Arendt, H. (1997) *¿Qué es la Política?*, Barcelona: Paidós.

———. (1993) *La Condición Humana*, Barcelona: Paidós.

Auyero, J. (2001) *La Política de los Pobres-Las Prácticas Clientelares del Peronismo*, Buenos Aires: Manantial.

Bonasso, M. (2002) *El Palacio y la Calle: Crónica de Insurgentes y Conspiradores*, Buenos Aires: Planeta.

Bourdieu, P. (1975) "La opinión pública no existe," *Revista Voces y Cultura* 10, II, Semester of 1996.

———. (1997) *Sobre la Televisión*, Barcelona: Anagrama.

Catterberg, E. (1989) *Los Argentinos Frente a la Política. Cultura Política y Opinión Pública en la Transición Argentina a la Democracia*, Buenos Aires: Planeta.

Cavarozzi, M., and J. M. Abal Medina (eds.) (2002) *El Asedio a la política*, Rosario: Homo Sapiens.

Centro de Opinión Pública de la Universidad de Belgrano (2003): "Sondeo de Opinión: Campaña Electoral Presidencial 2003. Efectos de la Campaña Sobre la Opinión Pública y Perspectivas Para el Ballotage." Available at <www.onlineub.com>

Cheresky, I. (1995) "¿Hay Todavía Lugar Para la Voluntad política? Consenso Economicista, Liderazgo Personalista y Ciudadanía en Argentina," paper presented at the Seminar "Desarrollo Institucional y Crisis de la Representación Política," ISEN, Buenos Aires.

———. (1997) "La Inadmisible Desaparición de Personas," D. Canton and R. Jorrat (eds.), *La investigación social hoy*, Buenos Aires: CBC.

———. (1998) "Régimen Estatal de Desaparición de Personas," *Sociedad* 12/13, Buenos Aires.

———. (1999a) "La Experiencia de la Reforma Constitucional," *Entre el Abismo y la Ilusión. Peronismo, Democracia y Mercado*, M. Novaro (ed.), Buenos Aires: Tesis-Norma.

———. (1999b) "Citizenship, Mass Media and Public Opinion. Changing Political Trends in Argentina and Other New Democracies," mimeo.

———. (2002) "Autoridad Política Debilitada y Presencia Ciudadana de Rumbo Incierto," *Revista Nueva Sociedad*, Caracas.

Cheresky, I., and J. M. Blanquer (eds.) (2003) *De la Ilusión Reformista al Descontento Ciudadano. Las Elecciones en Argentina, 1999–2001*, Rosario: Homo Sapiens.

Cheresky, I., and I. Pousadela (eds.) (2001) *Política e Instituciones en las Nuevas Democracias Latinoamericanas*, Buenos Aires: Paidós.

Colectivo Situaciones (2002) *Apuntes para el nuevo protagonismo social*, 19 and 20, Buenos Aires: Ediciones De mano en mano.

De Riz, L. (1993) "Los Partidos Políticos y el Gobierno de la Crisis en Argentina," *Sociedad*, N° 2, Buenos Aires.

Ducatenzeiler, F. "La Representación Política en los Tiempos del Neoliberalismo. Política con Políticos y Política sin Políticos," paper presented at Lasa Congress, Dallas, 2003.

Duverger, M. (1950) *L'Influence des Systèmes Electoraux sur la Vie Politique*, Paris: Lib. Armand Colin.

Feijoo, M. del C. (2003) *Nuevo País, Nueva Pobreza*, Buenos Aires, Fondo de Cultura Económica.

Ferry, J. M., and D. Wolton (1992) *El Nuevo Espacio Público*, Buenos Aires: Gedisa.

Fitoussi, J. P., and P. Rosanvallon (1997) *La Nueva Era de las Desigualdades*, Buenos Aires, Manantial.

Gellner, E. (1991) "Civil Society in Historical Context," *International social Science Journal* 129.

Giarraca, N. (2001) *La Protesta Social en Argentina*, Buenos Aires: Alianza.

Godio, J. (2003) *Luces y Sombras en el Primer Año de Transición*, Buenos Aires: Biblos.

Gorz, A. (1977) *Misère du Présent. Richesse du Possible*, Paris: Galilée.

Habermas, J. (1996) *Between Facts and Norms: Contributions to a Discourse Theory of Law and Democracy*, Cambridge, MA: MIT Press.

Hall, J. (ed.) (1995) *Civil Society: Theory, History, Comparison*, Cambridge, UK: Polity Press.

Hardt, M., and A. Negri (2002) *Imperio*, Buenos Aires: Paidos.

Kohan, A. (2002)*¡A las calles! Una historia de los Movimientos Piqueteros y Caceroleros del 90 al 2002*, Buenos Aires: Colihue.

Kymlicka, W. (1996) *Ciudadanía Multicultural*, Barcelona: Paidós.

Kymlicka, W., and W. Norman (1997) "El Retorno del Ciudadano. Una Revisión de la Producción Reciente en Teoría de la Ciudadanía," *Agora* Nr. 7.

Lefort, C. (1985) "La Cuestión de la Democracia," *Revista Opciones.*

———. (1986) "Les Droits de l'Homme et l'Etat Providence," *Essais Sur le Politique*, Paris: Esprit/Seuil.

———. (1990) *La Invención Democrática*, Buenos Aires: Nueva Visión.

Levitsky, S. "Chaos and Renovation: Institutional Weakness and the transformation of Argentine Peronism," 1983–2002, paper presented at Lasa Congress, Dallas, 2003.

———. (1997) "Crisis, Party Adaptation, and Regime Stability in Argentina: The Case of Peronism, 1989–1995," paper presented at Latin American Studies Association, Guadalajara, México, April 1997.

Mainwaring, S., and T. Scully (eds.) (1995) "Introduction: Party Systems in Latin America," *Building Democratic Institutions: Party Systems in Latin America*, Stanford: Stanford University Press.

Manin, B. (1998) *Los Principios del Gobierno Representativo*, Madrid: Alianza.

Marshall, T. H. (1950) "Citizenship and Social Class," *Citizenship and Social Class*, T. H. Marshall and T. Bottomore (eds.), London: Pluto Press, 1996.

McGuire, J. W. (1995) "Political Parties and Democracy in Argentina," *Building Democratic Institutions: Party Systems in Latin America*, S. Mainwaring y T. Scully (eds.), Stanford: Stanford University Press.

Mora y Araujo, Manuel (1995) "De Perón a Menem. Una Historia del Peronismo," *Peronismo y Menemismo: Avatares del Populismo en la Argentin*, Atilio Borón et al. (eds.), Buenos Aires: El Cielo por Asalto.

Morlino, L. (2003) "The Quality of Democracy: Improvements or Subversion? Introductory Remarks," Stanford, mimeo.
Mouffe, Ch. (1999) *El Retorno de lo Político. Comunidad, Ciudadanía, Pluralismo, Democracia Radical*, Barcelona: Paidós.
MTD de Solano y Colectivo Situaciones (2002) *Más allá de los piquetes*, De mano en mano, Buenos Aires.
Novaro, M. (2002) *El Derrumbe Político en el Ocaso de la Convertibilidad*, Buenos Aires: Norma.
Novaro, M., and V. Palermo (1998) *Los Caminos de la Centroizquierda: Dilemas y Desafíos del Frepaso y de la Alianza*, Buenos Aires: Losada.
Nun, J. (2000) *Democracia ¿Gobierno del Pueblo o Gobierno de los Políticos?*, Buenos Aires: Fondo de Cultura Económica.
O'Donnell, G. (1997b) "Ilusiones y errores conceptuales," *Agora*, Nr. 6, Buenos Aires.
———. (1992) "¿Democracia Delegativa?," *Cuadernos del CLAEH*, Nr. 61.
———. (1996) "Otra Institucionalización," *Agora* Nr. 5, Buenos Aires.
———. (1997a) "The (Un)Rule of Law and Polyarchies in Latin America," paper presented at APSA meeting, Washington DC, 1997.
O'Donnell, G., O. Iazzetta, and J.Vargas Cullell (eds.) (2002) *Democracia, Desarrollo Humano y Ciudadanía: Reflexiones sobre la Calidad de Democracia en América Latina*, Rosario: Homo Sapiens.
Orléan, A. (1999) *Le Pouvoir de la Finance*, Paris: Odile Jacob.
Oviedo, L. (2001) *Una Historia del Movimiento Piquetero*, Buenos Aires: Rumbos.
Palermo, V., and M. Novaro (1996) *Política y Poder en el Gobierno de Menem*, Buenos Aires: Editorial Norma.
Paramio, L. (1993) "Consolidación Democrática, Desafección Política y Neoliberalismo," *Cuadernos del CLAEH*, Nr. 68, Montevideo.
Peruzzotti, E., and C. Smulovitz (2001) *Controlando la Política*, Buenos Aires: Temas.
Przeworski, A., S. Stokes, and B. Manin (eds.) (1999) *Democracy, Accountability and Representation*, Cambridge: Cambridge University Press.
Romero, L. A. (1994) *Breve Historia de la Argentina Contemporánea*, Buenos Aires: Fondo de Cultura Económica.
Roniger, L., and C. H. Waisman (eds.) (2002) *Globality and Multiple Modernities: Comparative North America and Latin American Perspective*, Brighton, Portland, OR: Sussex Academic Press.
Rosanvallon, P. (1988) "La Représentation Dificil," F. Furet et al. (eds.), *La Republique du Centre*, Paris: Gallimard.
———. (2000) *Le Peuple Introuvable*, Paris: Gallimard.
———. (2003) *Por una Historia Conceptual de lo Político*, FCE, Buenos Aires.
Sartori, G. (1989) "Videopolitica," *Rivista Italiana di Scienza Politica*, Nr. 2, Anno XIX, Bologna.
Schnapper, D. (2000) *Qu'est-ce que la Citoyenneté?*, Paris: Gallimard.
Stiglitz, J. (2002) *El Malestar en la Globalización*, Buenos Aires: Buenos Aires.

Strasser, C. (2000) *Democracia y Desigualdad. Sobre la Democracia Real a Fines del Siglo XX*, Buenos Aires: Clacso.

Svampa, M., and S. Pereyra (2003) *Entre la ruta y el barrio*, Buenos Aires: Biblos.

Tocqueville, A. de (1988, 1969) *Democracy in America*, edited by J. P. Mayer, Translated by George Lawrence, Harper Perennial.

Torre, J. C. (2003) "Los Huérfanos de la Política de Partidos. Sobre los Alcances y la Naturaleza de la Crisis de Representación Partidaria," mimeo.

Touraine, A. (1995) "Comunicación Política y Crisis de la Representatividad," J. M. Ferry, D. Wolton et al. (eds.), *El Nuevo Espacio Público*, Barcelona: Gedisa.

Virno, P. (2002) *Grammatica de la Moltitudine*, Roma: Derivi Approdi.

Waisbord, S. (1995) *El Gran Desfile. Campañas Electorales y Medios de Comunicación en la Argentina*, Buenos Aires: Sudamericana.

———. (2001) "Interpretando los Escándalos. Análisis de su Relación con los Medios y la Ciudadanía en la Argentina Contemporánea," E. Peruzzotti and C. Smulovitz (eds.), *Controlando la Política*, Buenos Aires: Temas.

CHAPTER 6

ARGENTINA AFTER THE NINETIES: CHANGES IN SOCIAL STRUCTURE AND POLITICAL BEHAVIOR

Manuel Mora y Araujo

INTRODUCTION

In most Latin American countries the 1990s were a period of economic reforms and reorientation of foreign policy. Governments adopted market-oriented policies whose main aims were stabilization, deregulation, more open economies, and a shift from international "nonalignment" to a pro-Western approach. Generally, those policies received significant degrees of popular support. In Argentina the reforms resulted in the elimination of the sustained inflationary process, which affected the country for many years, a radical modification of the institutional framework regulating economic activities, a process of privatization of public utility companies to an extent almost unknown in the world, which in turn attracted huge amounts of foreign capital. They also resulted in a new era of friendly relations with the United States. Besides, the reform had an impact on the reduction of public spending, which was only partial due to its failure to meet budgets at the provincial level.

Those reforms—in Argentina and in other Latin American countries as well—were undertaken by fully democratic governments, a fact that disproved the idea that orthodox policies could only be implemented by military regimes. Argentina was, during those years, a paradigmatic case. Having redemocratized in the 1980s, Argentina was able to undertake profound changes in its public policies under a democratic government along with the backing of a high social consensus.[1]

However, the cycle of "neoliberal" reforms—as they have been called by many—did not have a happy ending. Problems of unemployment and public debt remained unsolved by these policies; when the economies entered into recession they proved to be unable to curb them and in many cases aggravated them. In Argentina this cycle ended in an abrupt and painful way: the fall of a democratic government, massive protest and political violence, confiscation of bank deposits, default of the public debt and a pronounced devaluation of the peso. All the evils of the country were then attributed, by the new government and by many analysts, to the so-called 'neoliberal' model. In April 2003 the presidential election gave way to a new constitutional government. Although at least 40 percent of the votes supported, beyond any doubt, the candidates whose proposals were close to that same "model," the elected government continued to attribute the country's problems to "the model" and presented its new policies as a radically different alternative.

In this chapter I will assess the impact of the reforms of the 1990s on Argentine social structure and its civic culture. Before that, I will refer briefly to the historical context of the reforms of the 1990s and their impact on Argentine society.

THE 1990S AND AFTERWARDS: SOCIAL PERCEPTIONS

The Argentine Pattern: A story of Disappointments

During the 1980s, Argentine society was enthusiastic about democracy. Then, after a few years, this enthusiasm collapsed, although society maintained a constant commitment to the democratic system. The most apparent element in the change of mood was a transformation in social demands, to which neither the government nor the opposition were able to respond.

The main issue in the new agenda of the 1980s was inflation. Secondly, as there was a crisis of confidence in the state, privatizations were also in strong demand. Carlos Menem emerged as the leader able to break with the Peronist tradition and lead the new agenda.

The processes that took place during the 1980s and the 1990s are part of a long story of unsolved problems and of long-term decline.

Argentina's decay is prior to "liberalism." The "neoliberal" experience of the 1990s just added a new disappointment to this frequently frustrated society.

Between 1950 and 1990, Argentina was one of the countries that showed the poorest performance worldwide. In fact, only countries belonging to a far more undeveloped category (Haiti, some African countries) showed worse positions than Argentina in economic, social, and even political indicators of change. In 1983, when Alfonsín was elected president, the prevailing mood in Argentine society was that this underperformance should be attributed to a combination of a "corporatist" power structure[2] and military intervention in political life. The democratization process then initiated was meant to trigger the end of both aspects. Alfonsín's government soon produced deep frustration: the "corporatist" power structure—identified mainly with strong trade unions and the military—was back influencing public policies on the side of the unions, and the government in order to survive was forced to compromise with the military.

Then, the time of "liberalism" arrived, with Menem's election in 1989. This new approach, led by a Peronist government, produced: a) greater integration of the Argentine economy into the world—something that in turn resulted in new opportunities for the more educated and qualified sectors of the population; b) stability—a new experience for society as a whole, and one particularly good for the poor, allowing them higher incomes, better standards of living, and access to credit; c) serious damage to the traditional well-being of the middle classes. Those middle sectors of society, to whom the solutions for the *malaises* under Alfonsín had not been good, thus became more and more angry with political leaders and began to abandon political parties and demand leadership renovation.

As indicated above, those reforms implemented during the first years of the 1990s were strongly supported by the population. Once the reforms goals were accomplished, however, society's agenda continued changing. The emphasis moved then to aspects of the political institutions. Corruption was the most relevant issue, but others related to the quality of institutions were also at stake. De la Rúa was elected president under those new demands. Once again, the government was unable to comply with the new agenda. De la Rúa's elected vicepresident—Chacho Alvarez—represented a new, less corrupt, more sensitive position; but soon, Alvarez resigned alleging corruption in the government and retiring from political activity. A few months later, De la Rúa appointed Domingo Cavallo as his minister of economy—something Alvarez had already demanded. At the end of

2001, this ended in complete disaster opening the way to a complex process that finally led Congress to nominate an interim president, Eduardo Duhalde. At the beginning of the interim administrations that followed De la Rúa's dismissal, the government produced the default that left Argentina isolated from the rest of the world and the peso was devaluated. A very deep recession followed.

So, this is a story of disappointments: first Alfonsín, then Menem, then Alvarez (De la Rúa's vicepresident) and, finally, De la Rúa and Cavallo with him.[3]

The 1990s: Low Confidence and Political Changes

The economic reforms and the new approaches to foreign policy introduced by Menem after 1989 received strong support from Argentine society. But the enthusiasm for those reforms lasted only until 1996 (after Menem's reelection). Menem's failure to meet the new demands and to modify some of his own behavior patterns in order to adapt to the new set of public values, to some extent account for this. His insistence on a second reelection also contributed to the same effect, as far as it showed he was much more committed to power than to strengthening institutions. But another decisive factor was the declining enthusiasm the reforms themselves aroused in significant sectors of the society. By the second half of the 1990s the losers began to be aware that they were, in effect, the losers.

In the balance, during the second half of the 1990s, Argentine society experienced a high degree of pessimism. The government approval rate under Menem's second term was extremely low. That situation deteriorated even more after the short honeymoon with De la Rúa, and went from bad to worse during the first six months under Duhalde.[4]

During those years, the public agenda was dominated by the issue of unemployment. If inflation was the main issue in the 1980s, it was unemployment in the 1990s, and it still is the main topic on the agenda. There is also a strong demand for political reforms—that is, improvements in the quality of political institutions.

Stability was, and continues to be, a major concern. The "convertibility" was very popular during the 1990s, and it still is—or, at least, the preference to a fixed exchange rate is. A fixed exchange rate is seems to be the only tool known to Argentines to generate stability. Argentina was, and still is, a society very sensitive to price instability.

In 2002, an important proportion of the population thought the years under Menem's administration (particularly, but not exclusively, during his first term) were economically the best in Argentina's history. But only a third of the population acknowledged that their personal situation was better in the 1990s than at that moment. In fact, another third thought they were worse off then.

The evaluation people make of their personal situation in the 1990s is not strongly correlated to social position or personal qualifications (education). To the extent there is a trend, it suggests that the 1990s has been more harmful to people who had medium personal qualifications (middle-middle classes) or temporary jobs (occupationally unstable) more than it did other groups. There is a trend among people who belong to the lowest socioeconomic segments to evaluate the 1990s as a period in which they were better off than in any other.

During the 1990s Argentina enjoyed a remarkable high "privatist" consensus (probably one of the highest worldwide). However, by 1996 "statist" attitudes began to increase. At present, they are stronger than "privatist" attitudes. However, there is no new consensus in favor of the state—we identify now a "new statism," a set of preferences for a greater but different role of the government in the economy: controlling, regulating, refereeing.

Social groups with a high favorable image include: producers (farmers, manufacturers, merchants), knowledge workers (scientists, intellectuals), and journalists (those responsible for making transparent the dark side of public life). During the 1990s, the situation was much the same; only, some of the "bad guys" (namely, politicians, and bankers) enjoyed a better image then than they do now. The image of the military is stable at relatively low levels; the image of trade-unionists was quite high at the beginning of the 1980s but by the 1990s it was already at the bottom of all the social groups, where it remains today.

In summary, Argentine society holds in high esteem those social groups that produce goods, those that know, and those that contribute to public transparency. On the contrary, it holds in poor esteem those who perform in activities defined as political or "politicized"—bankers being another story, related mainly to deposit confiscation at the end of 2001 (See Appendix, Table 6.A6).

A dramatic shift in power distribution preferences

A scheme of multivariate segmentation of the population allows us to identify three strongly differentiated periods (see table 6.1):

(a) The 1980s, when preferences relative to power distribution were widely dispersed. "Corporatist" preferences—a strong concentration

Table 6.1 Segments of Power Distribution Preferences

Segments	1985 (%)	1989 (%)	1992 (%)	1994 (%)	1998 (%)	2000 (%)	2002 (%)
S U M **"Corporatists"**	15	9	4	5	7	6	3
S U **"Classic statism"**	13	7	3	3	5	6	4
S M **"Statism with military"**	5	4	6	7	7	8	17
S **"Noncorporatist state"**	10	6	9	14	26	31	40
P S M **"Desarrollista"**	21	20	12	12	9	5	1
P S **"Neo-Peronists"**	13	1	8	6	4	4	3
P M **"Neo-Pinochetists"**	10	21	20	19	11	8	8
P **"Neoliberal"**	13	22	38	34	31	32	24
Total	100	100	100	100	100	100	100

[a] This segmentation is based on preferences on the role of the state vs. private companies (S, P), the trade unions (U, not U) and the military (M, not M). To facilitate communication, the segments have been labeled according to our own interpretation.
[b] All the survey information presented in this paper belongs to Ipsos-Mora y Araujo.

of power in trade unions and the military, both with and without a central role in the state—although not dominant, were the first plurality;

(b) The 1990s, when promarket, "neoliberal" preferences were higher;
(c) The current first years of the twenty-first century, when "anticorporatist" preferences dominate, with a bias in favor of more power to the state than to the private market.

Interestingly, at the beginning of the 1990s, "neo-Pinochetist" (market economy, weak trade unions, strong military) preferences were also quite significant.

The segmentation presented in table 6.1 speaks for itself. By 1985, Argentine society preferred strong "corporatist" power (trade unions, military, with or without a big state—mainly big). At the beginning of the 1990s, the preferences shifted toward the market (private sector); thus, "neoliberal" preferences predominated, but so did "neo-Pinochetist" ones (that is, powerful armed forces in combination with a market economy). By 2002, "neoliberal" preferences were still high, but the predominant segment was the "non corporatist statist."

On the political side, there has not been any move towards antidemocratic preferences during all these years. By 2002, confidence in democracy as such was in the order of 85 percent of the population, a figure a little bit higher than it was in 1984. However, the way civil society organizes itself in order to allow for political participation has

Table 6.2 Participation in Political Parties

Year	Members (%)	Feels affection (%)	No relation (%)	NA (%)
1984	26	47	22	5
1986	20	44	33	3
1988	24	35	35	6
1990	26	35	37	2
1992	22	29	46	3
1995	22	26	44	8
1996	19	23	53	5
1997	19	22	54	5
1998	18	18	59	5
1999	25	19	50	6
2000	19	24	53	4
2001	14	20	68	6
2002	19	8	69	4

changed. At the beginning of the 1980s, 73 percent of the population expressed membership in or sympathies towards political parties; that figure is no higher than 27 percent today (table 6.2). In the place of political parties, the "third" (or social) sector is growing[5] and it includes not only standard NGOs aimed at alleviating poverty, helping health and education, and protecting the environment, but also civic organizations whose aim is to improve different aspects of the quality of political institutions. Some of these proposals are modifications of the system of proportional representation and closed lists, procedures to hold more transparent primary elections, electronic voting, formal facilities to help the creation of new parties and the nomination of independent candidates, and the improvement of financial controls of campaigns.

More and more political processes are becoming the field where battles between civil society and the political parties take place year after year.

A Fragmented Society

The reforms of the 1990s had an impact on Argentina's social structure. In turn, changes in social structure created divergences in social expectations; society thus became more fragmented. What was traditionally a typical middle-class society enjoying homogeneous lifestyles—with only relatively marginal sectors at the top and at the bottom of the social structure—quite suddenly changed into a heterogeneous, fragmented society. At present not only do expectations differ widely from one segment to another, but the responses to political crisis and the ways through which each sector creates new forms of organized participation vary widely among different areas of the society.

Our individual competitive capabilities index captures one of the relevant dimensions of stratification (table 6.3).[6] It accounts for significant diversities in lifestyles, expectations, and social demands. The index was formed by adding up different indicators such as education, access to internet, ability to work with personal computers, and fluency in English. Education was weighted more than the other indicators. Three main segments (containing approximately a third of the population each) were identified: (1) people with high competitive capabilities; (2) people with low competitive capabilities; (3) people with no competitive capabilities.

1. *People with high competitive capabilities.* They are prepared to perform in any modern economy; so they expect a modern economy for their own country, a society integrated into the modern world, opportunities for careers involving upward mobility. As far as Argentina does not offer those conditions, many people in this segment—particularly among the youngest—are prepared to leave the country.

Table 6.3 Individual Competitive Capabilities Index

Segmentation according to individual competitiveness	(%)		Correlates
Highly competitive	*36*		* Prepared to perform in a "knowledge society"
Very high		6	* Demand for a modern economy
High		15	* Propensity to emigrate
High-medium		15	* Low political commitment
Not very competitive	*30*		* Worst-off under globalized economy * Some incidence of corporatist protection in part of this segment
Medium-low		20	* Growing nationalism
Low		10	* Some appeal of left-wing ideas
No competitiveness	*34*		* Economic and social exclusion * Dependence on government help
New poor		19	* Demand for antiinflationary policies
Backward		15	* Peronist territory
Total	*100*		

For them, the devaluation of the peso was a tremendous shock that contributed to isolating the country from the world and reducing attractive labor opportunities. It was one of the many frustrations and disappointments produced either by governments they had voted for or by the ones they had not.

These people do not have political leaders, they do not feel politically represented, they do not trust institutions, governments, and politicians. Among them we find the main stream of volunteers and leaders of NGOs and civic organizations, and the emergence of new technocratic groups of well-educated people looking for influential positions in governments and new political organizations.

2. *People with low competitive capabilities.* They are the losers of the 1990s: their income decreased significantly, their unemployment grew, and their perception of labour instability became weaker.

They do not like the globalized world, they prefer a relatively closed economy, and do not trust multinational companies and foreign capital. In this segment, nationalism is growing, protectionism is more and more accepted, free market concepts inspire mistrust, and old left-wing ideas once again find fertile grounds.

Although in this segment there also exists a generalized mistrust of politicians and political parties, there is here a greater propensity than in the former to vote for candidates coming from the old parties, particularly in provincial political environments.

3. *People with no competitive capabilities.* They are formed by two groups (each of the same size): the traditional poor and the new poor—formerly lower middle class, now lacking any kind of skill. These people are excluded from the labor market, they do not qualify to perform in any formal activity. They feel that the current economic conditions are clearly worse than those of the 1990s; at present their incomes are irregular and uncertain, many of them suffer hunger, and they are more dependent on political "clientelistic" structures. Having experienced the effects of inflation and hyperinflation over decades and the results of stabilization policies in the 1990s, their main economic demand at present is stability (they therefore tend to vote for Menem, in spite of some superficial anticapitalist stereotypes to which they subscribe).

The dependence of these people on the food and money distributed by governments under the Households Program (*Jefes y Jefas de Hogar*) makes them less likely to be part of any form of independent, political or civic activity. However, as they also have a need to belong to social groups of some kind (be they political, religious, or local criminal groups), Argentina is now experiencing the emergence of new manifestations of civic society among the poor. *Piqueteros* (violent, small organizations of unemployed prepared to dig road cuts, invade the streets in big towns, and demonstrate with different degrees of violence and vandalism) as well as local NGOs, local branches of wide-scope NGOs, and very small but quite powerful organizations oriented to cultivate and disseminate radical ideas, all seem to be the seeds of renovation of Argentina's civic life.

POLITICS AND CIVIL SOCIETY

The implications of this analysis on the current state of Argentina's civil society can be summarized in a simple way: though most of the population will continue to be alienated from politics as usual, it could develop new forms of political/civic participation; the growing confidence in the "social" sector together with the sustained commitment to democratic values is an indication that weaker political parties do not necessarily imply a weaker democracy. And lastly, society is in search of new styles of political leadership, and is producing new leaders out of the same processes that are changing the way people become connected to political life.

Politics and the "Social" Sector

The number of people linked to political parties—both in terms of membership and of sympathies—decreased dramatically over the last two decades. In fact, this is the most dramatic change that can be registered in dimensions related to public affairs and political life. This process of growing alienation of the population from the structures and organizations supporting representative democracy is a major challenge to the possibilities of improving the quality of political life in Argentina.

As trust in political parties declines, there is a growing process of acceptance of civic organizations, NGOs, and, generally speaking, the organizations of a civil society that are perceived as unpoliticized. Prevailing values concerning political life are defined more and more in terms of search for consensus, importance attached more to common aspects than to dividing ones, de-ideologization, and emphasis on goals and results rather than an emphasis on general values and visions of the world.

This process does not involve a majority of the population, but it is certainly growing in terms of the number of people connected to it. It is increasingly becoming a source of new leadership.

New Leadership

The profile of the new leaders Argentine society seems to be looking for strongly differs from what the usual leader profile was twenty or more years ago. One main aspect in the new leadership profile is that strong links with political parties today seem to be a liability rather than an asset to potential leaders. Among the leaders ranking at the top of any table of politicians approval rates, none appear to come from the core of the structures controlling the old parties. This fact, already true with respect to former presidential candidates—both Menem and his rival Angeloz or, more recently De la Rúa, were all perceived as opposing those powerful cores controlling their own parties—is now a far more generalized phenomenon.

A second aspect of the new leadership profile is that a lack of charisma seems to be a strength rather than a liability. The new leader has to have the look of a *primus inter pares*, as distant as possible from the character of semigod (a quite common image of new candidates is that they run their own cars without a driver or even make use of public transportation; this can easily be labeled as pure marketing, but it certainly goes beyond that). The new leader is not a providential man; rather, he is an interpreter of expectations and demands, somebody capable of translating them into government decisions and making use of political capabilities to make them viable.

A third aspect is that the leader has to show a good record of honesty and a commitment to normal moral values.

Where do these leaders come from? Eventually, they come from any of the three main segments referred to above. There are three kinds of new civil leaders in Argentina today:

1. Young people educated for the knowledge society, active in civil organizations and NGOs, looking for new spaces in political parties, think-tanks, and government structures.
2. Leaders of competitive low middle-class sectors, fighting for the survival of the "corporatist" statutes that guarantee privileged labor and wage stability to its members. They can either give voice to these goals or be a kind of new radical union leader.
3. The leaders of the new poor, either left-wing oriented (*piqueteros*) or local NGO oriented.

Their common characteristics are that they all mistrust politics as usual, they reject the traditional Argentine patterns of political behavior and they tend to concentrate on concrete, particular issues rather than on general, abstract ones.

In the competitive segment most of the new leaders come from NGOs and civic organizations. Most of them are typical members of the knowledge society, with an educational background in good universities; some of them are experienced managers of private companies. They are, quite typically, the kind of people who could chose to leave Argentina and perform without difficulty anywhere in the world but prefer, instead, a political commitment to help their country solve its problems.

In the middle-middle classes, political leaders are now more inclined to radical proposals, to aggressive or combative attitudes—normally in connection with trade-unions of public employees and teachers. In some provinces, political party leaders still prevail as usual, with a clear trend toward adopting the new attributes of the profile now preferred by most of the population. In some cases a new kind of nationalist/ populist leader gains ground, appealing to lower middle classes in a way that is quite similar to modern populism in some European countries.

Among the poor, the most common type of political leader is still the local boss, or his boss at a higher level, whose main capabilities lie in administrating clientelism. Competing with them there are, on one side, "new left" leaders—either violent or opposed to violent methods—and on the other, local NGO leaders (administrating distribution of food, local health centers, community centers, helping the local school). Interestingly enough, a new phenomenon has emerged: new bridges are being built connecting the poor with the upper middle classes through the cross-sectional structures of broad-based NGOs. (This is good for the poor but is even more beneficial to the educated middle-class volunteers and managers who thus obtain the first direct contact in their lives with poverty and the cultures of poverty.)

Nevertheless, consensus among these different sources of leadership looks problematic and will not be achieved easily. Time, opportunities of communication and the experience of attaining and making use of political power could produce a reversal of those conditions. It is too soon to predict the developments of those processes.

CONCLUSION

After democracy was reestablished in 1983, Argentine society seemed to go back to the political traditions that neither Peronism nor military governments ever completely destroyed. The Argentine model of the 1980s (a model enjoying high social consensus at the time) consisted of a democracy based on political parties, a central state that was overextended but at the same time quite weak, and a power structure sustained on strong noninstitutional power factors; that is, a representative, party-based and corporatist system. Under such a model, the link between citizens and politics operated through party membership or party sympathy; the fact that a significant proportion of citizens neither belonged to nor felt sympathy towards any party was, in the eyes of many political leaders, a phenomenon difficult to deal with.

That model had a short life. Different reasons account for its decay. On the one hand, Argentina was already in a process of cultural change, moving from the original Rousseaunian paradigm to more Machiavellian patterns prevailing in the world at the beginning of the post 1970s globalization: a less ideological world with a stronger orientation toward political regimes prepared to be judged in terms of results rather than in terms of values. On the other hand, more specifically domestic circumstances also played a role: the incompetence of Alfonsín's government in dealing with macroeconomic problems and its inability to balance different noninstitutional power factors possibly accelerated Argentina's move toward more effective governments. By the end of the 1980s Argentine citizenship was becoming more pragmatic and that made it less resistant to Menem's government in spite of its Peronist origins.

The changes in preferences reflected in table 6.3 suggest a growing acceptance of an economy based on private firms as well as a decline in the levels of confidence in trade unions and the political role of the Church. The expectation of effective governments still divided society in terms of the political role of the military, but this soon became a minor topic in relation to other power factors.

Now, the model of effective government also enjoyed a short life. During the 1990s, again the joint effect of world trends and local circumstances had an impact on Argentine politics. The successful results reached during his first term allowed Menem to be reelected in 1995; a large part of society was still afraid of putting the stability achieved under any risk. However, new demands were rising, aiming at power decentralization and new leadership styles; they held a strong element of mistrust in political parties and expected a renewal of political practices—a less divisive, less confrontational, less ideological way of doing politics—which the model of civic NGOs served better than the old model of political parties. Along with the deep loss of prestige of trade unions, the prestige of political parties began to fall again.

The new model society seemed to be looking for was more "Jeffersonian": citizenship should have a stronger voice, and political parties a less monopolistic control of the mechanisms of representative democracy. Menem was reelected in 1995, but before that, as early as

1994, the electorate voted to elect the Constitutional Assembly in a way that already revealed expectations of a wide dispersion of power. Moreover, Menem's approval rate fell quickly after his reelection and never recovered. Under the new model, neither trade union leaders nor politicians are expected to perform an important role, let alone foreign companies, the military and the bishops.

As party membership fell there was a growing trend to perceive citizens' political commitment as something that could—or should—be nonpartisan, even unpoliticized. The new values attached to political life that are increasingly gaining acceptance in Argentina are the following: consensus, growing importance paid to aspects that unify over those that divide, and emphasis on results rather than on principles. These values are at the root of the emergence of new leaders.

* * *

The idea that society is moving towards an "alternative model" is a conceptual construct, useful to understand reality, yet conjectural and perhaps a fantasy. We lack data to verify this idea; nevertheless, there is certain evidence that could support it.

1. The strong decline in party membership and party supporters.
2. Society's sustained commitment to democracy.
3. The growing number of people belonging to NGOs and civic organizations and the number of such organizations.
4. The growing fragmentation of the electoral body in terms of electoral behavior, the preference for a greater power distribution in congressional and provincial elections, the growing dispersion of vote in most of the instances.
5. The growing independence of the vote from party influence and loyalty. This phenomena, increasingly prevalent in the middle classes, is expanding to the upper classes and beginning to appear in the lower classes too. An indication of this is that, in spite of a lot of talk—not without good reason—about the influence of political machines and "clientelistic" relationships on the vote of lower-class people, in many elections lower-class voters did not vote for the candidates supported by the "clientelistic" apparatus but for those who had little to offer in terms of a particularistic link with voters.
6. The adoption of new institutions, such as public hearings—particularly active in dealing with topics such as those related to privatized companies—plebiscites at the local level for taking some decisions, and mechanisms for hearing the public opinion before

the nomination of candidates to the Supreme Court, forcing the Senate to take those opinions into account.

Elements like these show that it is possible to talk about a new wave of expectations concerning the kind of democracy and the style of public life desired: reduced concentration of power, more channels open to the direct participation of citizens in order to have at least a voice in public decisions, and decreased politicization—namely, party politicization—in dealing with public issues. All this is reflected in the style of leadership the society is selecting: people lacking "charisma," in many cases with well-known backgrounds previous to their political career, whose honesty is beyond reasonable doubt and whose power ambitions seem to be mitigated by their vocation of service.[7]

I think a strong civil society is a necessary condition for the emergence of a strong political order and for it to be able to provide acceptable collective solutions and at the same time guarantee a good environment for the search of legitimate particular objectives. Argentina has not had a strong civil society in the past—probably never in its history. It is too soon to assess whether society is now moving in the direction of becoming a stronger civil society; however, I am tempted to interpret though these encouraging indications that it is. At least, new forms of political action that could be typified in those terms can be identified.

To the extent that there is something like a "model" orienting Argentine society at present, it is rather close to the liberal ideal: high distribution of power; an organized, active civil society, whose individual members are free from coercion; legitimate political power, effective in making public decisions; and weak power factors influencing political decisions from outside political institutions. This chapter is an attempt to explore some of the causes that could account for the hypothetical evolution of Argentine society in that direction.

APPENDIX

Table 6.A1 Opinions on the Years Under "Convertibility" (December 2002)

Those years have been . . .	
Good for the country	43%
Fairly good for the country	29%
Bad for the country	28%
	100%

Table 6.A2 Opinions on the Decade of the 1990s (December 2002)

How would you say your personal situation was in the 1990s in comparison with the present?	
Better than now	35%
Same as now	27%
Worst than now	38%
	100%

Table 6.A3 Opinion on the Decade of the 1990s According to Position in the Competitive Capabilities Index (December 2002)

	CCI (%)		
	High	Medium	Low
Better	38	32	34
Same	28	26	26
Worst	34	42	40
	100	100	100

Table 6.A4 Preferences on Exchange Rate Policy (December 2002)

Which of the following alternatives is the best for Argentina?	
Free market exchange rate	25%
Fixed exchange rate	65%
Dollarization	10%
	100%

Table 6.A5 Argentina's Best Economic Period (December 2002)

Years under Menem's administration	36%
Perón's first administration	15%
Military administrations	8%
Alfonsín's administration	8%
Other	21%
None	4%
DK/NA	8%
	100%

Table 6.A6 Social Groups Images

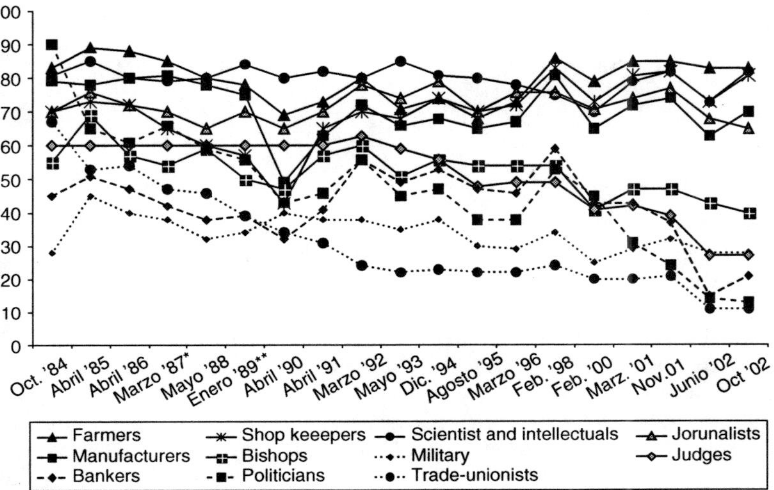

Notes

1. For an analysis of the first wave of reforms in the 1990s from the perspective of society and public opinion see Manuel Mora y Araujo (1993). The book also contains an analysis of public policies at the time from different perspectives.
2. Corporatism here means "a system of interests and/or attitude representation (. . .) for linking the associationally organized interests of civil society with the decisional structures of the state," Schmitter (1979).
3. The experience with Duhalde's short term—which was even shorter than scheduled due to his decision to call for anticipated presidential elections—and the more recent one with President Kirchner, are both beyond the scope of this paper.
4. However, there has been a remarkable recovery of confidence since the last months of 2002, which saw a surge of confidence after Kirchner's inauguration in May 2003.
5. There is a study by Gallup Argentina documenting the increasing and significant proportion of people active in social sector organizations. Another study shows that many people perceive the development of the social sector as a consequence of growing citizen consciousness, see María Braun (2003).
6. This segmentation was first presented, in more detail, in Manuel Mora y Araujo (2002).
7. At the moment of writing, the eight politicians at the top of the popularity ranking are: President Kirchner and Vice-president Scioli,

three ministers: Lavagna, Béliz, Bielsa (the three perceived as having a technical profile rather than an ideological one), two opposition leaders: Carrió and López Murphy, and one particular politician (neither opposition nor officialism): Carlos Reutemann. None of them were active in politics ten years ago; many of them were already well known for having been successful in other activities.

BIBLIOGRAPHY

Braun, María (2003) "ONGs en Argentina. Sobre el papel de las ONGs y su relación con el estado y las agencias internacionales," working paper, Buenos Aires.

Mora y Araujo, M. (1993) "Las demandas sociales y la legitimidad de la política de ajuste," *Reforma y Convergencia. Ensayos sobre la Transformación de la Economía Argentina*, F. A. M. de la Balze (ed.), Buenos Aires: Manantial.

——. (2002) *La Estructura Social de la Argentina: Evidencias y Conjeturas acerca de la Estratificación Actual*, Santiago: CEPAL.

Schmitter, P. C. (1979) "Still a century of corporatism?" Schmitter and G. Lehmbruch (eds.), *Trends Toward Corporatist Intermediation*, Beverly Hills: Sage.

Chapter 7

Sem Reforma Agrária, Não Há Democracia: Deepening Democracy and the Struggle for Agrarian Reform in Brazil

Wendy Wolford

In the two decades since Brazil's formal transition to democracy in 1985, a contentious civil society has become a celebrated (if not always welcome) political actor (Dagnino 2002; Gohn 1997; Rossiaud and Scherer-Warren 2000; Slater 1985). Organized expressions of discontent such as roadblocks, *ocupações* (occupations) of rural properties and government buildings, and marches through public spaces have become increasingly commonplace in the Brazilian understanding—or "repertoire" (Tilly 1978)—of resistance. Although often characterized as illegal or ill-advised by the government, in the context of widespread poverty and increasing disillusion with "actually existing democracy" in Brazil (Alvarez 1997), such actions are now widely accepted as legitimate forms of political participation (Navarro 2002:18).[1] Well-known musicians, actors, and politicians often publicly lend their support and talents to the various causes, contributing to a sense of popular acceptance (and even celebration) of opposition to the government.

One of the most visible, well-organized, and contentious actors in Brazilian civil society today is the rural grassroots social movement, *O Movimento dos Trabalhadores Rurais Sem Terra* (The Movement of

Rural Landless Workers, commonly referred to as the MST). The MST was officially formed in 1984 as landless farmers and rural workers mobilized to pressure the newly elected civilian government for access to land (Fernandes 1999). A year later, over 1,600 delegates from twenty-three states came together for the movement's first National Congress. Grounded in the belief that "land belongs to those who work it," the MST's methodology centers around occupations of properties considered unproductive and eligible for expropriation under Article 186 of the 1988 Federal Constitution (Panini 1990:181–208; Wright and Wolford 2003).[2] Even as Brazilian democracy has taken hold over the past twenty years, movement leaders continue to argue that the extreme political, economic, and social marginalization of the poor majority in Brazil necessitates deliberate acts of civil disobedience or contention: government leaders negotiating the institutions and culture of a "feckless" or "difficult" democracy (Mainwaring 1995; Hooper n.d., respectively) do not easily promulgate the Constitution if doing so means going against entrenched interests. The issue of land distribution, in particular, has a long history of creating both popular unrest and elite-sponsored repression: in this context, the MST advocates disrupting the regular political and social order (or routine) as a way of making the poor visible (or "legible," see Scott 1998).

In this chapter, I make two main arguments. First, I argue that through its opposition to the state, the MST is building channels for the constitution of "social capital." The concept of social capital has a long and not-altogether enlightening history (Woolcock 1998), but I use it here in the very narrow sense of civic engagement. Membership in the MST means participation in—or, at least, exposure to—the movement's formal and informal social networks. These networks provide fluid sites for political participation, the flow of information, and construction of a group identity, or what Portes and Sensenbrenner (1993) call "bounded solidarity." Although one cannot argue that this engagement necessarily engenders "trust" between movement members (as Charles Sabel, 1993, pointed out in his work on the U.S. manufacturing sector, participation in social networks may be less an expression of a consensus, than an attempt to create one), participation, access to information, and group identification all reduce the distance between state and citizen in Brazil. MST members have collectively generated a new way of thinking about and being political, and this has led hundreds of thousands of poor people throughout the country to demand the "right to have rights" (Dagnino 1998). The social capital accumulated by MST members has in turn generated both economic capital (particularly financial resources from the state such as credit, public services, and extension assistance) and what Bourdieu (1986) calls "cultural capital" (primarily education, but also accepted practices of political participation). That this comes through a movement that at least discursively opposes the government is indicative of the exclusionary nature of contemporary democracy in Brazil.

Second, I argue that although the MST requires the state for its continued reproduction (Novaes 1998: 178–179), the movement has been able to maintain its autonomy as a social movement by "jumping scales" (Smith 1993) from the local level to transnational and national civil society.[3] The MST has been able to defend its contentious behavior and maintain its independence from the government even as movement members demand public resources from the government (including land, credit, and basic services). Links to civil society at the transnational and national level are critical in creating this political space. Nongovernmental organizations, development institutions, and other social movements all contribute financial, political, and cultural resources that help MST members win access to land, credit, and services even in the face of significant government repression. The state remains the MST's main political referent, of course, but the movement gains considerable political leverage by going around the state and retaining its contentious demeanor.

In what follows, I describe the MST's formation and construction of an oppositional identity. I then analyze how the movement's strategies of opposition have created new forms of social capital and deepened the lived experiences of democracy in Brazil. Finally, I describe how the practice of "jumping scales" enabled the movement to keep its autonomy and access state resources.

Sem Reforma Agrária, Não Há Democracia

The MST's early opposition to the Brazilian government was constituted in the historical-material conditions of land tenure rights in Brazil. In advocating for the egalitarian distribution of land, the MST directly challenged one of the most politically and socially entrenched groups in Brazil: the rural land-owning elite (Martins 1981). Nowhere was control of civil society by the state (in this case, political domination by a minoritarian elite) as complete as it was in the countryside (Martins 2000). Colonial society, based on large plantations organized for export production, produced a hierarchical and personalistic political culture that still exists in much of the rural area today (Schwartz 1992). The overriding dynamic of plantation society was the search for an obedient, productive labor force: from the beginning, land was abundant while labor was scarce. This unfortunate ratio turned Brazil into the single largest importer of African slaves in the world. When the Brazilian monarchy finally abolished slavery in 1888 (the last country in the western hemisphere to do so), agricultural exports accounted for the vast majority of the country's gross domestic product and the search for a new labor force was a vital political and economic issue. Some politicians argued that land distribution was a necessary means of addressing both racial and economic discrimination in the country, and meager attempts were made to distribute land to new immigrants from Europe (Dean 1976; Holloway 1980; Stein 1987; Viotti da Costa 2000), but in general freed slaves and the rural poor were forced onto plantations as the new labor force (Fernandes 1965:20).

Rural elites continued to dominate presidential politics to such an extent that the presidents from 1889 to 1930 were referred to as "café com leite" (coffee with milk) because they came from either the dairy ranches of Rio Grande do Sul or the coffee plantations of Minas Gerais. In the 1950s, Caio Prado Júnior argued that the potential for revolutionary change was the greatest in rural Brazil because injustice and inequality were most prevalent there (Prado Jr. 1967; see also Navarro 1996). Conditions in the countryside worsened for the rural poor during the rule of the military government (1964–1982). The military promoted a "conservative" agricultural modernization through mechanization, capitalization, and vertical integration that increased production without altering the distribution of land or wealth (Graziano da Silva 1982). Modernization reduced the need for labor in agricultural production and many people left the countryside for the cities in the 1960s and 1970s. This alienation from the land not only generated an informal working sector in the large cities such as São Paulo and Rio de Janeiro but also created a "landless class" that could be mobilized around the struggle for agrarian reform (Navarro 2000; Stedile in Rossiaud and Scherer-Warren 2000).

This landless class was particularly strong in southern Brazil, a region with as long a history of peasant production as any in Brazil (Papma 1992; Seyferth 1990). As the agroindustrial production of grains expanded in southern Brazil and the spatial frontier came to an end, it was harder for the sons and daughters of small farmers to find land. Those who valued farming as a way of life and were unable to find new land of their own joined the MST (Wolford 2003a).

Their "cultural toolkits" (Swidler 1986), established in the historical practice of colonizing empty land by squatting, resonated with the MST's call to occupy illegitimately owned land. These landless farmers provided the material and ideological resources that transformed the squatter settlements of the 1970s into a national movement in the 1980s.

The MST's decision to oppose the Brazilian government at a time when there was considerable optimism about the transition to democracy came out of movement leaders' analysis of the relationship between "democracy" and agroindustrial capitalism in the countryside: they argued that the government would not willingly carry out a distributive agrarian reform because it was too closely allied with the interests of domestic and foreign capital. The most influential and visible leader of the movement, João Pedro Stedile, argued that, "the minimal rights of citizenship will not be given to us by the capitalism that we have. If it had wanted to give them to us, it would have already . . ." (Stedile 1994:319). Movement leaders argued that the optimism surrounding the transition to democracy was premature if there was no plan for a comprehensive agrarian reform project. At the first National Congress in 1985, the movement changed its slogan from "land for those who work it" to "without agrarian reform, there is no democracy." Over the next eighteen years, the movement's oppositional identity was solidified by two main political battles: the debate over the National Plan for Agrarian Reform (PNRA) and the Collor administration (1990–1992).

The PNRA, commissioned by Tancredo Neves (the civilian president elected in 1985) and written by the left-leaning intellectual, José Gomes da Silva, was intended to create a dialogue around the distribution of land. Land reform was a priority for the Tancredo administration, and the PNRA Gomes originally drafted was surprisingly liberal, promising to settle seven million people in fifteen years. The plan was opposed, however, by rural landowners who organized an effective opposition group, the *União Democrática Rural* (the Rural Democratic Union, or the UDR) that vowed to fight agrarian reform and the MST by any means necessary. As a result of their organization, agrarian reform legislation included in the final draft of the federal constitution (1988) was considerably less ambitious in terms of the amount of land eligible for expropriation and the number of families to be settled (see Veiga 1990; Gomes da Silva 1987).

In the early 1990s, the movement entered into another difficult period with the Collor administration (1990–1992). Although Fernando Collor de Mello was president only for two years before being forcibly removed from office, his term in office was difficult for the movement. Under Collor's administration, the number of land expropriations was negligible and federal armed guards were called on to discipline MST members in squatter camps. As João Pedro Stedile said, looking back,

> Collor wanted to crush us. He set the Federal police on us—for two years we had to eat whatever bread the devil kneaded, as we say. Many of our state-level headquarters were raided. There was even an attempt to kidnap me from outside our national office. A comrade from the CUT who looks a lot like me was seized, taken away and tortured. He was only released when they looked at his documents and realized they had the wrong person. The UDR had grown in strength, and there were a lot of assassinations between 1990 and 1992. They were terrible years for us. There was little organic growth, it was more a question of keeping going. Instead of our slogan "Occupy, Resist, Produce", it was more like "Get beaten up and hold out." (Stedile 2002:91)

Grounded in this long history of explosive land–labor relations, and receiving little assistance from the national government, the MST rejected every new presidential administration from 1985 to 2002 on the grounds that they represented "a bourgeois state . . . invested with class interest" (Stedile and Fernandes 1999:36, 51). On the eve of the 1994 presidential elections that would bring in Fernando Henrique Cardoso, the next democratically elected president to follow Collor, MST leaders warned movement members that Cardoso would be allied with economic interests that were not theirs: "[the present government of Brazil] represents the bourgeoisie, the powerful, the banks, the multi-national corporations and the large farmers . . . If state and economic power are intertwined, along with the media, it will be difficult to build a democratic life" (*Jornal Sem Terra* September 1994:2 and October 1994:3).

The MST's decision to advocate opposition as a form of political communication was a popular one in the immediate aftermath of Brazil's transition to democracy. The so-called new social movements formed during the transition and the subsequent battle over the drafting of a new constitution were distinguished from "old social movements" by their distaste for traditional political institutions (such as parties and trade unions) and traditional political ideologies (such as Marxism) (Hellman 1992; Slater 1985). Autonomy and opposition to the government were embraced in part because the new movements had been forged during military rule when the privileged spaces of organization were necessarily outside the formal purview of the state (Mainwaring and Viola 1994; Martins 2000). The new social movements, including the MST, valued their organizational independence and prided themselves on relatively eclectic theoretical interpretations of the national context (Gohn 1997; Scherer-Warren 1993).

As democratic institutions in Brazil solidified, however, social movements increasingly altered their strategies, making the decision to work with the government rather than against it and taking what Dagnino (2002:13) refers to as a "posture of negotiation," grounded in the belief that participation would work in their favor. The opportunity to access financial resources through state development agencies provided an incentive to play by the rules of the legal-institutional game (Gohn 1997; Hall 1993; Scherer-Warren 1993).

Even as more civil society actors chose to cooperate with the state, however, the MST adamantly maintained its "outsider" status, consciously and consistently deploying opposition and autonomy as important political tools. Longtime leftist supporters argued that the MST ought to work with(in) the government instead of against it (Martins 2000, 2003; Navarro 2002), but movement leaders refused to rework their discourse of autonomy and opposition.

Confronted by such powerful political opponents, the MST adopted methods intended to utilize the movement's most powerful resource—bodies—to greatest effect. The MST's strategy for forcing the government to take the demand for land seriously involves physically inserting landless bodies into unorthodox spaces: occupying private property or a government building or an urban plaza and agitating for the right to be heard (Fernandes 1999; Martin 2002). As a resource-poor social movement, this ability to recast spaces of private property and large-scale production as illegitimate while claiming a moral right to land for small farmers, is a powerful organization tool (Sewell 2002), and in the years since the movement's formation, the MST has carried out over 2,000 land occupations as well as hundreds of occupations of public buildings and private banks. The movement is affiliated with an estimated 1,100 land reform settlements that bring together over one and a half million people.

Deepening Democracy—Behind the Government's Back

Even as the MST opposes the government, it has broadened the spaces for political expression and contributed to a deepening of democratic political values within its membership. The MST has done this in part by creating avenues for the construction and articulation of "social capital," or what Robert Putnam (1993:167) describes as the "networks of civic engagement," which are thought to constitute a valuable asset in the production of democracy (also see Wolford 2001:307–312). Two aspects of the voluminous work on social capital are useful here: one derives from Tocqueville's enthusiastic discovery of the American "art of association," perhaps best exemplified in contemporary work by Putnam's optimistic evaluation of social networks in Italy, and the other derives from Bourdieu's (1986) more cynical conceptualization of social capital as resources available to members of a group, where appropriation is based at least in part on a strategic calculation of individual advance. In the case of the MST, both perspectives are useful: formal and informal networks created by movement members provide social resources (through the practice of association, flow of information, and identification with a group) to movement members who participate. The networks incorporate people who have traditionally remained outside of the state's "welfare net" into a parallel social system (Sorj 1998; Scherer-Warren 1993), and the social capital produced within in turn generates economic and cultural capitals that lessen the distance between MST members and the Brazilian state. Although social capital is not necessarily a sufficient condition for economic or democratic growth, it is potentially productive. As Peter Evans said: "if people cannot trust each other or [at least] work together, then improving the material conditions of life is an uphill battle" (Evans 1997:2).

The MST's social networks can be loosely divided into formal and informal networks. When the movement's rapid spread across Brazil generated internal concern over cultural and productive differences within the member community (Poletto 1997), the movement created an impressive organizational infrastructure capable of disseminating information, distributing resources, mobilizing participation, and monitoring behavior on settlements throughout the country. This organizational infrastructure is set into motion through formal networks that consist of MST activists who travel constantly between settlements bringing with them information, resources, and ideas. The activists have created "webs" (Alvarez 1997) that connect the settlements to one another and to the movement's center. These activists have the difficult job of being constantly in motion, but they are the physical embodiment of the movement's philosophy, and they provide critical links between the settlers and "the movement." As one activist who left the rural trade union to join the MST said, "[As an MST activist], you work directly with people. So you notice an improvement in their quality of life instead of always reading union contracts and documents."[4]

The activists are usually land reform settlers who have been "liberated" from their settlements by the other MST members in the community. They receive basic training in a number of organizational fields, the funds for which come from their home settlements and are channeled through the main movement. They are often called back to their settlements, either for a short period to help with temporary tasks such as the harvest or so that another settler may be chosen for liberation. The formal networks are also constituted by less frequent visitors to the settlements, such as university professors, high school teachers, clergy members, politicians, college students, all of whom bring with them experiences, suggestions, moral support, and sometimes, financial support. These people provide MST participants with a new set of "weak" social ties that widens their possible sphere of influence and provides contacts for further economic, political, and cultural opportunities (Granovetter 1973).

The informal networks consist of the settlers themselves who interact within the settlements and also encounter other members during regional and national meetings or mobilizations that are held regularly. The settlers attend frequent meetings on their settlements, both because as state land beneficiaries they are required to form a settlement association that meets regularly and because MST activists often visit and call meetings to gather and spread information about/to the settlers, disseminate the movement's official interpretation of the new economic and political context, and organize the settlers' contributions for future events, such as demonstrations or new occupations.

Association

People come together, or associate, through the movement in a number of ways. The most important activities the settlers engage in are ongoing land occupations, public demonstrations, and meetings.

MST activists recruit members who have already won land to participate in new land occupations because the movement has learned from experience that occupations have a greater chance of succeeding if they are attended by a large number of people—preferably families, men, women, and children.[5] People participate in occupations even after they have won their own land because they remember the act of entering the land as a particularly powerful symbolic moment in the struggle for agrarian reform (Fernandes 1999). Settlers often speak of that moment when they cut the fence and entered the farm as the time when they took their future into their own hands and defied what had always seemed like all-powerful forces, the government and the landed elite. Living in an encampment can be incredibly difficult and tiresome, but that moment of occupying is remembered—and retold—as a victory. As one settler who spent almost three years in an occupation camp said: "It was the best thing ever—everyone was united, and that way, people are able to achieve their goal."

The settlers also participate in successive occupations as a way of showing their support for the movement. Occupations are probably the most dangerous activity that the movement organizes and the settlers contribute to a special sort of solidarity by renewing their support through participation in a dangerous ritual. As one settler in the northeastern town of Água Preta (Pernambuco) said: "If the [MST] said, 'let's go occupy another area for another group of people,' I would leave here and go there because others are suffering the way that I used to suffer. They want to get land too, to have some peace, and if I could lend some strength (*força*), I would."

Those who do not participate directly in new occupations often help the families in the encampments by providing food and basic supplies.[6] Many settlers refer to this as an opportunity to pay back those who helped them when they were in a similar situation:

> We pay the MST because when we were camped out the activists explained to us that . . . the food we were eating was coming from another settlement. And they said that when we were all settled we were going to have a meeting so that everyone could contribute with some money, to help those who are still waiting to be settled and need food.

The settlers also participate frequently in public demonstrations such as statewide marches and urban rallies. MST regularly organizes such demonstrations to display the movement's strength and apply pressure on the government in relation to specific demands. In the town of Água Preta, a settler described a hunger strike in which he had taken part. The strike had made a powerful impression:

> I was at the big demonstration in Recife, in the Princess Palace . . . . We were demanding that our land finally be formally divided and that we be given our credit for food . . . We spent nine days on a hunger strike locked up there in the INCRA offices. Every now and then people left for the hospital without eating . . . but even if one person had died, INCRA and everything would have gone up in flames—no-one would have run.

Another settler in Campos Novos (Santa Catarina) had taken part in the national march of 1997. He said proudly that his legs still hurt and displayed his bruises, although there was nothing to see. He said that the march had been "a little bit of suffering, a little bit of happiness." Settlers who are not able to participate in the marches are able to hear about them in the news, and through the stories of those who go.

The third avenue for participating in the MST's social networks is through meetings. Attending meetings and expressing opinions in front of the other settlers represents an important step toward independence and a sign that the settlers exercise some authority over their own lives. Participation in the meetings is highly symbolic: as one settler who was previously a sugarcane worker in Água Preta said, he became much more involved in the community after receiving land because when he worked for the plantation boss "there were no workers' meetings. At that time, a meeting was to do forced labor."

Outside of the individual settlements, meetings are held throughout the year at the local, regional and national level. Perhaps the most important meeting is the National Congress, which brings together representatives from every affiliated encampment and settlement every five years to reformulate long-term goals. The National Congress is generally attended by several thousand people (11,000 in 2000) and receives significant attention in the media. Details about the Congress—both beforehand and afterward—are written up and sent out to each of the individual settlements either through the movement's newspaper or through a settlement's delegates. Other meetings include the yearly preparations for the statewide meeting that is intended to evaluate the previous year and establish goals for the future. These meetings take place first at the level of the individual settlement or encampment, then a regional meeting is held with selected members and, finally, the statewide meeting is conducted over a period of three days with hundreds of representatives from across the state. Although MST members are extremely heterogeneous, attending a regional, statewide or national meeting allows them to share their thoughts about the movement and about life on the settlements. Many times, MST members from one part of the country referred to customs practiced by settlers in another part of the country that they witnessed during a national meeting. MST members generally attend several such meetings (at the local and regional levels) every year.

Through their experiences of participation, MST members demonstrate a new faith in the power of collective action. As one settler said, "Alone, you wouldn't get anything. Without the movement, the settlements wouldn't be created. You need pressure on the government." Long after they win their land, many remain committed to the movement because they believe that organization is necessary for their interactions with the government, "The MST still helps us [now that we are on the land], without the movement, we won't get anything. How many times have they been to [the capital of this state] to fight for us? If we leave the movement, we leave everything. The movement is all of us, not just [the leaders]." Most movement members believe that poor Brazilians could only solve their problems through organized struggle, "If I could talk to a landless person, a poor person, I would say, 'you have to fight—what we've got, we got through the movement.' "

Information

The MST's social networks have also become a primary source of information for movement members. As one woman said, "[the movement] helps me—they explain how things are. And if there's something we don't know how to do, they help." The information disseminated throughout the country is remarkably similar as activists meet frequently and receive constant bulletins from the movement's center.

Information regarding local market and agronomic conditions passes between the settlements, generated both by people whose training has been supported by MST and by those who are committed to settler education. Until 2000 when the state-funded program Lumiar was cancelled, the MST contracted agricultural extension agents who were responsible for training the settlers to plant nontraditional, high-quality crops. Information about one settlement's experience planting a new crop, such as watermelon in southern Brazil, is talked about in other settlements as the agricultural extension agents make their rounds. Universities and vocational schools also provide rich sources of information for the settlements. In 1995, for example, a group of students from the Federal University of Rio Grande Do Sul collaborated with a settlement in promoting the use of sustainable agricultural practices (*Jornal Sem Terra* Vol.151:6). Similar examples of collaboration can be found on many settlements as settlers pass along their experiences to other settlers.

MST activists are also an important source of political information. MST activists travel to the settlements to inform movement members of new government policies regarding credit, technical assistance, and more. As an older woman on the settlement said, "other people my age don't know so many things about the government, politics." The activists travel to the settlements regularly with prepared "economic and political analyses" to deliver. In the winter of 1998, the economic analysis included a stinging repudiation of Fernando Henrique Cardoso's term in office, particularly his involvement with the financial institution, the International Monetary Fund. In the days immediately following the militant's political lecture, the settlers frequently repeated what they had heard: "Our government is against us. For all these four years [of Fernando Henrique Cardoso's presidency], we are the ones who are going to lose. We have to fight or the beast will get us!"

The activists also bring news of what is happening within the MST. They describe any meetings that take place beyond the level of the settlement so that everyone can discuss the conclusions arrived at during the meeting. The settlers are given the chance to discuss how and in what ways new developments will affect their own lives. Although the activists are the main source of this information, MST also operates its own newspaper, *O Jornal Sem Terra*, which carries information about recent occupations, the progress of affiliated settlements, and various legal negotiations to approximately 3,500 people. Many settlements also have access to a weekly radio program hosted by movement activists. One settler said she and her husband listened to the radio program every week: "We make our kids keep quiet. We sing the songs. We feel emotional."

Bounded Solidarity . . .

Through these networks, and the information they provide, the MST has also generated a third element of social capital: "bounded solidarity" or positive identification among group members (Portes 1995:15). MST leaders try to emphasize the importance of social equality among movement members. This sense of social equality is embodied in the concept of "union," or unity. Because members across the country are theoretically equal, they are encouraged to feel a bond with their fellow comrades. As one settler said: "*è a união que faz a força*" (it is unity that makes us strong). In a country characterized by political and economic exclusion, the stress on equal treatment may be one of the most important components of democracy (Dagnino 1998:53–54). Taking part in occupations, mobilizations, and meetings is a way of publicly confirming one's membership and identity as a *Sem Terra*. Distinguishing themselves in this way generates a sense of internal solidarity through external difference. When the settlers join in a march to the state capital, they walk in strict lines. They wear their cleanest MST T-shirts and caps, and they wave the MST flag as they march. The mobilizations disseminate the movement's message both outwards to society and inwards to its own membership.

. . . and Political Empowerment: Closing the Gap between State and Citizen

Participation in the social networks as described above is generating a sense of empowerment among some of the most marginalized people in the country. MST members attribute the success of agrarian reform in Brazil today to the movement's activities. As one settler said, "The government only wants to finish us. But we want agrarian reform. . . . .agrarian reform only began after the MST entered the picture." The process of learning movement ideals and practices is a slow one and not everyone participates equally—or even at all. But those who do participate have a sense of being able to pressure the government for accountability and transparency. As a settler who only joined the MST when the plantation he was living on was expropriated (Wolford 2004) said, "before I entered the movement, I didn't know anything about it, but now I understand more and I know that the movement is pretty strong, that they fight and they even negotiate—until we get what we want." Another settler who rarely joined in MST meetings or events after receiving land said, "I think that the movement helps us, I think that they give us a lot of strength. They confront, they confront the [National Institute for Agrarian Reform], INCRA. They pressure the government, even to make the [investment] projects happen for us, it's always the strength of the movement."

Participation in the MST's networks has reduced the distance between state and citizen in part because the movement has made internal democratization a constant, if difficult, goal.[7] At the First National Congress in 1985, the members decided against electing people to individual positions, such as president or leaders, and instead chose a national coordinating committee to be the highest political unit within the movement (Branford and Rocha 2002; Fernandes 1999). The committee consists of one elected member per state, each of whom serves for a two-year period. By creating a committee of representatives, delegates at the meeting hoped to keep particular individuals from dominating positions of power.[8] From the settlements up to the national coordinating committee, the MST is relatively decentralized, consisting of hierarchical nested levels that carry decisions from individual households to *nucleos* (groups of ten to fifteen families) to settlement associations, to regional associations, to state committees, and, finally, to committees, at the national level. MST activists travel regularly between households and settlements to try and keep everyone informed and actively participating. Although there are inevitably accusations of favoritism, neglect, and elitism, this emphasis on democratic decision-making has a positive influence on how people see the political space around them.

The MST also emphasizes the connection between the struggle for land and the struggle for citizenship. When MST members occupy a farm, they frame their actions as the right of every Brazilian citizen to adequate land and food for subsistence. As Jaime Amorim, the MST state leader in Pernambuco, said: "We want to turn the farmer into a citizen, with a bank account, a credit card, voter registration, in essence, an entrepreneur." Within the physical space of the occupation camp, movement leaders symbolically and materially support the vision of an alternative Brazil characterized by social equality, production for subsistence, and democratic decision-making (Wolford 2003b). An MST activist who took part in one of the earliest occupations in the southern state of Santa Catarina spoke of his experience in the movement as a foundational one in which he developed the sense of belonging to a community he could be proud of:

> when we were in the occupation, we were very discriminated against by the other people, even the poor people in the community. The occupation was in the beginning, when the movement was just getting started, and people didn't know anything about us and so they called us vagabonds, said that we didn't want to work and et cetera. I remember that I went around getting food . . . and a lot of people wouldn't give us anything because they said "their parents have enough food to give them and now they come asking food from us . . . ." For you to have an idea . . . I was one of the main leaders of the community, but after we left there I stayed away for three years because everyone looked at me differently, and it was humiliating. You know when someone is looking at you differently, you just know. Today, however, this has changed. And so on Mothers' Day I went back to the community, and when people saw me—well, I still don't know if it was pride or jealousy.

Another movement activist characterized the MST's work as producing citizens:

> We work with the people who are marginalized by the bourgeoisie, they are the . . . thieves, the people who lie around, the idiots. The

> movement takes those people and turns them into citizens. The person who was living there in the city, going around making trouble—well, when the movement goes back [to the city] with him in two years, the people who used to not care about him at all, they begin to see him as an authority, where before he lived without a voice in society.

This "voice" comes in part from movement members' ability to access resources not possible otherwise.[9] MST members also express a sense of responsibility for other Brazilians who are in a situation similar to their own. They regularly echo the MST's argument that the movement's activities are not only directed at the material gain of its members but at Brazilian society as a whole, "the movement fights for equality, for a better life for everyone." They approve of the movement's work even when it does not directly affect them. As one woman said, defending the movement against accusations that the activists did not come to a settlement often enough,

> I think that the movement helps us, if it didn't help us, we wouldn't be receiving our credit [from the government], because the movement always fights for us. There are people who said that the movement is helping . . . other people who want to occupy land. And so I always say, "no, they are helping us, they are always giving us strength . . . . And if we don't help them, if we don't contribute, they also aren't going to be able to help us . . ." Today I have what I have because of the movement. And they do have to fight for [the whole state].

Membership in a movement that is working for the good of Brazil as a whole gives the MST settlers a sense of confidence and pride in their relationship with the rest of society and the state, "We are trying to transform society. Today the movement is respected because we have won some of the things that we wanted. Our credit is subsidized, for example, not even the union got that!" The movement's methods are recognized as effective, even by non-MST members living near the settlements (many of whom denounce the act of occupying someone else's land). As one person living in the small town of Campos Novos, Santa Catarina, surrounded by agrarian reform settlements said disapprovingly, "They (the Landless) are living well! They have everything, they invade the land and now they're rich—and look at us!" This person did, however, believe that the MST was right in invading the property, "the Landless are right because there are owners who don't plant and they should have come here." A small farmer living in the area said "The movement has to exist because you don't get anything for free. But there need to be people who are responsible." Another small farmer said that he had considered joining an MST occupation because he would be treated better by the government as a settler than a small farmer, "They are united, they are organized. They get a lot of things."

Deepening Democracy: In Spite of the Government

In the twenty years since the MST began, the movement has had to balance the demand for state-led distribution of land with fear of cooptation through cooperation with state officials and institutions. One of the ways in which the MST has been able to secure both resources and its autonomy is by "jumping scales" from the local grassroot level to the level of national and transnational civil society. In 1993, Neil Smith defined jumping scales as a mobilization strategy in which organizations countered hegemonic institutional practices by subverting the conventionally understood scalar hierarchy (local:regional:national:global; see also Keck and Sikkink 1998). The MST, like the Zapatistas in southern Mexico, have been extremely successful in building and coordinating support at the national and international levels—something that seems to have surprised movement activists, Brazilian politicians and academics alike. James Petras (1997) referred to the MST as the most effective and organized movement of the so-called New Social Movements in Latin America's third wave of democracy. In a speech at the 2003 World Social Forum, Noam Chomsky referred to the MST as "the most important and exciting popular movement in the world." This praise is both recognition of and constitutive of the MST's success in building ties with other social movements, NGOs, academics, and politicians.

These ties were initially constructed in the early 1990s when the MST began to actively organize in urban areas of Brazil, expanding the struggle for land to the urban poor and the middle classes. As João Pedro Stedile said: "The fight for agrarian reform takes place in the countryside but will be won in the cities" (quoted in Linhares and Teixeira de Silva 1999:232). In 1995, the movement changed its slogan yet again, this time from "occupy, resist, produce" to "agrarian reform is everyone's struggle." And in 1999, the MST presented a new set of organizational goals that was much more inclusive than those established in 1985. The goals now included a guarantee of work for everyone, social justice, and an end to all forms of discrimination including gender-based discrimination. This appeal to a universal notion of citizenship rights is very different from the personalistic politics, what DaMatta (1991) calls "relational politics," which have historically characterized many of Brazil's political institutions and relationships (see also Mainwaring 1994).[10] As a result of the MST's ideology, methods, and organizational structure, the movement has become one of the key figures in the struggle over deepening democracy in Brazil: "the MST, with its incredible capacity for organization and mobilization, has been giving force and continuity to the still-weak process of democratic negotiation over questions tied to the restructuring of the Brazilian society" (d'Incão and Roy 1995:210). By the late 1990s, groups as diverse as teachers, bus drivers, students, and political parties all supported agrarian reform as one of the most legitimate expressions of opposition to the status quo. A study in 1997 showed that over 85 percent of those polled supported both the need for redistribution and the MST's methods in pursuing reform (IBOPE 1998). The struggle for land has become part of not only "national political culture," but also an alternative political culture. The third stage of the Citizenship Action against Hunger and Poverty, announced in 1995, is the National Campaign for the "democratization of land." This campaign brings together a number of different celebrities and political groups—of which the MST is only one (Novaes 1998).

In expanding—or "massifying"—the struggle, MST successfully framed resistance to the state as a legitimate defense of democratic ideals, or the "right to have rights" (Dagnino 1998). This framing has pushed the MST into the transnational spotlight. MST members have made connections to farmers' movements across Latin America and the Global South. The movement's ideology is shared by many other farmers' movements, and perhaps most eloquently espoused by Vandana Shiva (also see Gupta 1998; Thurow and Kilman 2003). The movement is highly respected in Latin America—new movement actors in urban areas and in other countries seek out MST leaders for tactical advice.[11] MST activists go on regular speaking and solidarity tours in Mexico, Cuba, the United States, Europe, the Philippines, India, and South Africa (among other countries).[12] In 1997, farmers' movements from around the world agreed to designate April 17 "International Farmers Day" in commemoration of the day in 1997 when military police killed nineteen landless workers marching to the state capital of Pará, in northern Brazil. The MST participates actively in the international farmers' movement, Via Campesina, founded in 1992, and movement representatives joined the Inter-Continental Caravan that traveled across western Europe in 1999 (see Featherstone 2003 for an excellent analysis). Along with these and other agrarian movements, the MST is an important actor in the worldwide counter-globalization movement. The MST has had a significant presence in organizing and maintaining the People's Global Action network (PGA) and the World Social Forum (WSF).

These national and transnational connections have provided financial, cultural, and moral resources to the MST and in so doing have helped the movement establish itself as an important political actor in Brazil.

Social movements and NGOs such as Christian Aid, Global Exchange, Friends of the MST, UNICEF, and the Institute for International Cooperation and Development have donated considerable funds to the MST: charitable donations constitute the largest (and overwhelming) part of the movement's budget. International letter-writing campaigns organized by the MST have played a key role in pushing for the relocation of human rights trials to the national level rather than keeping them at the local level—or in local courts—where elite interests tend to exert a more conservative influence. Awards such as the Right Livelihood Award (also called the Alternative Nobel Prize) and the King Balduin prize for international development, as well as recognition from UNESCO for an innovative educational campaign provide financial resources as well as external legitimacy. Funds from UNESCO help pay for 1,200 MST teachers who offer literacy classes to over 25,000 adults. International donations have also sponsored an "itinerant school" where teachers travel between occupation camps providing basic education to children who are taken out of school so that they can occupy land. Cultural icons such as Chico Buarque (the Brazilian singer and writer) and Sebastião Salgado (the Brazilian photographer) have also contributed to the movement's fame and familiarity by appearing at social events honoring the movement and contributing to artistic endeavors in the movement's name. Funds from the sale of *Terra*, a musical collection produced by Buarque and a series of photographs taken by Salgado, are all donated to the MST. These funds are considerable: the photo exhibit was shown in approximately 800 cities worldwide. All of these public displays of solidarity are extremely important not only for their material contribution, but also for maintaining the movement's popularity among a public as quick to doubt as it is to hope.[13]

These network ties and resources have turned the MST into the privileged representative of landless(ness) in Brazil. Although there are dozens of movements throughout the country, as well as a long history of militant trade unionism, it is MST leaders who are regularly asked to define the "agrarian problem" in Brazil and quoted in newspaper articles and books on the subject. It is the MST that every politician from the national level to the local level has to meet with in order to reassure the voters that an agrarian reform agenda exists. The MST's struggle—its ideology, organizational structure, and methods—has been successfully scaled up into "*a luta de todos*"—the struggle by and for everything and everybody. A prominent MST leader from Santa Catarina (who moved up to the Northeast when the movement began mobilizing there) put it this way: "we picked an issue that united everyone—the land. [Land] is a necessity. Land is the word that unifies. Land became the element of the struggle. You offer the workers the opportunity to have land—but through an occupation [that they participate in]."

Conclusion: The MST and Lula in the Fight for Brazil's Democracy

In October 2002, the political left in Brazil won a significant victory. After running in three previous elections, Luis Inâcio "Lula" da Silva was elected president of the country.[14] As a member of the Workers' Party and widely considered the candidate of the common people, Lula's overwhelming victory in 2002—he received a higher percentage of the popular vote than any previous candidate in Brazilian history—was indicative of the tremendous desire for economic, political, and social change in the country. His election was also indicative of the support for the Workers' Party itself.[15] Since its formation in 1984, the MST has supported both Lula and the PT. In 1989, almost 40,000 people attended a campaign rally for Lula at an MST settlement in Rio Grande do Sul (Branford and Rocha 2002:54). Movement members and leaders have publicly (and privately) campaigned for party candidates at both the local and the federal level.

Lula's election presents a challenge for the MST. On the one hand, Lula is sympathetic to the movement's concerns and has consulted the movement extensively in implementing his new agrarian reform project. Lula appointed Miguel Rosseto, a former communist party activist and enthusiastic public supporter of the MST, to be the minister in charge of agrarian development. Lula met with MST representatives and solicited their opinion regarding appointees to state INCRA (National Institute for Colonization and Agrarian Reform) offices. Lula has also made the rural areas and the eradication of hunger a key element of his new administration. The head of Lula's much-touted *Zero Fome* (Zero Hunger) program, José Graziano da Silva, is a leading left-wing academic supportive of agrarian reform, although he has been critical of MST's actions at times. These programs and new political attitudes are, in part, a response to the social capital deployed by movement members: participation in the MST has helped to reduce the distance between the people (or demands and rights) represented by the movement and the state, and the state has responded with continued attention to agrarian reform and the rural poor.

At the same time, the space available for acceptable civil disobedience is also reduced. Opposition to Lula is less broadly palatable than opposition to the Cardoso government, as Cardoso was increasingly unpopular toward the end of his eight-year administration. Observers have already rushed to present MST's continued practice of land occupations as traitorous to the Lula administration. As one journalist wrote: "Invading land is like brushing your teeth! The MST is as much an enemy of the PT government as it was of the FHC government—or more. In the first three months this year, there have already been 44 land invasions, as opposed to 10 in the same period last year" (reported in the Estado de São Paulo 04/20/03, p.1). Brazilian academics such as José de Souza Martins (2000) and Zander Navarro (2002) have been vocal in their opinions that MST needs to work more closely with the government or it will have to be considered an obstacle to democratic development and to the wishes of the people. Martins argues that the transition to democracy provided a window for civil society to challenge the domination of the Brazilian state, but the window will shut if civil society refuses to work within the state and allows official political institutions to be co-opted by right-wing forces much more comfortable with the state-driven rhetoric of democracy and reform.

The MST has worked with Lula to assist the government in implementing its campaign promises for agrarian reform. At the same time, the movement has always insisted on maintaining its autonomy from official politics in general and the PT in particular. Even as the movement supports the PT administration, it has maintained the use of opposition as an important political tool. In 1998, when it seemed that Lula might win the presidency, a news reporter asked João Pedro Stedile where he would be on the day of the inauguration. Stedile answered that he would be coordinating a massive round of land occupations. During the 2002 elections, Lula expressly asked MST not to "support" him in this way.[16] Ultimately, the MST did support Lula's nomination for the presidency, but the movement will continue to use opposition as an important tool for representing the poor vis-à-vis the government.

When Lula was inaugurated in January 2003, the MST promised the PT a six-month reprieve from organized resistance, but by March 7, 2003, the movement had already announced that "the honeymoon was over," and declared its intention of initiating a new wave of land occupations that would challenge the Lula administration to demonstrate its true loyalties. Those MST members who supported a new wave of occupations were following a hard line against the government, demanding that Lula choose between a radical platform of social redistribution and the more moderate platform of growth with distribution. As João Pedro Stedile said: "If the Lula government understands the people's message, then it will strengthen the process of change. If, on the other hand, he tries to fool the people by asking for patience, then he will [be expelled] like [Argentina's ex-president] De La Rúa."

It is clear that even as the MST continues to fight for agrarian reform by working more closely with Lula's government, the movement will still maintain its capacity and threat of opposition as a strategic tool in its struggle for state resources. The movement's oppositional ideologies and strategies were forged in the country's history of land tenure relations and in the movement's early relationship with the Brazilian state, and this identity will not easily change.

Notes

1. Another example of technically illegal actions being excused by the social context of poverty and inequality is the *saque* or the practice of looting a supermarket or truck for food. During the drought of 1997–1999 that affected northeastern Brazil, the MST was a highly visible organizer of *saques*. The governor of Pernambuco in 1998, Miguel Arrães, stated that: ". . . to confuse *saques* with assault or a robbery is to treat a very serious social issue as if it were violence." High-ranking members of the Catholic Church also justified the practice, arguing that: "Those who take something that does not belong to them in order to survive do not sin." This comment by the Archbishop of João Pessoa was immediately criticized by Brazil's president, Fernando Henrique Cardoso, but it did prompt the federal government to expedite the transferal of emergency aid funds to the Northeast.
2. Occupying private and public property is permitted under Article 186 of the 1988 Constitution, which states that land has a social function to fulfill such that rational and adequate use of land and labor is observed in accordance with the adequate utilization of all other natural resources and preservation of the natural environment. The idea of land having a social responsibility to be productive became constitutional

law in 1946, but its origins can be dated back to Portuguese land law of the fourteenth century (Holston 1991). Properties may also be occupied if it can be established that ownership is uncertain or improperly obtained. In 1999, INCRA estimated that approximately 100 million hectares of land were held with suspicious titles.

3. David Lehmann (1990) has argued that social movements can either engage in rent-seeking behavior in order to receive highly regulated favors from the government, or they can miss out on the official benefits and try to work alone (Lehmann 1990:155; also see Zamosc 1986).
4. All direct quotes in this paper come from field research conducted in Santa Catarina and Pernambuco between 1998 and 2003 unless otherwise indicated.
5. The two main advantages of a large group of people are that violence is less likely and the federal government is more likely to step in. Violence is less likely because a large group of people draws attention. The townspeople often come out to see what is happening, the media often interviews participants and local leaders feel they need to get involved. Both public and private gunmen are reluctant to resort to violence as a means of intimidation when there is a large group assembled for an occupation. A large group also increases the likelihood that the movement's case will be tried at the Federal level for resolution. The Federal government only becomes involved in land disputes if the land itself is property of the Federal government, or if there is sufficient disturbance to warrant assistance. An occupation that is tried at the Federal level has an initial advantage over an occupation tried at the local level because the Federal Constitution guarantees the social responsibility of land while judges at the local level prioritize the Civil Code which protects the sanctity of private property.
6. The settlers also provide assistance for movement activities not related to land occupations. They are often asked to put together whatever food they can for MST members who are taking part in long mobilizations. Being able to participate in this way is not always an easy thing, but when the settlers are able to, it often makes them feel like they were able to participate in the actual event. In Água Preta, a young settler said that he was rarely able to leave the settlement and join in MST demonstrations, but he did pay the movement regularly and so "it's as if he went." The settlers also argued that the movement was working for them and so they had an obligation to be supporting the activities: "I am settled, but they are fighting for us. So today, we put together food for people [mobilizing] in Chapeco."
7. In spite of the movement's insistence on decentralization and democracy, there have been consistent allegations (and some evidence) of a Leninist style of decision-making (Navarro 2002).
8. Even though the National Coordinating Committee is run by elected representatives who serve limited terms, there are six MST leaders who have occupied influential positions since the movement began.

This "old guard" is extremely influential in movement policy and decision-making.

9. MST members first receive assistance from the state during the occupation period when local governments send in supplies of food and medicines. Activists organizing occupations often tell participants to bring enough food to last a few days, until the government and other settlers begin to contribute. MST's success in winning expropriations is such that new recruits and squatters consider it extremely unlikely that they will not win access to land (Deere and Leal 1999; Hammond 1999). The Cardoso administration has even consulted with MST—and the country's largest rural union, the Confederation of Agricultural Workers (CONTAG)—over what properties should be expropriated. The government also passed legislation in December 1996 that strengthened the Rural Property Tax (ITR), which was an important step toward eliminating regressive tax evasion in the countryside. Legislation was also passed that expedited land reform claims by allowing resources to be made available for the purchase of land within twenty-four hours.
10. As Warren Dean has written, "the exchange of state patrimony for the short-term gain of private interests is a constantly repeated theme in Brazilian history, so ingeniously and variously pursued and so ingrained as to appear the very reason for the existence of the state" (Dean 1995:276).
11. The MST's assistance in the technical business of organizing other movements was most visible in the urban "sem-teto" (homeless) movement in Rio de Janeiro and São Paulo, as well as in the Movimiento Sem Tiera of Bolivia. Land-based movements such as the Movement of Small Farmers (the MPA), and the Movement of Women Cultivators have all benefited from the spaces of opposition and representation that the MST has opened in relation to the state. MST's support for these movements is intended to be a public expression of discontent with the state's inability to respond to the political and ideological vacuum created by the defeat of the authoritarian state (Sorj 1998).
12. See the Web site maintained by the nonprofit organization, Friends of the MST (part of Global Exchange). Available at <www.mstbrazil.org> for details on MST tours and solidarity activities in the United States.
13. Almost everyone in Brazil agrees that agrarian reform is necessary, but the disagreements over "on whose land" and "for whom" are tremendous—and often violent.
14. Born in the northeastern state of Pernambuco, Lula traveled to São Paulo as a child and eventually found work as a machine operator in an automobile factory. Lula's political career began in the late 1970s when he helped to coordinate the automotive workers' strikes that played a key role in bringing an end to the military dictatorship.

In 1980, Lula became a founding member of the Workers' Party and served as its first president (French 1992; Keck 1992). He ran for president in 1989, 1994, and 1998, and came very close to winning each time although his left-leaning agenda scared many mainstream and conservative Brazilians.

15. The PT has grown rapidly since the early 1980s, nearly doubling its representation in the Chamber of Deputies in 1982, 1986, and 1990. The party won several key city and state elections in the late 1980s, including the position of mayor in São Paulo, Porto Alegre and Belo Horizonte. The PT is attempting to change a clientelistic political culture and civic disengagement by establishing popular participatory mechanisms, the most visible and important of which is the *orçamento participativo* (participatory budget, or OP). The OP brings together "nonelites" who would normally be excluded from the political process and allows them to determine priorities for the allocation of local investment spending (de Souza Santos 2000). Although the number of people who actually participate in the OP is a small fraction of those represented by the party, the existence of a space for participation is an important step toward building a more active citizenry (Avritzer 2002; de Souza Santos 2000; Nylen 2000).
16. The MST did not support Lula's candidacy unanimously; several MST leaders openly expressed a preference for Olivia Dutra, the popular PT governor of Rio Grande do Sul and were disappointed when he was not nominated.

BIBLIOGRAPHY

Alvarez, S. E. (1997) "Reweaving the fabric of collective action: Social movements and challenges to 'actually existing democracy' in Brazil," *Between Resistance and Revolution: Cultural Politics and Social Protest*, R. G. Fox and O. Starn (eds.), Brunswick, NJ: Rutgers University Press.

Avritzer, L. (2002) *Democracy and the Public Space in Latin America*, Princeton: Princeton University Press.

Bourdieu, P. (1986) "The Forms of Capital," *Handbook of Theory and Research for the Sociology of Education*, J. Richardson (ed.), New York: Greenwood Press, 241–258.

Branford, S., and J. Rocha (2002) *Cutting the Wire: The Story of the Landless Movement in Brazil*, London: Latin American Bureau.

Dagnino, E. (1998) "Culture, Citizenship, and Democracy: Changing Discourses and Practices of the Latin American Left," *Cultures Of Politics/Politics Of Culture: Re-Visioning Latin American Social Movements*, S. E. Alvarez, E. Dagnino and A. Escobar (eds.), Boulder, CO: Westview Press.

———. (2002) "Sociedade Civil e Espaços Públicos no Brasil," *Sociedade Civil e Espaços Públicos no Brasil*, E. Dagnino (ed.), São Paulo: Editora Paz e Terra S/A, 9–17.

DaMatta, R. (1991) *Carnivals, Rogues and Heroes: An Interpretation of the Brazilian Dilemma*, Indiana: University of Notre Dame Press.

Davis, D. E. (1999) "The Power of Distance," *Theory and Society* 28:585–638.

De Souza Santos, B. (2002) "Participatory Budgeting in Porto Alegre: Toward a Redistributive Democracy," *Produzir Para Viver: Os Caminhos da Produção não Capitalista*, B. de Sousa Santos (ed.), Rio de Janeiro: Civilização Brasileira.

Dean, W. (1976) *Rio Claro: A Brazilian Plantation System, 1820–1920*, Stanford, CA: Stanford University Press.

———. (1995) *With Broadax and Firebrand: The Destruction of the Brazilian Atlantic Forest*, Berkeley: University of California Press.

Deere, C. D., and M. León De Leal (1999) *Towards a Gendered Analysis of the Brazilian Agrarian Reform*, Storrs, CT: Center for Latin American and Caribbean Studies, University of Connecticut.

D'Incão, M. C., and G. Roy (1995) *Nós, Cidadãos: Aprendendo e Ensinando a Democracia*, São Paulo: Paz e Terra.

Escobar, A., and S. E. Alvarez (eds.) (1992) *The Making of Social Movements in Latin America: Identity, Strategy, and Democracy, Series in Political Economy and Economic Development in Latin America*, Boulder, CO: Westview Press.

Evans, P. (1997) *State–Society Synergy: Government and Social Capital in Development*, Berkeley: University of California at Berkeley, International and Area Studies.

Featherstone, D. (2003) "Spatialities of Transnational Resistance to Globalization: The Maps of Grievance of the Inter-Continental Caravan," *Transactions of the Institute of British Geographers* NS 28:404–421.

Fernandes, B. M. (1999) *MST, Movimento Dos Trabalhadores Rurais Sem-Terra: Formação e Territorialização*, São Paulo: Editora Hucitec.

Fernandes, F. (1965) *A Integração do Negro na Sociedade de Classes*, vol. 1, São Paulo: Editora da Universidade de São Paulo.

French, J. D. (1992) *The Brazilian Workers' ABC: Class Conflict and Alliances in Modern São Paulo*, Chapel Hill: University of North Carolina Press.

Gohn, M. d. G. (1997) *Os Sem Terra, ONGs e Cidadania*, São Paulo: Cortez.

Gomes da Silva, J. (1987) *Caindo por Terra: Crises de Reforma Agrária na Nova República*, São Paulo: Busca Vida.

Graziano da Silva, J. F. (1982) *A Modernização Dolorosa: Estrutura Agrária, Fronteira Agrícola e Trabalhadores Rurais no Brasil*, Rio De Janeiro: Zahar Editores.

Gupta, A. (1998) *Postcolonial Developments: Agriculture in the Making of Modern India*, Durham: Duke University Press.

Hall, A. (1993) "Non-Governmental Organizations and Development in Brazil under Dictatorship and Democracy," *Welfare, Poverty and Development in Latin America*, C. Abel and C. M. Lewis (eds.), Oxford: Oxford University Press, 421–437.

Hammond, J. (1999) "Law and Disorder: The Brazilian Landless Farmworkers' Movement," *Bulletin Of Latin American Research* 18, 4:469–489.

Hellman, J. A. (1992) "The study of new social movements in Latin America and the question of autonomy," *The Making of Social Movements in Latin America: Identity, Strategy and Democracy*, A. Escobar and S. E. Alvarez (eds.), Oxford: Westview Press.

Holloway, T. H. (1980) *Immigrants on the Land: Coffee and Society in São Paulo, 1886–1934*, Chapel Hill: University of North Carolina Press.

Holston, J. (1991) "The Misrule of Law: Land and Usurpation in Brazil," *Comparative Studies in Society and History* 33, 4:695–725.

Hooper, A. (n.d.) "Democratic Consolidation/Democratic Crisis in Brazil? The Collor Presidency, 1990–1992." Available at <www.psa.ac.uk/cps/1994/hoop.pdf> (accessed September 27, 2004).

IBOPE (Instituto Brasileiro de Opinião Pública e Estatística) (1998) "Pesquisa de Opinião Pública Sobre a Reforma Agrária," summary of national poll conducted March 5–8, Rio de Janeiro.

Keck, M. (1992) *The Workers' Party and Democratization in Brazil*, New Haven, CO: Yale University Press.

Keck, M., and K. Sikkink (1998) *Activists Beyond Borders: Advocacy Networks in International Politics*, Ithaca, NY: Cornell University Press.

Lehmann, D. (1990) *Democracy and Development in Latin America: Economics, Politics and Religion in the Post-War Period*, Philadelphia: Temple University Press.

Linhares, M. Y. L., and F. Teixeira da Silva (1999) *Terra Prometida: Uma História Da Questão Agrária no Brasil*, Rio de Janeiro: Editora Campus.

Mainwaring, S. (1994) *Democracy in Brazil and the Southern Cone: Achievements and Problems*, Notre Dame, IN: University of Notre Dame Helen Kellogg Institute for International Studies.

———. (1995) "Brazil: Weak Parties, Feckless Democracy," *Building Democratic Institutions: Party Systems in Latin America*, S. Mainwaring and T. R. Scully (eds.), Palo Alto, CA: Stanford University Press, 354–398.

Mainwaring, S., and E. Viola (1994) "New Social Movements, Political Culture and Democracy: Brazil and Argentina in the 1980s," reprinted in *Social Movements in Latin America*, J. I. Domínguez (ed.), New York: Garland Publishing, 205–240.

Martin, J. Y. (2002) "Uma Geografia da Nova Radicalidade Popular: Algunas Reflexões a Partir do Caso do MST," *Terra Livre* 18, 19, June/July:11–37.

Martins, J. de S. (1981) *Os Camponeses e a Política no Brasil: As Lutas Sociais no Campo e seu Lugar no Processo Político*, Petrópolis: Vozes.

———. (2000) "As Mudanças nas Relações Entre a Sociedade e o Estado e a Tendência á Anomia no Movimentos Sociais e nas Organizações Populares," *Estudos Avançados* 14, 38:268–278.

Navarro, Z. (1996) "Democracia, Cidadania e Representação: Os Movimentos Sociais Rurais no Estado do Rio Grande do Sul, Brasil,

1978–1990," *Política, Protesto e Cidadania no Campo*, Z. Navarro (ed.), Porto Alegre: Editora da Universidade do Rio Grande do Sul, 62–106.

Navarro, Z. (2000) "Breaking New Ground: Brazil's MST," *NACLA Report on the Americas* 33, 5:36–39.

———. (2002) " 'Mobilization Without Emancipation'—Social Struggle by Brazilian Landless," *Produzir Para Viver: Os Caminhos da Produção não Capitalista*, B. de Sousa Santos (ed.), Rio de Janeiro: Civilização Brasileira.

Novaes, R. (1998) "A Trajetória de uma Bandeira de Luta," *Política e Reforma Agrária*, L. F. C. Costa and R. Santos (eds.), Rio de Janeiro: Mauad, 169–181.

Nylen, W. (2000) "The Problem of Low and Declining Rates of Participation in Participatory Mechanisms of Public Administration: Lessons from the Participatory Budgets of Betim and Belo Horizonte, Minas Gerais," paper prepared for delivery at the Brazilian Studies Association (BRASA) VI International Congress, Atlanta, GA, April 4–6.

Panini, C. (1990) *Reforma Agrária: Dentro e For a da Lei*, São Paulo: Edições Paulinas.

Papma, F. (1992) *Contesting the Household Estate: Southern Brazilian Peasants and Modern Agriculture*, Amsterdam: Centre for Latin American Research and Documentation.

Petras, J. (1997) "Latin America: The Resurgence of the Left" *New Left Review* 223:17–47.

Poletto, I. (1997) "O Movimento dos Trabalhadores Rurais Sem Terra e a Luta Pela Terra," *Cadernos de Estudos Sociologicos* 97:14–28.

Portes, A. (1995) "Economic Sociology and the Sociology of Immigration: A Conceptual Overview," *The Economic Sociology of Immigration: Essays on Networks, Ethnicity and Entrepreneurship*, A. Portes (ed.), New York: Russell Sage Foundation.

Portes, A., and J. Sensenbrenner (1993) "Embeddedness and Immigration: Notes on the social determinants of economic action," *American Journal of Sociology* 98, 6:1320–1350.

Prado, Jr., C. (1967) *The Colonial Background of Modern Brazil*, Berkeley: University of California Press.

Putnam, R. "The Prosperous Community," *American Prospect* 13:35–42.

Rocha, J., and S. Branford (2002) *Cutting the Wire: The Story of the Landless Movement in Brazil*, London: Latin American Bureau.

Rossiaud, J., and I. Scherer-Warren (2000) *A Democratização Inacabavel: As Memòrias do Futuro*, Petropolis, RJ: Vozes.

Sabel, C. (1993) "Studied Trust: Building New Forms of Cooperation in a Volatile Economy," *Explorations in Economic Sociology*, Richard Swedberg (ed.), New York: Russell Sage Foundation.

Scherer-Warren, I. (1993) *Redes de Movimentos Sociais*, São Paulo: Edições Loyola.

Schwade, E. (1992) *A Luta Não Faz Parte Da Vida . . . E A Vida: O Projeto Politico-Religioso De Um Assentamento No Oeste Catarinense*, Florianopolis, SC: Universidade Federal de Santa Catarina.

Schwartz, S. (1992) *Slaves, Peasants, and Rebels: Reconsidering Brazilian Slavery*, Chicago: University of Illinois Press.
Scott, J. C. (1998) *Seeing Like a State: How Certain Schemes to Improve the Human Condition have Failed*, New Haven, CT: Yale University Press.
Sewell, Jr., W. H. (2001) "Space in Contentious Politics," *Silence and Voice in the Study of Contentious Politics*, D. McAdam, S. Tarrow, and C. Tilly (eds.), Cambridge: Cambridge University Press, 51–89.
Seyferth, G. (1990) *Imigração e Cultura no Brasil, Brasília*: Editora Universidade Federal de Brasília.
Slater, D. (ed.) (1985) *New Social Movements and the State in Latin America*, Amsterdam: CEDLA.
Smith, N. (1993) "Homeless/global: Scaling places," *Mapping the Futures: Local Cultures, Global Change*, J. Bird, B. Curtis, T. Putnam, G. Robertson, and T. Tickner (eds.), New York: Routledge, 87–119.
Sorj, B. (1998) "A Reforma Agrária em Tempos de Democracia e Globalização" *Novos Estudos* 50:23–40.
Stedile, J. P. (ed.) (1994) *A Questão Agrária Hôje*, Porto Alegre, RS: Editora da Universidade Federal de Rio Grande do Sul.
———. (1997) "O MST e a Questão Agrária: Entrevista com João Pedro Stedile," *Estudos Avançados* 11, 31:69–98.
———. (2002) "Landless Battalions: The Sem Terra Movement of Brazil" *New Left Review* 15 (May/June):77–104.
Stedile, J. P., and B. M. Fernández (1999) *Brava Gente: A Trajetória do MST e a Luta Pela Terra no Brasil*, São Paulo: Editora Fundação Perseu Abramo.
Stein, S. (1985) *Vassouras: A Brazilian Coffee County, 1850–1900.* Princeton: Princeton University Press.
Swidler, A. (1986) "Culture in Action: Symbols and Strategies," *American Sociological Review* 51, 2:273–286.
Thurow, R., and S. Kilman (2003) "Food Sovereignty: Global Rallying Cry of Farmer Movements, a Food First" *Backgrounder* 9, 4 (Fall).
Tilly, C. (1978) *From Mobilization to Revolution*, Reading, MA: Addison-Wesley Publishing.
Veiga, J. E. da (1990) *A Reforma que Virou Suco: Uma introdução ao dilema agrário do Brasil*, Petrópolis: Vozes.
Viotti da Costa, E. (2000) *The Brazilian Empire: Myths and Histories*, Chapel Hill, NC: University of North Carolina Press.
Weyland, K. G. (1996) *Democracy without Equity: Failures of Reform in Brazil*, Pittsburgh, PA: University of Pittsburgh Press.
Wolford, W. (2001) "Case Study. Grassroots-Initiated Land Reform in Brazil: The Rural Landless Workers' Movement" *Access to Land, Rural Poverty, and Public Action*, A. de Janvry, G. Gordillo, J. Platteau, and E. Sadoulet (eds.), Oxford: Oxford University Press, 304–315.
———. (2003a) "Families, Fields and Fighting for Land: The Spatial Dynamics of Contention in Rural Brazil," *Mobilization* 8:201–215.
———. (2003b) "Producing Community: Geographies of Commitment on Land Reform Settlements in Brazil," *Journal of Agrarian Change* 3, 4:500–520.

Wolford, W. (2004) “Of Land and Labor: Agrarian Reform on the Sugarcane Plantations of Northeast Brazil,” *Journal of Latin American Perspectives* 31, 2:147–170.

Woolcock, M. (1998) “Social Capital and Economic Development: Towards a Theoretical Synthesis and Policy Framework,” *Theory and Society* 27, 2:151–208.

Wright, A., and W. Wolford (2003) *To Inherit the Earth*, Oakland: Food First Press.

Zamosc, L. (1986) *The Agrarian Question and the Peasant Movement in Colombia: Struggles of the National Peasant Association*, 1967–1981, Cambridge: Cambridge University Press.

Chapter 8

Civil Society and Political Decay in Venezuela

Daniel H. Levine

Civil society emerged as a self-conscious force in Venezuela in the context of extended political and institutional decay. The term itself was rarely heard in national life before the 1980s, as the country's powerful political parties monopolized all kinds of organization, incorporating and subordinating them to party networks. As the political party system and the institutions built around it entered a terminal decline, great hopes were placed in civil society as a potential source for reconstructing politics on more open and democratic grounds—democratizing the country's democracy that was widely perceived to be in crisis. These hopes have been frustrated and the energies that moved them have not found enduring form. The combination of high hopes for empowerment and a new kind of politics with frustration and disempowerment unites Venezuelan experience with much of the rest of Latin America in an unhappy pattern.

Why is continued citizen mobilization accompanied by growing disempowerment of those same citizens? Why do movements fail, leaders burn out, and members disperse, and what are the implications of this organizational failure for democratic representation? Reflection on the nature of empowerment and disempowerment can shed light on the peculiar mix of strengths and weaknesses that mark the relation of civil society to state and politics in Latin America. To the extent that the hopes placed in civil society for empowerment and positive political change are frustrated and the results are disempowerment and demobilization, the implications for stable and meaningful democratic representation are grave.

Throughout Latin America, large numbers of people have been mobilized over the last decade for sustained, repeated, and often risky collective actions including rallies, campaigns to collect and deliver signatures, marches, demonstrations, sit-ins, and the like. In Venezuela, the process has been particularly intense since the late 1980s, as a profusion of new and often short-lived groups combined with established organizations such as trade unions or business federations, political parties, and professional groups to manage and sustain the effort. Several factors together explain the relation of civil society to politics in this case. The precipitous decline of powerful political parties, and of the entire system of organizations and political norms built around it created a space for the emergence of groups referring to themselves as "civil society" and their rise to prominence and their political frustration in the course of the 1990s. Long-term economic decline gutted the capacity of the parties to sustain patronage networks, and of national state institutions to pay for, much less manage, social welfare programs. The decay of party control and state capacity opened the field to new groups, while laying the groundwork for a process of class and political polarization that have found full throated expression in the rise of Hugo Chávez Frias to political power, and in the regime and movement he leads (Roberts 2003; Márquez 2004). These factors underpin a trajectory of mobilization and counter mobilization, activism, and sustained protest that dominated national politics since the late 1990s.

The appearance of citizen movements (mostly urban) and civil society as independent political actors was part of a broad movement to open and "deepen" the country's democracy. Central to this process was the appearance of new capabilities and groups *outside the net of state and established political parties*, which fought to open and energize politics. They mounted steady pressure for broader citizen participation, greater accountability of politicians and institutions, easier access to politics, and far reaching institutional reforms including significant changes in electoral rules and systems of representation (Gomez Calcaño 1998; Levine 1998). Facing state and party structures and leaders identified as corrupt and unresponsive, citizens turned to civil society as an arena for participation and a platform for advancing demands about representation. The entire effort reflected and reinforced the decay of the political parties, whose control over organizations and procedures weakened in the face of changing social dynamics and extended economic crisis that made traditional clientelistic strategies no longer viable.

The kind of citizen mobilization at issue here involves more than simple "demand making," which then finds representation through established conventional channels. At stake is also a claim to representation that politicizes new spaces and groups in national life. The failure or short-circuiting of the movements raises questions about the possibilities of constructing enduring representation that starts and ends in "civil society."

"Civil society" as a collection of independent groups pressing claims for a place in national life and institutions emerged within Venezuela's well-established democratic system. The goal was not to overthrow authoritarian rule or to manage a transition to democracy but rather to "democratize democracy" and give it new life and breath by broadening citizen access and loosening the grip of the country's powerful political parties and dominant state apparatus. It has become common lately in academic discourse to cast doubt on the *bona fides* of the democracy established in 1958, to underscore its corrupt and exclusionary character. Elsewhere in this volume, for example, Oxhorn states "it is impossible to understand the level of support for Chávez among Venezuela's poor without recognizing the privileged, often corrupt nature of the same organizations typically associated with political democracy . . . . it is the exclusionary nature of Venezuela's pacted democracy that largely propelled Chávez to power."

It is important to confront this view directly. I would argue instead that the political system established in 1958 institutionalized universal suffrage, and popular representation while delivering on promises to improve the level of living of ordinary people, most notably in terms of health, education, and social mobility. The later crisis of this system, and in particular of its core political institutions, can be explained not by some original sin of "exclusion" but rather as the result of the deadly interaction of two elements: the devastating effects of a long-term economic decay and the inability of leaders and institutions to change as society changed around them. Political parties and state institutions created for a still rural, mostly illiterate and unmobilized society failed to adapt to an urban, educated, media-soaked, and highly active society.

This became painfully evident in February 1989, when massive urban rioting broke out in Caracas and other cities, in the wake of the government's economic restructuring "package." The *Caracazo* and its aftermath was a shock to the system not only because of the toll of violence, but also to the extent that it revealed how hollow the whole system of party and state dominated arrangements for social control through party organizations or unions had become. Leaders were out of touch and organizations could no longer "deliver" their base. López Maya (2003:136) writes,

> It was the weakness of the institutions designed in the past to contain and regulate political order and everyday life that explains the extension and violence of the protest. If the political actors and unions had been in tune with their constituencies they could have foreseen the scale of the discontent that was building up at the time, healthy parties and unions could have planned strategies to oppose or negotiate with the government on these measures. This in turn could have made possible some containment of the discontent and given some hope to the people which might have lessened their anger. However . . . political representation and mediating institutions had already been seriously eroded.

Efforts to reform the system and to open up institutions to greater and more varied citizen representation also began in the mid 1980s and gained urgency as signs of economic, political, and institutional decay began to appear and concerns rose over the need to "relegitimize" the country's political system (Levine 1998). An array of citizen movements arose demanding more authentic and accountable representation. From the beginning, the membership base and agenda of core urban movements has been predominantly middle class. Initial demands found expression in decentralizing reforms that devolved power to states and cities, reduced barriers to participation, and expanded the number of offices open to election (including most notably mayors and governors). But these and other reforms were swept away by the continuing political crisis and ultimately marginalized by the victories of Hugo Chávez who came to office with a very different agenda of total change (Levine 2002). The initial power of Chávez' movement was magnified by the collapse of older structures. As some of these recovered ground and citizen movements began to emerge again, opposition mounted, mostly in the form of civil society mobilizations, once again seeking political redress and accountability outside the formal structures of the political system.

By 2004, the continuing economic decline that began in the mid 1980s had left Venezuelans in 2003 with income levels and standards of living that barely equaled those of four decades earlier (Kelly and Palma 2004; Roberts 2003). Leaders and organizations were so entrenched that they managed to hang onto power into the mid 1990s. But the organizations they controlled turned out to be hollow shells, as rising levels of inflation, unemployment, public debt, and voter abstention combined with growing unrest, violence (in politics and also in daily life), and the shock of military rebellions in 1992 (the first in almost thirty years) to cast the entire political system into an extended crisis.[1] (Hernandez 2003; Levine 2002, 2003; Montferrante and Padilla 2004).

In sum, it was the discredit and decay of established leaders and parties combined with institutional failure and sustained economic crisis that opened the door for a wide range of movements to emerge and claim a voice as "civil society." Participants in these movements sought not only to satisfy immediate demands (say for housing or services) but also to express, by their actions, a claim to citizenship and equal status apart from established, conventional structures of representation. They project not only their demands, but also their image of themselves as citizens, forcefully onto the public stage. Their activism politicized urban spaces in new ways: creating new forms of action and building (often literally) new spaces for such activism. The long-term pay off of such activism, in terms of sustained benefits, new policies, or accountable leaders, has been problematic. The weakness, reversibility, and often open failure of so many efforts requires us to reconsider the possibilities and limits of democratic representation, and to search for possible solutions in ways that go beyond tinkering with electoral machinery.

The relation of empowerment and disempowerment to democratic politics is of central concern here. Discussions of empowerment tend to be people-friendly. They underscore the need to provide people with the skills and capabilities that make access to power possible—to empower them, and to enhance the "quality" and "authenticity" of representation. "Quality" and authenticity of representation entail more than the assurance that electoral results reflect votes accurately and fairly, according to whatever electoral rules are in place. Assuming universal suffrage and relatively free and open elections, representation that is authentic and of high quality further requires lowering barriers to organization, multiplying instances and arenas of political action, making voting easier, and representatives more accountable and more accessible. The goal of such reforms is to link new urban spaces, groups, and networks to the institutional structures of the political system in ways that allow social energies to "bubble up" and find representation (Avritzer 2002). In case after case, massive numbers of citizens have joined together and sought representation of their interests through public, often risky, mobilizations of all kinds. Politics and systems of representation should be capable of linking together these new networks and spaces, but with rare exceptions, this has not happened. Political leaders remain wedded to a top-down vision in which it is they who know what to do and how to do it.

They either do not make the links or they use them for a time and move on. Citizen movements are too often left stranded and divided, lacking enduring channels of contact or control into the political sphere.

The theoretical challenge is to rethink the relation between social movements and political representation in ways that preserve the energy and openness of both. The practical challenge is to confront the dilemmas of disempowerment in ways that limit the damage to the possibilities of citizen activism, and open representative politics. Addressing both of these challenges requires attention not to civil society alone, but also to the character of political leadership, institutions, and the kinds of ties that connect civil society with the politics.

POLITICAL DECAY AND THE RISE OF CIVIL SOCIETY

Although it is not easy to put a precise date on the beginning of the decline of the political system and its core institutions, most observers agree that by the early 1990s, the dominant parties AD (*Acción Democrática*) and COPEI (*Comité de Organización Política Electoral Independiente*) were shadows of their former selves (Molina 2004; Crisp, Levine and Molina 2003). Their weakened condition undermined the ability of leaders to respond effectively to the crisis created by the two attempted coups of 1992, and by the country's ongoing economic decline. Once legendary party discipline weakened, making secure interparty deals in the legislature was much more difficult to manage. COPEI divided, and its founder Rafael Caldera, waged a brilliant, antiparty campaign to win the presidency in a four way race in 1993. This was the first election since the restoration of democracy in 1958 that was not won by either AD or COPEI. Although the two parties continued to do well in regional and local voting, throughout the 1990s, the political scene witnessed continued growth of citizen organization (including insurgent unionism) escaping from party controls, rising levels of abstention, growing antiparty sentiment, and a series of intraparty divisions. The election of 1998 and subsequent national, regional and local votes confirmed the end of the old parties and of the political system built around them.

The political trajectory of Hugo Chávez Frías, his election to the presidency in 1998 (affirmed in subsequent voting under a new Constitution and with new electoral rules) and his overall political project challenged the legitimacy of the core political arrangements of the past four decades, and looked to build a new, and supposedly more democratic and participatory society and political system (Coppedge). Fiery populist rhetoric has been the daily bread of the "Bolivarian revolution" from the beginning, and mobilization of masses has been its core claim to legitimacy. Like Fujimori earlier in Peru, Chávez looked to destroy existing political parties (and associated groups, notably the trade unions), with the difference that Chávez wanted to rebuild politics in a "revolutionary" and "participatory" style, with a broad range of arenas and groups in direct contact with the leader and the state.[2] In practice this has meant attacking and dismantling old structures, restlessly inventing and reinventing new ones, including notably the regime's own political party and diverting state resources into vaguely defined "Bolivarian circles." This is a classic "movement politics," closely tied to the personal appeal of President Chávez, that operates in practical terms through an alliance between the left and key elements of the military.

Once in power, the Chávez government made an effort to put its rhetoric of participatory (as opposed to representative) democracy into practice through a series of provisions in the Constitution that make a place, at least in theory, for the active participation of "civil society" in politics. The 1999 Bolivarian Constitution, for example, provides that the legislative councils of the different states "consult with" civil society on matters of interest to the states (Article 206) and that "civil society" nominate three members of the National Electoral Council, charged with managing elections (Article 296). Similar provisions are scattered elsewhere in the constitutional text. As a practical matter, disputes about how to define "civil society" make it almost impossible to figure out who could and should be recognized as speaking in its name.

The steadily increasing polarization of the country has turned "civil society" into a highly contested term: both pro- and anti-Chávez groups claim to speak in its name, denying legitimacy and authenticity to the other. The results are occasionally anomalous. For example, although in theory civil society was to participate in evaluating candidates for the "citizen power," in practice the president took this task upon himself, on the grounds that because a majority of the population had voted for him, he was the proper representative of civil society. (Salamanca)! More often lately, the results are confrontational and too often deadly, with groups clashing in the streets.

It is not easy to come up with reliable estimates of the scale of groups and movements that constitute "civil society." Salamanca (2004) cites estimates for the total number of civic associations that range from about 25,000 to about 54,000. The largest proportion are neighborhood associations, along with a substantial number of groups devoted to promotion and development, working with government and international resources. There is also a strong, but regionally concentrated cooperative movement, and a significant, although numerically small, network of human rights organizations. To be sure, neither mobilization nor political action is central to the agenda of many associations. There are music groups, civic theaters, urban or regional cultural centers (*ateneos*), cooperatives, sports clubs, and a host of related groups whose logic and daily life needs have little to do with political confrontation (Gómez Calcaño 1998; Lander 1995; Levine 1998; Salamanca, 2004).

But even groups that see themselves as removed from politics are linked to the state (and thus to politics) in ways that draw them into the partisan arena. Many if not most seek and receive resources from the state. Even in times of economic decline, the Venezuelan state remains a powerful source of financing and material resources for groups of all kinds. Further, the accelerated rhythm of mobilization and polarization in the last decade and a half have made it hard for groups to stand apart from political division and on the margins of confrontation.

The years from 1989 to the present are arguably the most protest-filled period in the last hundred years of Venezuelan history: one massive urban uprising, two attempted coups, the impeachment and removal of one president, and a rising tide of marches, demonstrations, and violent actions in the universities and on the streets[3] (López Maya 2002; Hernández 2002). Levels of protest surged following the *Caracazo* of February 27, 1989, and after a short respite under the second government of Rafael Caldera (1993–1998), the rhythm of demonstrations, marches, and street protests picked up again as the country entered a new electoral cycle. To be sure, urban protests, often violent, had never completely gone away. Student activism, sparked by regular violent actions under the leadership of *encapuchados* (literally "hooded ones," students with hoods to shield their identity) regularly spilled over from high school and university campuses into the streets.

Protest and the scope of confrontation broadened with the election of Chávez as president. López Maya shows that among kinds of protest, confrontational actions showed the strongest increase in 1999. Her figures do not include events beginning in late 2001, when protest grew and mobilizations, marches, and clashes became the daily bread of urban life, not only in the capital city of Caracas, but throughout the country: mobilization and counter-mobilization, rally and counter-rally, with massive marches following one another at ever shorter intervals. Protests, occupations of buildings, and coordinated actions involving banging of pots and pans, creating a truly deafening noise (*cacerolazos*) along with blowing of whistles or car horns (*bocinazos*) became everyday occurrences (González de Pacheco).

Starting in 2001, the opposition consolidated and counter-mobilizations began to make themselves felt. The opposition consists of a loose alliance of remnants of the old political parties, the trade union movement, the Catholic Church, and a broad range of the groups and civic associations self identified as "civil society." The space in which conflict has been played out is largely urban and, as we shall see, both sides claim to be acting in the name of civil society, democracy, and the public good. Early steps in the rejuvenation of the opposition came with the defeat of government sponsored efforts to "take" the Central University (in Caracas) for the "people," and with the defeat of a government sponsored referendum to "renew" the leadership of the trade union federation. These were followed by a succession of marches, rallies, strikes and work stoppages (*paros*) that became a regular feature of the calendar in Caracas and other cities.

Protest techniques common in other countries, such as *cacerolazos* and caravans of cars honking horns were put to use and massive marches (long since abandoned in favor of television-centered campaigning) returned to center stage. A regime claiming legitimacy on the basis of its ability to mobilize was now running into massive counter-mobilizations. Fearing the appearance of weakness and losing control of the street, the regime began to put on its own massive marches. The process escalated from early December 2001 through to the tragic events of April 11–13, 2002, when a gargantuan march, heading through downtown Caracas to the presidential palace, was attacked by snipers. Many were killed, and in the ensuing crisis the government was replaced and then retook power as the military divided and different coalitions of citizens "took" and "retook" the streets. All sides then pulled back from the brink for a while, but after about six weeks the rhythm of marches and counter-marches began again, accelerating through the fall of 2002 and culminating in the remarkable but ultimately failed civic strike of late 2002 and early 2003.

It is instructive to compare the mobilizations that forced out Peru's Fujimori with those competing to oust, support, or restore Chávez (Levine and Romero 2004). The former were managed by a loose coalition of groups from across the country, knit together by local and national level activists with prior experience in mobilizations, energized by the OAS findings of fraud and irregularities in the 2000 reelection of Fujimori, and by growing revelations of corruption linked to Vladimiro Montesinos. Mobilizations were sparked first by students and women's groups, who began with symbolic acts such as sweeping the *plaza* of the Congress and regular washings of the flag (to cleanse them of corruption). As protests expanded, they were joined by NGOs and then by political parties who added financing and organizational reach. The campaign itself combined enormous marches (such as the Marcha de los Cuatro Suyos[4] in Lima, of July 28, 2000) with a series of regional mobilizations along with innovations like weekly public washings of the national flag. The organizations and political parties prominent in the 1980s disappeared from the political scene following Fujimori's "auto-coup" of 1992, and lost all legal status after elections to the Democratic Constituent Congress in 1993. They resumed a public role only once protests were well under way.

The contrast with Venezuela is noteworthy. The organizational backbone for sustained public opposition to President Chávez did not come from new groups. Instead, an unexpected but effective antigovernment alliance was formed between the trade union federation, the business federation, the Catholic Church, and the mass media. The first two provided organizational resources while the latter two gave legitimacy and an amplified public voice. That this coalition was able to put so many people into the street on such a regular basis depended less on the groups' own members, than on the motivation of a loosely linked net of neighborhood and human rights groups reinforced by the trade union movement and the media.

Despite regular reference to the role of "civil society," in neither country did the civic organizations of the previous decade, once seen as the basis for a new kind of politics, play a central role. Different kinds of organizations emerged to take the lead. Apart from human rights groups, which have grown throughout the region in the last fifteen years in response to dictatorship (Sikkink 1993), the key organizational players were either occasional coalitions gathered for a particular purpose around a specific leader or old line organizations such as trade union, business federations, or the Church. Mobilization and commitment were sustained less by groups as such than by multiple, overlapping loose or "weak ties" between groups and individuals that facilitated connections and the exchange of information, support, and resources, across groups, social sectors, and physical spaces (Granovetter 1973; Smith 1996). Clearly, mobilization, even massive and sustained mobilization, can take place without permanent organizational structures. Cellular telephones, faxes, and media saturation have changed the task of getting people together for collective action. Nonetheless, in the absence of enduring organization, it is difficult to consolidate gains, to monitor the progress of policies, and to enforce accountability from leaders, without an endlessly repeated round of institution challenging mobilizations. Those who bear the brunt of activism are vulnerable to division and betrayal by leaders. The path from empowerment to disempowerment is open.

Empowerment and Disempowerment

Empowerment is a plastic concept, often used in conjunction with equally protean terms such as "civil society" or "social capital". Like "accountability," "empowerment" has no easy equivalent in Spanish, and neologisms such as *empoderamiento* commonly fill the linguistic gap. The elasticity of these concepts reflects their multidimensional character: they point to processes that involve organizational growth, personal and collective identity, leadership skills, social trust, and the ability to secure goods and services, and operate simultaneously on a range of social levels.

"Empowerment" is a people-friendly concept. The term denotes a kind of social and political process and a pattern of structure and organization that provides citizens with a growing range of arenas for access to the public sphere, reduces barriers to action, and creates conditions that enhance a sense of self-worth and recognized personal as well as collective identity—that empowers them. The relation of empowerment to citizenship is straightforward. The women and men who come to see themselves as citizens with rights equal to others, are in that measure set on the road to individual and collective action as normal and possible.

The capacity to build and sustain organization is important to the process, for organization can enhance empowerment by linking individual and group capabilities and moving action to broader arenas. At the same time, however, by subordinating group efforts to leadership concerns and stifling independent decision, all-powerful and all-encompassing organization can also disempower ordinary people. In her classic work on Mexico's PRI, Susan Eckstein (1977) points to the irony of organization, noting that for many in Mexico, being organized within the PRI meant less, not more power. In his work on religion in the United States, Warner makes the general point that the empowerment that may come from organization is necessarily latent: more a by-product than an intentional goal. He states (1993:1070), "it is to be expected that the empowerment functions of religion are latent. At an individual level, those who seek well-being in religion tend not to find it; those who gain well-being from religion are not those who seek it." The logic of Warner's apparent paradox is that empowerment, like social capital, rests in the long-term construction of community, trust, and the skills and dispositions required for working together—not just in creating or joining organizations, and much less in simply "getting the goods."

As a concept and social process, empowerment is asked to do a lot, and it should be no surprise that many movements have failed to fill the bill. Even the most cursory review of recent theoretical and empirical work on urban social movements, empowerment, and politics in Latin America reveals a slow recovery from a hangover brought on by exaggerated expectations, laced with a heavy dose of idealization of the new movement. The autonomy of movements (vis-à-vis institutions such as political parties, state institutions, or church) was overdone, and a romantic image of the "small is beautiful" kind made many observers anticipate that a totally new kind of politics would arise from the seeds provided by these movements. This in turn would provide the basis for a different pattern of representation with new kinds of political parties, and altered institutions that would hopefully be more democratic and more fully empowering of citizens than what had hitherto existed (Hellman1992; Lander 1995; Oxhorn 2001).

This did not happen: in case after case, the new politics was easily absorbed into the old, and movements split, or simply fell apart. That movements fail and empowerment does not endure should be no surprise. Movements often fail: activism is costly and antinomian and the day-to-day pressures of economic and family survival make organization difficult to sustain (Piven and Cloward 1977, 1998). Anyway, as Stokes (1995) and others have shown for Peru, the emergence of more participatory (and therefore, in principle more "empowering") styles of organization does not necessarily replace older self-concepts and forms of action. People are practical, and new styles of action take their place as an alternative to be weighed and perhaps put to use, as circumstances seem to indicate.

What does disempowerment mean, and what is the path from empowerment to disempowerment? There is withdrawal from activism, often prompted by burnout and sometimes by family pressures (commonly gender specific, and affecting women in particular). There is also a failure of leadership replacement. Groups that campaign for democracy may remain authoritarian within, and leaders have problems letting new generations come to the fore. The problem is notorious in groups linked to the Catholic Church where dependence on clergy makes for enormous vulnerability if and when more conservative clergy arrive on the scene. Finally, of course, with the opening of new political spaces (through transitions to democracy or reforms within democratic systems) younger activists easily find other, perhaps more rewarding and less costly outlets for their energies. This is not to say that empowerment is necessarily illusory. Many have indeed acquired new skills and self-images, and imparted these to others in their communities. But the concept is incomplete, and the reality fragile. The linkage between civic spaces of empowerment and public spaces of political representation and state power remains problematic. The absence of stable links to larger structures also undercuts the visibility of groups in the public sphere, which is essential to their gaining recognition as legitimate actors and claimants to public rights, resources, and spaces.

The theoretical problem is to discern if there is something about the way in which empowerment was sought, organizations constructed, or connections built by urban movements that has self-limiting or self-destructive qualities. Venezuelan experience is instructive here. The country's long process of political decay freed potential clients from party controls while at the same time opening the field to new kinds of groups operating in newly created political spaces. Cases in point include the neighborhood movements, insurgent trade unions, new political parties, and a host of groups and federations self-consciously identified as civil society. Like many new groups, urban citizen movements arose to address specific needs created by the urban context and the deteriorating economic situation—crime, garbage collection, provision of services, zoning, and traffic, for example. Satisfying these needs required some rearrangement of the relevant institutions and political spaces, and led to campaigns for political and electoral reform. Building these connections and sustaining these campaigns led to a search for allies and patrons: leaders and groups capable of providing needed access to resources and institutions. There is a fine line here between sustaining empowerment and falling into time-honored clientelist patterns, and the line is easily blurred. One need not assume the complex pattern of dependence of PRI-controlled Mexico at its height (Eckstein 1977) to recognize that groups and communities require allies in the state and the larger political arena, and that these allies may and likely do have other agendas. State or party control of resources is critical here: hence the critical role often played by NGOs with autonomous resources in freeing groups from dependence on parties. It is this connection that has proved unreliable, leaving groups dependent on unaccountable leaders and institutions, even for groups (like most of the neighborhood movements) whose middle-class character offers some insulation from fiscal pressure.

The institutional reforms put in place in Venezuela in the 1990s opened new possibilities for organization, representation, and action. State and local governments were energized, new career paths opened for leaders, a host of new political groups appeared, carrying the promise of far reaching political dealignment and realignment. But the whole process was aborted and gains proved short-lived. The 1999 Bolivarian Constitution recentralizes power, and once in office, President Chávez has worked to recentralize politics, curtailing the reforms that had gathered force in earlier periods. This was a setback for the autonomy of social movements, as decentralization had had provided many local and regional groups with viable arenas for mobilization and action—places to get started without having to compete on the national level from the very beginning.

Under the Chávez regime so far, conventional processes of interest mediation or representation are commonly bypassed in favor of a direct relation between the leader and the people (Kornblith 2005; Levine 2003; Salamanca 2004). Much effort has been put into groups called *círculos bolivarianos* (Bolivarian Circles) depicted by the regime and its spokespersons as independent citizen networks. The only empirical study to date of the *círculos* (Hansen, Hawkins, and Seawright 2004) suggests otherwise, pointing up their dependence on state institutions and financing, and their role as transmission belts mobilizing support for the regime and its leader and delivering goods to loyalists.

Much contemporary work on urban movements and civil society in Latin America has framed the matters that concern us here in the context of transitions to democracy and democratization. Notable cases of transitions to democracy present the following anomaly: citizen mobilization and new citizen groups that were prominent in campaigning for democratization declined, split, and often simply disappeared with the restoration of democracy. The anomaly lies not only in the decline of specific movements, which makes sense given the availability of channels of action and the competition for resources and for supporters. Although decline may have been inevitable, the process was clearly accelerated by naive and unworkable understandings of politics, and by untrustworthy and unreliable political allies. With the possible exception of Brazil, where the PT has clear roots in the popular movements, and has grown steadily at all levels, the common experience has been one of division and betrayal (Blondet 1991; Lander 1995; Levine 1998; Levine and Stoll 1997).

The preceding comments suggest that more is at issue than regime change. Analysis of the anomaly presented by activism and disempowerment benefits from being situated in a larger context of thinking about social movements, civil society, and institutions. Movements commonly emerge, grow, succeed or fail, and decline, moving through what Tarrow (1994:156) terms cycles of protest. "What is distinctive about such periods," he writes, "is not that entire societies 'rise' in the same direction at the same time [they seldom do]; or that particular population groups act in the same way over and over, but that the demonstration effects of collective action on the part of a small group of 'early risers' triggers a variety of processes of diffusion, extension, imitation, and reaction among groups that are normally quiescent." In this light, the proper question is not so much why groups do not survive, but what if any legacy they leave in new rules, expectations, or capabilities. The opportunity structure that urban citizens face must also be taken into account—resources and institutional channels available, accountability, and access.

The record from Venezuela is mixed on both counts. The emergence of civil society within Venezuelan democracy reinforced and extended a culture of rights and activism, but has not provided the means for building enduring and representative connections of the kind once made through the political parties. Since the late 1980s, there has been widespread concern in the country with institutional design and institutional engineering (Crisp 2000; Crisp and Levine 1998; Levine 1998). But failures of accountability remain more the norm than the exception. The provisions of the 1999 Bolivarian Constitution that allow for referendum and recall of officials are an opening in principle, but as a practical matter the use of these instruments (like those for regulating the electoral system) has been caught up in the overwhelming polarization of the country (Kornblith 2005). Little or nothing has been done to open up the process of candidate selection, and all important matters such as access to court, control of the penal system, and the effective impunity of police and security forces remain untouched. In effect, in terms of mobilization for political action, the system taking shape now is a throwback to the personalistic politics of a leader who relies on movements and campaigns to implement policies. In such a context, activism tends to be episodic, leaving activists, at the end, at the mercy of a different charismatic leader—new face, same dependence.

URBAN SPACE AND URBAN CITIZEN MOVEMENTS

The preceding considerations bring me to a closer look at urban spaces and urban citizen movements: to the city as a stage or arena for action, and to city dwellers as actors. The urban scene in Venezuela (as in much of the Third World) is marked by a dominant capital city, explosive growth with bigger cities growing faster than smaller ones, and all cites faster than rural sectors. Internal migration has been the predominant motor of urban growth in Venezuela, where rural poverty, road construction, and urban investment paid for by petroleum sparked a process of migration, beginning in the 1930s, that emptied the countryside. In recent years, regional cities have experienced substantial expansion.

In Venezuela, urban space (above all the streets, *plazas*, and neighborhoods of the capital city) has long been a prime arena for political action of all kinds: from rallies, demonstrations, and marches to blockades, bus burning, and street fighting. Urban mobilizations were key to the overthrow of the country's last dictator, Marcos Pérez Jiménez, in January 1958. Urban land invasions and the formation of vast new shantytowns remained a prominent feature of city life through the early 1960s, but have since faded, although occupations of buildings have returned to the scene in recent years. The emergence of "civil society" as an actor in national politics brought a different kind of urban movement onto the national scene decades later in the form of the neighborhood movement. The first such groups were created to defend property rights and control urban development. Their agenda soon expanded to include pressure for greater municipal autonomy, and the fiscal and electoral reforms this entailed (Garcia Guadilla and Silva Querales 1999; Gómez Calcaño 1998; Lander 1995; Levine, 1994, 1996, 1998; Salamanca 2004).

The urban geography of Caracas has shaped the specific way in which organization, protest, and confrontation have evolved. Caracas is separated from the Caribbean Sea by a mountain range whose slopes give the city a northern frontier. The city itself is contained in a large east-west valley with extensions to the south, east, and west along similar valleys. This makes the social geography of the city something like a sandwich, with business and wealthier districts in the center and east, flanked by poorer urban areas, including housing projects, *barrios*, older, now urbanized invasion areas on the eastern and western edges in the hills and ravines. The class segregation suggested by this arrangement of space has been undermined in recent years by the city's metro system, which facilitates daily class mixing in urban spaces of a kind unknown thirty years earlier.

The well-known class polarization of support and opposition to President Chávez, and his own predilection for polarization as a strategy, gave political conflicts of the 1998–2005 period a markedly spatial character: political protest in Caracas has been as much territorialized as expressed in votes. Most opposition marches begin in the east and move to the center: the regime mobilizes support in the western and eastern extremities of the city.[5] The intensification of conflict and polarization, visible in a continuous stream of marches and counter-marches, has if anything reinforced class segregation, as neighborhoods organize in self-defense and greet outsiders and unknown faces with fear and suspicion. García-Guadilla points to the "kidnapping of public spaces along with strong processes of spatial segregation and social polarization: in a word, the de democratization of the city" (2003, 6–7). Her analysis is worth quoting at length.

> "The consequence of this has been the creation of closed spaces and ghettos within the city that respond to social and political differences, the territorialization of political conflicts, the appearance of highly segregated urban spaces, the loss of liberty to move about within the city with the risk of being identified as "one of them", and the rise of spaces of fear and violence. In short, the loss of rights to the city, exclusion, de democratization, and the loss of citizenship. (García-Guadilla 2003:10)

The original role of urban spaces is replaced by one of struggle.

> Highways no longer serve to move vehicles and persons to daily activities but rather for massive manifestations, to keep extended vigils (with tents and all the gear of modern camping), plazas no longer exist for rest or recreation but rather to express political support or rejection of the President. Young people of the middle classes who once followed north American recreational patterns are the first in reinforcing this new subculture which is not limited to marching but also to the clothes one wears in a march (in the colors of the national flag), national folkloric music that animates them, and a host of nationalist symbols and placards. (García-Guadilla 2003:17–18)

More is lost in this process than the use of urban sense and a hitherto notable ease in the mixing of people of different class and race in most public spaces. There is also a loss of citizenship in the original sense of the term that, of course, derives from being part of a common city. Sustained polarization has also gutted the democratizing thrust of key groups within civil society. Many of the very same neighborhood organizations that once fought to extend and democratize the country's democracy have now morphed into semimilitarized local self-defense groups with elaborate plans for defending home space from "the other" (Garcia-Guadilla, 2003:20).

Conclusion: Is Disempowerment the Future of Empowerment?

The combination of activism and massive citizen mobilization with disempowerment that marks the social and political trajectory of Venezuela over the past decade and a half does not augur well for citizen empowerment or representation and does not provide clear lines for gauging the likely future dimensions of "civil society" or its possible roles in the political system. The decay of political institutions, including but not limited to political parties, leaves citizens with space for the creation of civil society—a space they have filled with enormous energy and creativity. But in the absence of reliable and trusted political intermediaries—either formal institutions or political parties—these energies are rarely converted into sustained and authentic representation. Is disempowerment the future of empowerment? Reading back from recent waves of massive, mostly urban mobilizations may provide some clues.

Avritzer (2002:103) states that in transitions from authoritarian rule to democracy, a general problem has been "how to connect the newly emerged public sphere with the recently reempowered political society." Solutions, in his view, have focused either on restraining mobilization (to avoid undue "strain" on fragile systems) or on devising new systems of accountability. Neither has succeeded well, and Avritzer argues for,

> an alternative framework for the study of democratization that I call participatory publics [grounded in the introduction of] stronger deliberative devices as the result of political renovation. . . . Only a change in strategy can lead to a different perspective according to which the institutional problem ceases to be solved by following the first postulate of the democratic elitist tradition, the narrowing down of politics to the activities of government. As long as the democratic impulses in Latin America remain insulated at the societal level, democratization strategies are bound to fail. Democratic designs in the new Latin American democracies are dependent on their capacity to move democracy from a societal practice into a form of public deliberation. (Avritzer 2002:166)

Avritzer's points bear reflection in the case of Venezuela. New citizen movements and the very idea of "civil society" as an autonomous space for organization and action, emerged as a potential force in Venezuela within an already established democracy, advancing the goal of democratizing and relegitimizing the country's stagnant political arrangements. The deep and widespread discredit of parties, party elites, and governing institutions appears to have inspired elements of the 1999 Bolivarian Constitution that address, at least in principle, the concerns Avritzer outlines. The Constitution avoids mention of representative democracy, but is lavish with projects for a wide array of deliberative and participatory instances including but not limited to referenda, citizen assemblies, cooperatives, shared enterprises, educational communities, public participation in nominations for national bodies, and the like. The whole process, and indeed the general appeal of Hugo Chávez and the movements gathered around him, makes sense as part of a broad assault on the old system, its institutions and operative rules. As a practical matter, this has translated into a dismantling of older institutions and routines and a reliance by the regime on episodic mobilizations, "campaigns," and above all, on the military institution, for the implementation of policy and the delivery of services (Trinkunas 2004).

The consultative and deliberative processes outlined in the 1999 Constitution have had only limited use on a national scale: notably in the trade union referendum (an early defeat for the government) and most importantly in the August 2004 referendum to recall the president, which was a major defeat for the opposition. Limitations of space preclude a full discussion of the process leading up to the presidential recall and the vote itself (Kornblith 2005, McCoy 2005). But even a brief account illustrates how overwhelming polarization and personalist politics can trump formal constitutional provisions. The August 15, 2004 vote was the culmination of well over a year of mobilization and effort by the opposition coalition, including two national signature drives, a related effort to "verify" signatures initially disqualified under rules adopted midstream by the National Electoral Authority, and sustained harassment of those who signed recall petitions, including but not limited to loss of employment. The body governing elections (Consejo Nacional Electoral, National Electoral Council) was itself highly polarized with a government majority. Kornblith writes, "The government girded itself stoutly for the struggle by putting a pro-Chávez majority on the CNE board and packing the Council at all levels with the president's sympathizers. The institutional resources came from the government's control over the public bodies whose decisions would shape the referendum's design and organization" (Kornblith 2005:133). The wording of the question on the ballot made no mention of the concept of recall which is in the constitution (*revocación* in Spanish) asking instead, "Do you agree with rendering ineffective the people's mandate given through legitimate democratic elections to the citizen Hugo Rafael Chávez Frias as president of the Bolivarian Republic of Venezuela for the current presidential period?" The options presented to voters reversed the normal order in such elections: with NO (to keep the president) placed before YES (to recall him) on the ballot.

The ultimate victory of the president, by a broad 59–41 Percent margin, surprised many observers, and explanations of the outcome are shaded by the polarization of the country. Opposition figures point to the extended difficulties of the process itself and suggest fraud, while progovernment figures cite effective mobilization by the regime's own forces. Indeed, opinion polls had tracked a steady growth in support for the president over the year leading up to the vote, support that was reinforced by a sustained series of "missions and campaigns" delivering a wide range of resources to supporters. One strong critic of the process reflects on the more general implications in these terms.

> The so-called participatory democracy enshrined in the 1999 constitution devalues representative democracy, dilutes the prominence of political parties as articulators of collective will, and converts the armed forces into a crucial actor with the ability to insert itself and its influence into any sphere of national life. In this model, elections are instruments to be used at the service of a personality cult and a sociopolitical model with long-term hegemonic aspirations, deeply tied to a politicized armed forces and connected to a population mobilized by means of plebiscites and patron–client mechanisms. It is a bitter irony that elections have served so often and so well to promote the ambitions of a group and a political project that oppose democracy, its principal institutions, and its crucial values. In the process, those who are committed to liberal democracy believe less each day in the effectiveness of elections as mechanisms to articulate collective preferences and to produce power relations that can adequately express collective sentiment. (Kornblith 2005:136)

In the wake of the referendum, the regime has hardened its stance with aggressive moves to control the mass media, expand the armed forces, implement more radical programs (including land seizures), and further limit the opposition.

* * *

The dilemmas of mobilization with disempowerment are not limited to middle-class groups or opposition movements. The Chavez regime manages its own support organizations in classic populist terms, with independent organization and representation subordinated to and mediated through the leader. It will not be easy to solve the puzzle of mobilization with disempowerment. Part of the difficulty is practical: obstacles of all kinds litter the path of those who try. There are also theoretical problems to address. Much thinking about empowerment, citizenship, and representation is caught somewhere in between reflection on social movements and analysis of institutional design, and a desire to expand citizen access and participation in already existing arenas. The problem is how to give enduring and legitimate form (to institutionalize) to this new participation. Continued polarization, sustained economic and institutional decay, and the newly aggressive stance of the regime have if anything accentuated the fragmentation of political forces to such a point that agreement on such spaces (let alone on who should participate in them) seems very unlikely. The future of civil society does not look as good as it used to, and optimists (apart from those in the regime) are scarce on the ground.

Notes

1. Molina (2004) provides another perspective on the decline of the once all-powerful party system of the parties, and argues that the decay of parties of this type makes rebuilding of any kind of stable political institutions all the more difficult.
2. Instead of "representative," Venezuelan democracy in the 1999 Constitution "is and always will be democratic, participative, elective, decentralized, alternative, responsible, pluralist, and with revocable mandates" (Article 6).
3. CF the 1991 annual report of PROVEA (Programa Venezolano de Educacion y Accion en Derechos Humanos) which states that "in contrast to earlier years, and basically during and after the national protests of February 1989, it was possible to confirm that *the social spectrum participating in protests is widening. Now participation in organized protests has opened fields of action for new groups: along with students and workers one finds a range of professional associations and social groups: doctors, nurses, peasants, Indians, firemen, police, cultural workers, housewives, and neighborhood groups actively joining in defense of basic rights*" (italics in original) PROVEA, 114–115.
4. The term comes from the four regions, or Suyos, of the Inca Empire, Tahuantinsuyo. The name suggests that the march gathers force from all corners of the country.
5. A well-recognized and commercialized *kit del marchista* (a marcher's kit) hit the market by 2001, including at a minimum, sun visors, flags, whistles or pots, and banners (Gonzales de Pacheco 2004).

BIBLIOGRAPHY

Avritzer, L. (2002) *Democracy and the Public Space in Latin America*, Princeton University Press.

Blondet, C. (1991) *Las Mujeres y el Poder. Una Historia de Villa el Salvador.* Lima: Instituto de Estudios Peruanos.

Coppedge, M. (2002) "Soberanía popular versus democracia liberal en Venezuela," Marisa Ramos Rollón (ed.), *Venezuela: Rupturas y Continuidades del Sistema Politico (1999–2001)*, Salamanca, Spain: Ediciones Universidad.

Crisp, B. (2000) *Democratic Institutional Design. The Powers and Incentives of Venezuelan Politicians and Interest Groups.* Stanford. Stanford University Press.

Crisp, B., and N. Silva Querales (1999) "De los movimientos sociales a las redes organizacionales en Venezuela; estrategias, valores e identidades," *Politeia* 23, Segundo Semestre, 7–27.

Crisp, B., D. H. Levine, and J. E. Molina (2003) "The Rise and Decline of COPEI in Venezuela" *Christian Democracy in Latin America. Electoral Competition and Regime Conflicts*, Scott Mainwaring and Timothy Scully (eds.), Stanford: Stanford University Press, 275–300.

García-Guadilla, M. P. (2003) "Politización y Polarización de la Sociedad Civil Venezolana: Las Dos Caras Frente a la Democracia," paper presented at meetings of the Latin American Studies Association, Dallas, Texas, March 2003.

Gómez Calcaño, L. (1998) "Civic Organization and Reconstruction of Democratic Legitimacy in Venezuela," D. Canache, and M. Kulishek (eds.), *Reinventing Legitimacy: Democracy and Political Change in Venezuela*, Westport CT: Greenwood Press.

González de Pacheco, R. A. (2004) "Encuestas, Cacerolazos, y Marchas," *En Esta Venezuela Realidades y Nuevos Caminos*, Marquez, P., and R. Piñango (eds.), Caracas: Ediciones IESA, 337–356.

Granovetter, M. S. (1973) "The Strength of Weak Ties," *American Journal of Sociology* 78, 6:1360–1380.

Hansen, D. R., K. A. Hawkins, and J. Seawright (2004) "Dependent Civil Society. The Circulos Bolivarianos in Venezuela," presented at meetings of the Latin American Studies Association, Las Vegas NV.

Hellman, J. A. (1992) "The Study of New Social Movements in Latin America and the Question of Autonomy," A. Escobar and S. Alvarez (eds.), *The Making of Social Movements in Latin America: Identity, Strategy, and Democracy*, Boulder: Westview Press.

Hernández, T. (2002) "El desafío de la violencia en el actual sistema político venezolano," M. Ramos Rollón (ed.), *Venezuela: Rupturas y Continuidades del Sistema Político (1999–2001)*, Salamanca, Spain: Ediciones Universidad.

Kelly, J., and P. Palma (2004) "The Syndrome of Economic Decline and the Quest for Change," *The Unraveling of Representative Democracy in*

Venezuela, Jennifer McCoy and David J. Myers (eds.), Baltimore, MD: The Johns Hopkins University Press, 202–230.

Kornblith, M. (2003) "Representación y Personalismo: Una Dificil Combinacion (con particular referencia al caso venezolano)," A. M. Bejarano and E. Pizarro (eds.), *The Crisis of Democratic Representation in the Andes* (forthcoming).

Lander, E. (1995) *Neoliberalismo, Sociedad Civil, y Democracia. Ensayos Sobre América Latina y Venezuela*, Caracas: Universidad Central de Venezuela, Consejo de Desarrollo Científico y Humanístico.

Levine, D. H. (2003) "El Consenso Democrático Venezolano en Dos Tiempos, 1972–2002," *Politeia* (forthcoming).

——. (2003) "Debate: Undemocratic Venezuela," *Bulletin of Latin American Research* 22, 3:231–236.

——. (2002) "The Decline and Fall of Democracy in Venezuela: Ten Theses" *Bulletin of Latin American Research* 21, 2:248–269.

——. (1998) "Beyond the Exhaustion of the Model: Survival and Transformation of Democracy in Venezuela," D. Canache and M. Kulisheck (eds.) *Reinventing Legitimacy: Democracy and Political Change in Venezuela*, Wesport, Connecticut: Greenwood Press.

——. (1994) "Goodbye to Venezuelan Exceptionalism," *Journal of Inter American Studies and World Affairs* 36, 4:145–182.

Levine, D. H., and B. Crisp (1998a). "Democratizing the Democracy? Crisis and reform in Venezuela," *Journal of Inter-American Studies and World Affairs* 30, 2:27–62.

Levine, D. H., and C. Romero (2004) "Movimientos Urbanos y Desempoderamiento en Perú y Venezuela," *America Latina Hoy* 36:47–77.

Levine, D. H., and D. Stoll (1997) "Bridging the Gap between Empowerment and Power in Latin America," S. Hoeber Rudolph and J. Piscatori (eds.), *Transnational Religion and Fading States*, Boulder, CO: Westview Press.

López Maya, Margarita. (2003) "The Venezuelan Caracazo of 1989: Popular Protest and Institutional Weakness" *Journal of Latin American Studies* 35:1 (February) 117–138.

——. (2002) "Venezuela after the *Caracazo*: Forms of Protest in a Deinstitutionalized Context," *Bulletin of Latin American Research* 21, 2:199–218.

Márquez, P. "Vacas Flacas y Odios Gordos," *En Esta Venezuela Realidades y Nuevos Caminos*, P. Marquez and R. Piñango (eds.), Caracas: Ediciones IESA, 29–46.

McCoy, J. A. (2005) "The Referendum in Venezuela One Act in an Unfinished Drama," *The Journal of Democracy* 16, 1:109–123.

Molina, J. E. (2004) "The Unraveling of Venezuela's Party System. From Party Rule to Personalistic Politics and Deinstitutionalization," *The Unraveling of Representative Democracy in Venezuela*, J. McCoy and D. J. Myers (eds.), Baltimore, MD: The Johns Hopkins University Press, 152–178.

Montferrante, P. (with the assistance of J. R. Padilla) (2004) "La Cotidianidad del Venezolano: Entre el Miedo y la Violencia," *En Esta*

Venezuela Realidades y Nuevos Caminos, P. Márquez and R. Piñango (eds.), Caracas: Ediciones IESA, 269–288.

Oxhorn, P. (this volume) "Conceptualizing Civil Society from the Bottom Up: A Political Economy Perspective."

——. (2001) "When Democracy Isn't All that Democratic: Social Exclusion and the Limits of the Public Sphere in Latin America," Miami: North South Center.

——. (1994) "Understanding Political Change after Authoritarian Rule: The Popular Sectors and Chile's New Democratic Regime," *Journal of Latin American Studies* 26:3.

Piven, F. F., and R. Cloward (1998) *The Breaking of the American Social Compact*, New York: The New Press. (Especially Part IV "Disruptive movements and their electoral impact" #17, "Normalizing collective protest," 345–374).

——. (1977) *Poor Peoples' Movements. Why they Succeed. How They Fail*, New York: Vintage.

PROVEA (Programa Venezolana de Educación y Acciān en Derechos Humanos), selected years *Situación de los derechos humanos en Venezuela. Boletín de derechos humanos y coyuntura*, selected years, Caracas.

Roberts, Kenneth (2003) "Social Polarization and the Populist Resurgence in Venezuela," *Venezuelan Politics in the Chávez Era. Class, Polarization, and Conflict*, Steve Ellner and Daniel Hellinger (eds.), Boulder CO: Lynne Reinner, 55–72.

Salamanca, L. (2003) "Civil Society: Late Bloomers," 55–70, J. McCoy and D. J. Myers (eds.), *The Unraveling of Representative Democracy in Venezuela. Toward a New Model of Participation*, forthcoming.

Sikkink, K. (1993) "Human Rights, Principled Issue Networks, and Sovereignty in Latin America," *International Organization* 47:411–441.

Smith, C. (1996) *Resisting Reagan. The U.S. Central America Peace Movement*, Chicago: University of Chicago Press.

Stokes, S. (1995) *Cultures in Conflict. Social Movements and the State in Peru*, Berkeley: University of California Press.

Tarrow, S. (1994) *Power in Movement: Social Movements, Collective Action, and Politics*, Cambridge: University Press.

Trinkunas, H. A. (2004) "The Military: From Marginalization to Center Stage," *The Unraveling of Representative Democracy in Venezuela*, McCoy, J., and D. J. Myers (eds.), Baltimore, MD: The Johns Hopkins University Press, 50–70.

Warner, R. S. (1993) "Work in progress towards a new paradigm in the sociological study of religion in the United States," *American Journal of Sociology* 98, 5:1044–1093.

Index

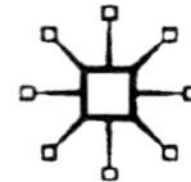

First published in 2006 by
PALGRAVE MACMILLAN™
175 Fifth Avenue, New York, N.Y. 10010 and
Houndmills, Basingstoke, Hampshire, England RG21 6XS
Companies and representatives throughout the world.

PALGRAVE MACMILLAN is the global academic imprint of the Palgrave Macmillan division of St. Martin's Press, LLC and of Palgrave Macmillan Ltd. Macmillan® is a registered trademark in the United States, United Kingdom and other countries. Palgrave is a registered trademark in the European Union and other countries.

ISBN 978-1–4039–7228–6

Library of Congress Cataloging-in-Publication Data

Civil society and democracy in Latin America / edited by Richard Feinberg, Carlos H. Waisman, and Leon Zamosc.
p. cm.
Includes bibliographical references and index.
ISBN 1–4039–7228–1 (alk. paper)
1. Civil society—Latin America. 2. Democracy—Latin America. 3. Latin America—Politics and government—1980– I. Feinberg, Richard E. II. Waisman, Carlos H. (Carlos Horacio), 1943– III. Zamosc, Leon.

JL966.C58 2006
320.98—dc22 2005056461

A catalogue record for this book is available from the British Library.

Design by Newgen Imaging Systems (P) Ltd., Chennai, India.

First edition: April 2006

10 9 8 7 6 5 4 3 2 1

Printed in the United States of America.

Transferred to Digital Printing in 2008

Index

Printed in the United States
151597LV00001B/22/P

9 781403 972286